To Elena,

SYSTEMIC EVIL

MAT PEREZ v. THE FBI

My heart went into the struggle for ethical investigations and truth. I was glad to be part of the restoration.

Sam Martinez

SAMUEL C. MARTINEZ

SYSTEMIC EVIL: MAT PEREZ v. THE FBI

Samuel C. Martinez

Published by Samuel C. Martinez

Cover Design by Adriana Avila

ISBN-13: 978-1503052611
ISBN-10: 1503052613
Library of Congress Control Number: 2014919795
CreateSpace Independent Publishing Platform
North Charleston, South Carolina

SYSTEMIC EVIL: MAT PEREZ v. THE FBI
IS DEDICATED TO

Bernardo Matias "Mat" Perez,
Who stood on his feet in the face of defeat.
Antonio "Tony" V. Silva,
Who persevered what he feared.
Jose "Joe" Angel Silva,
Who swung the sling of David at the FBI to save it.
Lucius Desha Bunton III,
Who represented justice, leaving his legacy with us.
Don Haskins,
Who played the right players despite the naysayers.
Mentors,
Who are there for others in a world of brothers.
Yvonne "Bonnie" Martinez Jaquez,
Who was and still is.

FOREWORD

Dr. Josiah Heyman
University of Texas at El Paso

Systemic Evil tells an important and fascinating story. The FBI is a significant institution in contemporary American society. It has a high level of recognition and prestige. It holds considerable power in criminal justice. And it represents an important opportunity for individual social mobility. The term "glass ceiling" represents barriers to upward career progress inside organizations and corporations. The glass ceiling for Hispanics (to use a common, if flawed, label) in the FBI thus harmed them personally, and it also caused a loss in all the capabilities they could offer to the public safety of society. Of course, it offends our sense of justice. Yet it could and did change. It changed not because society woke up one day and decided to do things the right way. It changed because of the courageous lawsuit by Hispanic agents, undertaken at considerable risk to them. We often shy away from conflict, from upsetting the accepted order, but it is just such efforts and struggles that bring about improvement over the long run. Yet much more improvement still is needed in the condition of Hispanics in the United States.

To understand the issues involved, and to place this book in a wider context, it helps to review briefly the history of Hispanics in the United States. Of course, many details will be bypassed, but the basic stages are informative. The United States seized half the territory of Mexico at the end in 1848 of a war of aggression, with a small purchase to follow in 1853. We should always remember that much of this territory was the independent possession of Native Americans, but what matters to the present story is that there were numerous settlements of former Mexican citizens in this territory. Despite treaty provisions that ensured such people U.S. citizenship and legal rights, there ensued a second kind of conquest, a long period of violent force and legal chicanery designed to rob the Mexican-origin inhabitants of their lands, possessions, resources, and political power.

Puerto Rico likewise was essentially a conquest, a colony of Spain striving to be independent that discovered itself transferred instead as a colony to direct U.S. rule after the Spanish-American war of 1898 (in 1952, it assumed an ambiguous status as a "commonwealth" in the United States). Cuba did become quasi-independent after the Spanish-American war, although the United States retained for itself the power to veto Cuban laws and intervene in the island. In each site, the legal system was largely a foreign imposition, set up in opposition to the community rather than part of it. Overt racial discrimination divided Euro-Americans and their institutions and privileges from Hispanics, though there was always ambiguity over the whiteness of some Hispanics.

Setting aside Cuba, which was independent and had a revolution in 1959 that eventually resulted in alienation from the United States, the main political struggles of Puerto Ricans and Mexican Americans (to use a flawed but useful term) gradually shifted from the outside to the inside, with Hispanic citizens and residents claiming civil rights and fighting against discrimination in the surrounding society. Previously, the struggles for justice concerned people on whom the United States had been imposed, and whose property had been stolen under the guise of law. But increasingly, Hispanics arrived as working immigrants, in the case of Mexicans (and later Central and South Americans) as immigrants to the United States, and in the case of Puerto Ricans, already U.S. citizens, as migrants to the mainland. Their struggle was for fair treatment in the new society: non-discrimination, good wages and working conditions, open housing and good schools, political representation, and so forth.

An immense and admirable profusion of struggles followed, making our society better and better, though hardly perfect. Three main sorts of struggles ensued, all of them important. First, initially relegated to backbreaking labor, Hispanics fought to enter white-collar jobs such as FBI agents. Once inside those organizations, they fought to break through glass ceilings. This brings both personal upward social mobility, and involvement in the powerful and prestigious organizations in society. Stepping into these new organizational roles proves that Hispanics are not just "hewers of wood and drawers of water." Such forward steps are resisted because of entrenched assumptions of racial hierarchy and tight networks of inside privilege, relegating Hispanics to the zones of least power and most exploitation. But courageous struggles change these patterns. This is the story told in *Systemic Evil.*

Second, in laboring roles, which after all are honorable and good work, Hispanics and other have and continue to conduct struggles for fair pay and benefits, safe conditions, occupational advancement, and so forth, and more widely for a good quality of life for self, family, and children. Indeed, this groundwork of prosperity for working families often precedes advancement into businesses, professions, and white-collar jobs. Third, the struggles of Hispanics are not just matters of those already inside the United States and established at various levels in its economy and society. Because immigration from Latin America and the Caribbean continually renews the U.S. Hispanic population, the conditions surrounding migration and border-crossing deserve attention and struggle. These include improving life opportunities at home, in Puerto Rico, Mexico, the Dominican Republic, Cuba, Central America, and so forth, so that people do not have to migrate. Should they migrate, it is best if they can move legally and openly, free of the risks of criminal organizations and death in the desert. National security also benefits from people moving openly, not covertly. And application of laws and regulations should respect constitutional and human rights, and officials should be held accountable, be they non-Hispanic or Hispanic.

Through struggles such as that recounted for the FBI, Hispanics are better represented (if still inadequately) in the dominant institutions of society. It thus bears remembering that subtle but powerful "structural biases" remain. For example, when young people—Hispanics and others—drop out of school to earn money in service or laboring jobs because, say, a father is deported to Mexico, they never reach the point of being able to struggle for advancement into management. We need to resolve the biases and prejudices at all stages of the life course; we need people to be able to arrive at the point of deservedly knocking on management's door. When evil is systemic, the change must be also.

PREFACE

When I worked in the Denver Federal Bureau of Investigation (FBI) office, Special Agent Jim Horn said, "I used to think that racists were uneducated." He identified a Denver agent friend and added, "He is one of the smartest, most educated guys I know, and he sure blew my theory." My relationship with this educated friend included exchanging greetings in passing, but never working or socializing together. Most agents in Denver, a medium-sized office, hung out in circles of friends with the circles intermixing many times, yet he was absent from his circle when my circle mixed with his. This coexistence was acceptable to both of us. Had Jim never commented about his friend's racist feelings, I would have been unconscious of his avoidance.

No one lives without discrimination, whether it is incidental or deliberate. Discrimination lives with us every day on the receiving or giving end, intentional or non-intentional. To discriminate means to make a distinction in favor of or against a person, item, or thought. The development of humans for survival relied on prejudging persons, situations or the unknown as friend or foe, fight or flight. In the twenty first century, differentiating families, schools, politics, religion, social economics, attire, art, culture and countries is common, with or without hostility. Google unfairness, prejudice, racism, or discrimination and you will find new articles of its existence along with articles denying discrimination exists. We are quick to choose the known rather than the unknown for comfort and security, rather than investigate the unknown for its individual merit or fine distinction.

Blessed with every day choices, we sometimes make innocent mistakes and do not recognize when our speech or actions negatively affect another. Discrimination becomes evil when a person or an organization fails to correct something said or an action where a victim of the negative statement or action is offended or finds unfair. When an organization fails to act on discrimination, and falls back defensively on what they perceive as their personal interests, needs or a noble cause, the lack of response becomes systemic discrimination. Willful neglect is evil.

During the lawsuit, the FBI workplace, with a few exceptions reflected the American corporate world and had an Anglo upper management that did not recognize discrimination. The plaintiffs in PEREZ v. FBI made equal opportunity their mission. Management was not perfect and they made mistakes. Minorities want the same opportunity to pass or fail. When minorities have the same opportunities to perform at the same level as good or mediocre Anglo managers and receive the same opportunities to succeed, then fairness in the workforce begins.

I felt compelled to publish the events of discrimination after the premature, cancer-related death of plaintiffs' attorney Antonio V. Silva on September 15, 2009. This history of *Perez v. FBI* represents the countless hours of interviews, many thousands of pages of transcripts, and FBI documented evidence. Personal interviews with witnesses and Hispanic agents in person, by telephone, and via email added to the information in the book. I have augmented these personal accounts with experiences from my twenty-six years of FBI service in the third person. The FBI Prepublication Unit vetted the names and content of this book, yet the public affairs' office denied my request to interview active FBI Hispanic agents in supervisory or executive positions to note the positive advances of Hispanics in career development. *Systemic Evil* is a tribute to FBI agents that voice and right wrongs.

The church backdrop of the cover illustrates the embedded values Mat Perez learned in the seminary that proved vital in withstanding management's biased allegations and abuse. Out of tradition of proper respect and gravity, law enforcement officers mourn fellow officers killed in action by wearing a black band over their badge. The black band surrounding the FBI badge speaks for the author and other agents mourning the demise of investigations in which a federal judge found the FBI EEO program bankrupt and guilty of discrimination.

Disclaimer:

Systemic Evil is the work of non-fiction documentary on the *Perez v. FBI* class action lawsuit. All authored materials in this book are the sole responsibility of the author. Except for the introduction and the last two chapters, the sources of information for this book were from testimony taken from court transcripts between August 15, 1988 and August 25, 1988 and from personal interviews. The author and publisher strove to make sure the information in this book was correct from court records, FBI documents, personal events and memories. All other sources of information or references appear in the Works Cited.

The materials are not the views or opinions of the Federal Bureau of Investigation or class members. Proper names in this work may be incorrect, as the court reporter obtained the names phonetically and did not obtain the correct spellings of a few during the trial. Proper identification and research corrected most names, yet phonetic spellings of names remained unidentified and uncorrected. Pseudonyms may appear for privacy reasons. As several agents of the FBI have similar names, the author identified agents further through office assignments and bureau records. This work has no intent to affect the privacy of individuals with similar names not associated with this case.

The following is from court transcripts of the Court Reporter's Certificate:

> Court Reporter in and for the United States District Court for the Western District of Texas, do hereby certify that the within and foregoing is a full, true, complete and correct transcript of the proceeding had in the above entitled and numbered cause at the time and place as shown herein, to the best of my knowledge, skill and ability. It was typed under my supervision and direction. I certify that the transcript fees and format comply with those prescribed by the Court and the Judicial Conference of the United States.

ACKNOWLEDGEMENTS

Each moment in life is graceful and precious, with many people contributing to this book. The project makes acknowledgements impossible to those individuals who provided good and bad thoughts, good and bad values, good and bad actions, and good and bad support through life's adventures. The interactions between the good and bad provided the opportunity to write the events. Thanks to those for the experiences.

This project proceeded with interest, encouragement and support for publicizing the events of the Mat Perez lawsuit from professors at the University of Texas at El Paso (UTEP). President Dr. Diana Natalicio and Dr. Dennis Bixler-Marquez relayed the events to Dr. Howard Campbell, who provided the information to Dr. Josiah Heyman and Richard Dugan, coordinator, Assistive Technology Lab, UTEP. Sandy Alexander, Mac Brantley, Dale Caldwell, Leo Gonzales, Rogelio Guevara, Ruth Martinez, Gil Mireles, Mat Perez, Rudy Valadez, Noemi Wilson, Albert Zapanta, and the FNW Group were very helpful in reviewing, editing or providing significant additions to the book. Tom Hilburger was responsive with court documents, as were the people interviewed for this project. A special thanks to deceased friend Eddie Gonzalez who served as the Director of the United States Marshal Service and supported this project. Muchas gracias for the support.

Table Of Contents

Introduction

"Humans are the only species that follow unstable pack leaders."
– César Millán Favela

José Manuel Miguel Xavier Gonzales, in a few short weeks it will be spring. The snows of winter will flee away, the ice will vanish, and the air will become soft and balmy. In short, José Manuel Miguel Xavier Gonzales, the annual miracle of the years will awaken and come to pass, but you won't be here.

The rivulet will run its purring course to the sea, the timid desert flowers will put forth their tender shoots, and the glorious valleys of this imperial domain will blossom as the rose. Still, you won't be here to see.

From every tree top some wild woods songster will carol his mating song, butterflies will sport in the sunshine, the busy bee will hum happy as it pursues its accustomed vocation, the gentle breeze will tease the tassels of the wild grasses, and all nature, José Manuel Miguel Xavier Gonzales, will be glad but you. You won't be here to enjoy it because I command the sheriff or some other officer of the country to lead you out to some remote spot, swing you by the neck from a nodding bough of some sturdy oak, and let you hang until you are dead.

And then, José Manuel Miguel Xavier Gonzales, I further command that such officer or officers retire quickly from your dangling corpse, that vultures may descend from the heavens upon your filthy body until nothing shall remain but bare, bleached bones of a cold-blooded, copper-colored, blood-thirsty, throat-cutting, chili-eating, sheep-herding, murdering son of a bitch.[1]

The 1881 court transcripts and the salient facts of the trial in New Mexico are not available, which makes it difficult to determine if the defendant understood the charges against him, had adequate representation, or deserved the guilty verdict; however, the sentence left no doubt of the outcome.

Now picture this copper-colored Mexican—José—herding sheep on his great-grandfather's land and eating chili for lunch in New Mexico long before it joined the Union in 1912. Along comes a frontiersman claiming the Surveyor General of New Mexico, who disallowed any land titles written in Spanish, has granted the frontiersman the land of José's family, and he threatens Jose with force, telling him to leave. José, understanding little English, defends himself and slits the man's throat. The court charges José with murder. Can we say the judge asked for all of the facts and rendered a fair decision that overlooked skin color, national origin, culture and language?

Judges, past and present, whom we have chosen to bring balance to our courts, have their personal interests and influences affecting judgment and fairness. This bias concerned Mat Perez. He needed a rational judge who could both analyze simple characteristics of disparate treatment and exhibit a virtuous character to issue a verdict of discrimination against one of the most reputable law enforcement agencies in the world. Mat shared his story with about four hundred potential class members and his attorney, Jose Silva. Three hundred and ten Hispanic FBI agents joined the class action lawsuit charging the FBI of employment discrimination. The large number surprised Mat, yet the FBI appeared unconcerned.

Mat Perez followed his heart, never thinking that he would lose the woman he loved. His point of reference to obligations, dedication and family was his father, who worked ten, twelve, and sixteen-hour days, and the home took care of itself. Mat could not let go of responsibility, the dangerous investigations, the development of exciting results or the heavy caseload that led to his divorce. He loved his work. The divorce devastated the former Catholic seminarian. While time diminished the emotion of his failed marriage, Mat's work responsibilities grew to such a degree that he became the Federal Bureau of

Investigation (FBI) Special Agent in Charge (SAC) of the San Ju-
Division, and this brought new life to him.

In Puerto Rico, he met and fell in love with FBI office assistant Yvonne Shaffer, but an unforeseen obstacle came from the pinnacle of the FBI. Orders came from the director's office that Mat was to stay away from Yvonne as the FBI suspected she was a Socialist. He fell in lockstep with the director's order and avoided Yvonne. Her eventual mistreatment by the FBI and the cleared allegations led Mat to abandon the director's order by marrying Yvonne. Mat became a target. The FBI demoted and transferred Mat to Los Angeles against the will of its Special Agent in Charge, Richard T. Bretzing. Mat's well-documented religious and ethnic disparate treatment and harassment resulted in repeated and ignored Equal Employment Opportunity (EEO) complaints, which led to retaliation against not only Mat, but also those who supported his complaint. Outnumbered and underfunded, Mat knew the FBI would smother him without help from fellow agents and the guidance of attorneys.

Hugo A. Rodriguez, an eighteen-year veteran FBI agent in Albuquerque, New Mexico, earned his law degree while he was an FBI agent. As a Cuban-American Spanish speaker, he knew the troubles Hispanic agents had in the bureau with deliberate and unconscious discrimination. There were also bigots who disparaged the self-worth of Hispanics, blacks and women. As a member of the Albuquerque "Palace Guard," in which he had unrestricted executive access, he enjoyed that access to the SAC and the Assistant Special Agent in Charge (ASAC) as their principal legal advisor, hostage negotiator and applicant recruiter. He overheard ASAC Rodney McHargue ask the SAC, "Did you hear what that fucking Perez is doing with the Hispanics?" The ASAC also told the SAC that Mat's wife was a Communist. The SAC displaced Hugo from access to the Palace Guard and curtailed his assignments after he received widespread media recognition for his and his wife's civic activities. The SAC told him, "I can't control your personal life, but I can control your professional life." He would later leave the bureau and join Jose Silva and Tony Silva as attorneys for the class action lawsuit. With the law on their side, they still needed support from Hispanic agents.

Two FBI agents, Jerry Dove and Ben Grogan, died in a hail of gunfire as five other wounded agents battled through the carnage of April 11, 1986, a crime perpetrated by two armed and dangerous US Army Ranger-trained killers. Faced with the superior firepower of assault rifles, the FBI agents stood as a team with a purpose and defended one another. Agents lay dead and wounded in the quick exchange as over 130 bullets created bloody chaos. As the two bank robbers attempted to escape in a stolen FBI car, Special Agent (SA) Edmundo Mireles, Jr., despite being dazed from one gunshot to the head and another that left his left arm paralyzed, while still under fire, sat up, supported himself against a nearby car, then, using his body, his knees and his right hand, cocked and fired all the rounds in his shotgun at the suspects. Faced with death, his fear dissolved into anger and determination to stop the two killers. Ed dropped the empty shotgun, pulled his revolver out, staggered toward the getaway car, shot and emptied all of his ammunition, leaving the perpetrators dead. Ed survived, and in recognition of his actions, the FBI awarded him the first-ever FBI Medal of Valor. Yet, even before that dark and tragic day, Ed had survived other shots—wounds of discrimination—when he sensed rejection within his FBI community. Ed would testify to discrimination in the bureau, but not as a class member. With evidence, law, and support on the side of Hispanic agents, there was still concern in finding a rational judicial decision and a judge who would render a guilty verdict against the powerful FBI.

Federal Judge Lucius Desha Bunton III, a conservative judge who presided over the *Perez v. FBI* trial in El Paso, Texas would be called to certify a class action lawsuit, to sit through a trial of accusations against an FBI he held in high esteem, and then to have the responsibility of rendering a fair decision. His friend William S. Sessions, a former Texas judge, was now at the helm as the director of the FBI, replacing Director Webster.

In the 1960s, the FBI, under the leadership of Director J. Edgar Hoover, the man who served as director for an unprecedented forty-eight years (1924 to 1972), produced remarkable results in combating violent acts of criminal discrimination engendered by hate groups and racial separatists.[2] Director Hoover ordered agents into hostile communities where politicians and law enforcement officers protected hate groups, violent acts of disparity, church and cross burnings, and systematic intimidation. The payoff to the US was a reduction in the number of hate crimes that targeted victims of a specific race, ethnicity, or religion.[3] For many in the FBI and around the world, the actions of the South defined the term discrimination.

The FBI, the agency charged with investigating discrimination and enforcing federal laws, did its part when the government passed Affirmative Action policy by hiring blacks, women and Hispanics in the late 1960s and early 1970s. Violations requiring Spanish-speaking investigators multiplied in part by cases developed by linguists and development of Spanish-speaking informants. FBI management, to the letter, swore Spanish-speaking agents were needed and vital to solve ongoing cases. To support the new recruits of minorities was the Equal Employment Opportunity Commission (EEOC) with oversight responsibility of unfair practices.

Mat Perez motivated three-quarters of the Hispanic agents to support the *Bernardo "Mat" M. Perez, et al. v. Director William H. Webster, the Federal Bureau of Investigation, and Attorney General Dick Thornburgh, et al.*, known as *Perez v. the FBI,* claiming that FBI management and the EEOC were both in theory and in practice discriminatory for a perceived noble cause—the needs of the bureau.[4,5] The Hispanic group composed of educated professionals, former military officers, police officers, detectives and corporate business managers gathered in attempt to reeducate the FBI, the DOJ, and the EEOC on the elements of employment discrimination. To move the FBI and the courts past discrimination as a hate crime, Hispanic agents needed to amplify the term of discrimination, which meant displaying examples in the degrees of discrimination—that discrimination is favoritism, bias, unfair policy or assignments, disparate treatment to policy, inequitable evaluations, inaction to issues, retaliation to complaints, bigotry and breaking laws. Judge Bunton and the court would answer questions to the issues of the lawsuit.

Can a verdict of conviction occur without hate or can the court find an agency guilty of discrimination when there is no malice or unfair intent of disparate treatment? Would the FBI backdown, regroup, and consider allegations of discrimination when three-quarters of the Hispanic agents certified the class action lawsuit or would the FBI retaliate against those agents? Would field agents who complained about management policies now turn against the Hispanic class members claiming a "Taco Circuit" of disparate treatment by management?

Would the testimonies of a Hispanic SAC, four supervisors, and thirty-seven Hispanic street agents outweigh the testimonies of all three FBI Executive Assistant Directors, a slew of SACs, ASACs and supervisors? Would the meager finances of the Hispanic agents and their attorneys be able to withstand the prolonged delays and deep pockets of the government? Would the Hispanic agents or the FBI accept an unfavorable verdict? Would the FBI make the necessary changes to a possible finding of discrimination, or would they resist and retaliate?

Would the court documents the FBI prepared provide factual data or errors, and would the documents contradict any testimony? Would there be exposure to violations of law other than discrimination, such as setting up sub-files on its employees or issuing grand jury subpoenas on administrative matters? Would there be evidence that the FBI tolerated badge-carrying agents to slur blacks, women and Hispanics? Are the needs of the bureau justified, and are they enough of a noble cause to warrant the violation of rights of individuals? Would the FBI be capable of intervening in employees' private lives? Would the FBI restrict an SAC of required resources, financial help, support and agents needed to address four Major Cases: a police corruption case and three other cases in which terrorists bombed United States military property, and ambushed and killed U.S. Navy sailors by machine guns?

Would the Equal Employment Opportunity Commission (EEOC) take corrective actions on allegations of complaints against the FBI or develop a systemic pattern of accommodating FBI investigations? Would the Hispanic agents' lawsuit against management practices on assignments and promotions benefit whites, blacks, women, and support employees?

No one lives without prejudgment or discrimination, incidental or deliberate. The story of *Perez v. the FBI* shows examples where coincidental discrimination turned evil, first by willful neglect, then by retaliation.

1

Sluggish Support, Heavy Harassment

Bernardo Matias Perez, known as Mat, is the oldest of the ten children of Ernestina Dornaletxe and Matias Perez. Mat grew up in a small California town called Lone Pine, a Mexican pueblo once known as *El Pueblito de las Uvas*, "the little town of grapes." Ernestina's family immigrated to California from Macaye, Labourd, in the French Pyrenees and near the Spanish border. Exiled during the French Revolution, the Dornaletxe family ended up in California as farmers and sheep ranchers before turning to gold and silver mining during the Gold Rush. Matias' family fled the Mexican Revolution from Jalisco, Mexico, and upon their arrival worked for the railroads and trekked across the west, ending up near Lone Pine.

Instead of watching television, Mat grew up attending daily rosaries. He was enveloped in the faith and liturgy of the Roman Catholic Church, which dominated his family's culture and the history of Lone Pine. At age thirteen, Mat left home to attend a new seminary, Ryan Preparatory College, in Fresno, in preparation to become a diocesan. Enrollment at Ryan was low, and classes were small—never more than five students per class. With the constant personal attention of his instructors, Mat excelled, becoming the first student to complete the intense six-year curriculum. After graduation from Ryan, Mat journeyed south to the major seminary of the Archdiocese of Los Angeles in

Camarillo, California, St. John Vianney, where he began his philosophy studies. However, by age twenty, Mat realized that, although his faith was still strong, the priesthood entailed sacrifices and commitments beyond those he was willing to make.

After a consultation with mentors, his parents, and his spiritual advisor, Mat left St. John Vianney in January 1960 and, at the suggestion of his uncle, Gilbert Dominguez, applied at the FBI and received a position as a clerk. His FBI mentors in the Identification Division convinced him to go back to school and complete a four-year college degree. Mat resigned from the FBI after working for a year and a half as a personal messenger for FBI Director J. Edgar Hoover to pursue a bachelor of arts degree in Spanish literature with a minor in classical languages—Latin and ancient Greek—from Georgetown University.

In April of 1963, just a month before graduation, Mat married Mary Margaret Bushwaller. Mary, the daughter of an American diplomat, grew up in Australia, Brazil, and Mexico. After Mary Margaret, then a freshman at Georgetown University, had dated Mat for a while, she decided she would quit school and work full time so the two could marry. Mat passed the Foreign Service Exam, but the US State Department declined to offer him a position. Mat returned to work for the FBI in a support capacity and met Jim Miller, another former seminarian, who convinced Mat he should become an FBI agent. In 1963, new FBI agents had a starting salary of $7,690 per year—a salary higher than his father ever made after forty years of work. With his Jesuit educational background and Georgetown degree, Mat breezed through the FBI Academy.

The physical requirements of Hoover's FBI were not rigorous. The FBI conducted pro forma background investigations and sometimes required specific work experience along with a "clean background," which meant no bad debts, no alcoholics, no homosexuals, no divorces, and no family histories of mental illness. At the time, Mat observed that there were no female agents, fewer than ten African-American agents (most served as Mr. Hoover's personal chauffeurs), fewer than ten Hispanic agents, and just a few Jewish agents. Mat saw no dark skinned Hispanics and believed he was the seventh Hispanic in the FBI.

The director ruled as supreme sovereign of this lily-white organization, through his handpicked subordinates. Mistakes were unacceptable. When the director ordered, "Fix responsibility!" it meant that someone was responsible, someone had to suffer, and that unfortunate someone could expect to be censured, demoted, transferred, or fired without haste. The FBI worked like a well-oiled machine, and when the director pressed a key or made a call, an immediate answer, never the wrong one, appeared. Hoover directed every important case nationwide, and nobody—not even the president—ever told him "no." He portrayed himself as "the Greatest Living American." The FBI placed its membership among the world's elite. The FBI even rejected an aspiring, young Richard Nixon, although the director made it a point to bestow an honorary FBI badge on the inaugurated President Nixon during his first official visit. Elvis Presley was not so lucky; when Elvis wanted an FBI badge and begged for an FBI assignment, "His Excellency" Hoover turned "The King of Rock 'n' Roll" down cold.

Everyone thought that FBI agents were lawyers or accountants. When Mat became an FBI agent, he was surprised to find few accountants and even fewer lawyers; instead, he found many former teachers, ex-military men and even some old Texans with mere high school diplomas whom the FBI had hired during World War II. Hoover's secretary, Helen Gandy, also had a say in promoting her "Gandy Boys." These were her personal, handpicked "natural-born leaders" whom she nurtured because she liked the "cut of his jib," which meant their general appearance and demeanor. Some of these "Gandy Boys" graduated from a two-year diploma mill and received the opportunity to rise to top positions, while other agents needed to have a four-year college degree. The agent who temporarily served as FBI Director after William S. Sessions and who entered the FBI after Mat did not have a four-year college degree but was a "Gandy Boy." Mat became a special agent and served in the following: Tampa Division, San Antonio, followed by the Washington Field Office, Miami, the FBI Headquarters, Mexico, back to Headquarters, Los Angeles, San Juan, back to Los Angeles, and ending in the West Texas town of El Paso.

Mat inquired about career development. He applied for a supervisory position in Miami only to face rejection. Mat surmised that he would have a dead-end career if he stayed on the so-called "Tamale Squad," a foreign counterintelligence group of Spanish speakers whose supervisor had been in place and had not been promoted for the previous eighteen years. He requested a squad transfer to take over the supervisory vacancies of other squads when they opened, but the FBI denied his requests. Mat did not have an FBI "Rabbi," nor did he belong to anyone's "fiefdom." The FBI terms "Rabbi" and "Hook" referred to high-ranking agents who helped aspirants move up the "corporate ladder." Through his faith, Mat believed in life's opportunities. He had FBI mentors, Anglo men who loved the work and who loved to talk about what they did, and Mat listened and followed their lead.

Mat did everything he could to secure a promotion. He possessed versatility, he developed good cases, he recruited reliable sources, he worked undercover, he worked bombing and terrorism cases, he translated tapes others could not interpret, and he assisted others with their own casework. He even volunteered to become a night supervisor even though the position offered no grade or pay increase. Then at last, he received a promotion to the Domestic Intelligence Division at FBI Headquarters (FBIHQ) and excelled. FBIHQ sent him to Hermosillo, Mexico, to liaise with the Mexican police.

When Mat's wife deserted him and their three sons because of his heavy workload and frequent road trips, coupled with the countless hours he worked and the kidnapping and murder of American Vice-Consul to Mexico John Patterson, it broke his heart. His wife refused to reconcile—Mat's work had cheated the family of his time, but Mat could not forgo his work. The failed marriage conflicted with Mat's Catholicism, but dedication to his full caseload pulled him through. Mat moved onto the Inspection Staff, in which top agents exchanged ideas and mentored one another.

After gaining inspection certification and hoping to become an ASAC, the bureau placed him in the Freedom of Information Section and gave him a black ink marker to redact and black out information that the FBI did not want the public to see. For Mat, editing documents held no vital importance, no FBI case serial number, no need for a badge or credentials—he missed investigations. He expressed this to Richard Held, Sr., the number-two man in the FBI, who was capable of making personnel decisions. Held listened and agreed. Mat left Held's office in high spirits.

Oliver "Buck" Revell, Held's assistant, stood listening on the other side of the doorway. Revell, a "Gandy Boy," had fast-tracked his way to a higher position, despite having far less seniority than Mat. Buck told Mat that he needed to become a supervisor before going out for the ASAC position. Mat asked, "Why should I have to take an extra transfer when other agents and peers with less time have become ASACs without being supervisors?" Revell cautioned Mat not to question him and to follow orders or he might find himself headed nowhere fast.

Mat, with silent protest, accepted the circuitous route, knowing it was possible that Revell could replace Held. Mat had seen careers ended over incurring the wrath of the director or one of his lieutenants. Revell added with confidence, "You are making my program work. I will not forget you. For this sacrifice and taking this job, I guarantee within one year you will be an ASAC." Therefore, Mat became one of "Buck's Boys" and looked forward to going before "the Buck board," a nickname in the FBI for the career board in which Buck handpicked his selection from the candidates. Mat later learned that Buck Revell had a stand-alone computer in his office he used to identify whom and whom not to promote, in violation of FBI policy. Mat's "Buck Boy" status became short lived.

Mat transferred to Los Angeles and supervised Squad 6, also known as the "Garbage Squad," which covered miscellaneous aspects of foreign counterintelligence and domestic intelligence. As a supervisor, Mat supported his agents and staff. Mat had undercover agents known as "beards" on his squad; they infiltrated the Weather Underground and other domestic terrorist groups. The Garbage Squad grew to about forty agents and had good support from SAC Elmer Lindberg. The US Attorney General recognized Mat in a prominent case involving a plot to attack President Jimmy Carter's wife, First Lady Roselyn

Carter, and other prominent women at the National Women's Caucus in Houston. Mat's two and a half years as a supervisor in LA served him well, and he had some of the FBI's best agents on his crew. He recognized that most of the experienced field agents handled investigations far better than FBIHQ managers ever could. Mat's squad also had top-notch, well-trained Los Angeles Police Department (LAPD) officers with equivalent capabilities, and this allowed him to develop and maintain a great working relationship with the LAPD.

The LA office announced an ASAC vacancy. Mat wanted it, but FBIHQ said no, that he had to go through the Management Aptitude Program (MAP). Revell's promise that Mat would become an ASAC within a year never materialized. Mat underwent MAP assessment and received a level 4 rating—considered high marks—with no contingencies, which meant he received an evaluation with no administrative weaknesses. Yet, despite Mat's success, Assistant Director Jim Adams told Mat he could not become an ASAC in LA.

Soon afterward, the bureau announced Mat's promotion to ASAC San Juan (SJ), Puerto Rico (PR). Mat flew to San Juan at once, excited about the promotion. He reviewed administrative, security, and criminal files and made suggestions to FBIHQ with the concurrence of his new boss. SAC John Hinchcliffe was a breath of fresh air—an open, honest, and positive leader who saw, as did Mat, that the San Juan Division was the "orphan child of the bureau."

The island of Puerto Rico, an unincorporated territory of the United States, located thirteen hundred miles from the US mainland, had endemic diseases such as dengue and monga that were common in the underdeveloped nations of the Third World. Fecal matter contaminated their water supply, homes had burglar bars on their windows, the police were often undertrained and corrupted, and the island had some of the highest murder rates in America. The San Juan Division had a two-year transfer policy, which resulted in ten agents rotating in while ten agents transferred out, which led to a lack of continuity. Agents often transferred to San Juan to get away from more expensive and undesirable locations and then sought their office of preference (OP) just as soon as they accomplished the required two years of service. Almost half of the agents did not even speak Spanish, so the Spanish-speaking Hispanic agents on the streets conducted the investigations while the non-Spanish speakers staffed the air-conditioned office.

In 1979, FBIHQ transferred SAC Hinchcliffe to the Phoenix Division. Director Webster appointed Mat SAC San Juan. Eight months earlier, Mat had been at FBIHQ and had gone through the protocol of meeting with all of the division heads and chiefs following his appointment as ASAC San Juan. He felt he understood their expectations, so he did not return to DC as the appointed SAC of San Juan just to shake hands and receive their benediction. Mat called the director to thank him and told Webster he would perform at his best.

Mat thought that perhaps as the SAC of a field office, he would deliver speeches at Rotary Club luncheons, learn to play golf, and do all of the things that other SACs did. However, just seven days into his new assignment, terrorists machine-gunned a US Navy bus and killed two sailors, leaving ten in critical condition. Volcanic chaos erupted. The assault became a "Major Case," codenamed after Navy Murders (NAVMUR). The bureau gives Major Cases in the FBI short code names to facilitate written communications. For incidents designated as Major Cases, the bureau spares no expense in pursuing justice, as witnessed by the Patty Hearst kidnapping case, Wounded Knee, the St. Francis Tavern Bombing, the Mariel Boatlift, the 9-11 investigation, Waco Siege, Ruby Ridge, and organized crime or terrorism cases such as the Boston Marathon Bombing. Major Cases are the top priority in the FBI with lots of investigators, reams of paperwork, and extra resources assigned. FBIHQ knows that failure occurs when resources are restricted.

In San Juan, the many non-Spanish speaking agents assigned to the office compounded the difficulty of the management and investigative problems related to the murderous act perpetrated against US Navy personnel. Mat recalled reading an FBIHQ communication that stated that assignment to San Juan, Puerto Rico, did not require Spanish-language proficiency. Some Anglo and Hispanic agents in San Juan had attended Spanish-language schools, which enhanced and padded the statistical record, but it did not reflect on the agent's actual ability to function in Spanish on the street. Non-Spanish speakers most often became coordinators, received special jobs at the office and shuffled paperwork, while Spanish-speaking agents worked the streets. San Juan had an unstructured model of more coordinators than investigators.

Years earlier, Mat, as an inspector's aide, wrote up the administrative shortcomings inherent in the lack of Spanish speakers in the San Juan office, but the lead inspector ordered him to tear up his report. Mat followed those orders, but kept a copy for record. He also recalled that, once in DC, the chief inspector questioned him about the low number of write-ups he had submitted as an aide. Mat produced his copies of unapproved write-ups that addressed a whole litany of issues: a SAC's drinking problem, an agent who failed to conduct proper investigations, and the lack of Spanish-speaking agents in San Juan, among others. The chief inspector asked if any other copies of those reports existed. Mat provided him with all of the trusted copies. The chief inspector then praised Mat for his fine work and dedication while he disregarded the unregistered write-ups. Mat knew that FBIHQ was aware of the lack of Spanish speakers in San Juan, yet the problem remained unaddressed.

While managing the Major Case NAVMUR and other ongoing investigations, and besides his regular administrative duties, Mat reintroduced to FBIHQ the continuing problem of the two-year transfer policy and the assignment of non-Spanish speaking agents to San Juan. The San Juan office also had the lowest clerk-to-agent ratio in the FBI. No long-term investigative experience in San Juan existed, as agents arrived on duty, took about six months to get on board, and then would provide a good year of service before becoming "short timers" preparing to transfer out. While some extended their assignment, San Juan had a reputation for being the office with the youngest agents and with no real old-timers. There were only a handful of General Schedule (GS)-13 level agents of the fifty-five assigned agents in San Juan. Field agents have ratings from GS-10 through GS-13, whereas supervisors begin at GS-14.

A few dedicated agents put their hearts into learning Spanish, but the majority maintained a strategy that got them out of an undesirable office, into San Juan for a short period, then into their office of preference (OP). Partnering non-Spanish speakers with Spanish-speaking agents in the field was a necessity, since in San Juan the conduct of proper investigations requires the ability to speak fluent Spanish. Mat had a clear duty to report his office's needs. Of the fifty-five agents assigned to the San Juan Division, some worked in small resident agencies in towns throughout the territory: Roosevelt Roads, St. Thomas, Aguadilla, and Ponce.

Major Case NAVMUR created huge problems. Mat met with the Chief of Police of Puerto Rico (PPR) at the bloody crime scene on the naval base of Sabana Seca. Mat called the director and requested additional Spanish-speaking agents, clerical staff and resources such as automobiles, radios, telephones, typewriters, and increased funding. Mat bypassed the usual chain of command because of the emergency. Back at FBIHQ, Mat had bruised egos by going straight to Director Webster. Mat, keeping an open mind, may have been the first SAC to tell a director he did not know who was responsible. Mat at first had the full support of Director Webster and Associate Director Dr. Lee Colwell, telling them and others that the San Juan office was under siege. However, delays tangled Mat's requests for material items. The FBI responded with retorts such as "proper resources are unavailable," "there are priorities above San Juan," and "we will get back to you." This insufficient action upset and shocked Mat.

Mat asked to handpick veteran agents he wanted assigned to San Juan for ninety days Temporary Duty (TDY). Instead, he got other TDY agents for thirty days at a time. While Mat did not want to create undue hardship for agents by asking FBIHQ to require agents to work TDY in San Juan for ninety days, he knew that agents would accept the ninety-day assignments. Agents train to prioritize "the needs of the bureau," and as faithful patriots, they work 60- to 120-day TDY assignments, yet the bureau was obstinate in approving and limiting TDYs for 30 days.

Mat and the FBI needed to solve the murder of the Navy personnel to prevent follow-up atrocities. The office spent an inordinate amount of time explaining the case to the thirty-day agents and orienting them on suspect terrorist groups, all the while ensuring the visiting agents received lodging, transportation, briefings and preparation before investigations. Orientation presented a unique problem because of local customs, terms, security, the muddled Puerto Rican street address system, and the other unique cultural aspects of Puerto Rico.

The lack of support and concern FBIHQ showed for Mat's requests astonished him. Then, hot on the heels of NAVMUR, came three more Major Cases in San Juan: the National Guard Base Bombing (NAGBOM), a Police Corruption case (POCO), and the attack on a US Navy ship at Vieques Island (CHOWBOAT). A flood of Major Cases such as this was unheard of in FBI history for any regional office, let alone a small office like San Juan. NAGBOM occurred when a terrorist group blew up nine aircraft on the ground on Muniz Air Base. POCO sprung up, alleging forty top police officials took bribes. CHOWBOAT just added to the overload.

No SAC had ever led four FBI Major Case investigations with fifty-five agents assigned to a peripheral office with limited resources—an impossible task. The lack of headquarters support, coupled with the constant turnover, prevented the Puerto Rico office from working properly. Repeated requests for assistance went unanswered. Offsite management commanded from afar rather than allowing the onsite SAC to take control and manage the fast-moving events. Inexperienced agents, agents on TDY, and a support staff lacking the necessary tools may have been of some concern to headquarters, but their actions reflected not. San Juan agents knew they were on their own. Under such siege conditions anywhere in the continental US, the FBI would fly in hundreds of agents overnight to handle the situation, but not for the "orphan child field division" or for "Orphan Mat" drowning in the blood of US military personnel and the US government's loss of millions of dollars of valuable fighter planes. FBIHQ responded with a Band-Aid.

San Juan identified several Puerto Rican terrorist groups that changed names to avoid identification and misdirect their pursuers. Mat sought to identify specific individuals as targets and go after them. Instead, the bureau requested general reports on the Puerto Rican terrorist and nationalist groups, of which there were a multitude. Report writing stifled the ongoing investigations and created delinquencies, which created still more bureau demands. Mat thought it much more important to identify the prime suspects and the people with whom the prime suspects met, those with whom they slept, their habits, their individual weaknesses, their use of drugs, etc.

Instead, the FBI prioritized the required paperwork on the suspect groups so that headquarters could make the big decisions. Mat had worked a rash of bombing cases in Miami with Special Agent (SA) Richard "Dick" Castillo and had hit the street and ferreted out information that pointed to good leads, arrests, and confessions, but the Miami field office had investigative continuity with its agents and plenty of support and resources.

Additional problems surfaced in the day-to-day running of the office. Other SACs had a say in selecting their supervisors. Without Mat's consent, FBIHQ appointed Rodney McHargue the San Juan terrorism supervisor. Mat, threatened with a charge of insubordination, could not replace him; such is the power of a well-placed "Rabbi." Mat had various issues with McHargue, who spoke no Spanish and took sick leave when he suffered from migraine headaches or when bombs went off. According to Mat, McHargue took sick leave, missing supervision of over 150 bombing investigations in a single year, in addition to having anger management issues and the appearance of avoiding responsibility. McHargue transferred to FBIHQ with the help of Buck Revell, who served as McHargue's "Hook." Now, McHargue instructed Mat on terrorism cases.

In spite of FBIHQ's denial of resources to address the Major Cases NAVMUR, NAGBOM, POCO and CHOWBOAT, headquarters still demanded immediate results. When a terrorist group claimed responsibility for toppling a television (TV) tower on top of a remote mountain, the bureau demanded an immediate investigation. Mat did not want his agents removed from other investigative work to trek two days up a mountain to verify that someone had bombed a TV tower. Mat wanted his agents where the terrorists were, rather than where they had been. The bureau would have no part of Mat's strategy, not because the bureau knew of the conditions in San Juan, but because Mat's strategy did not fit into their program. Had the situation been normal in San Juan, Mat would have had no problem telling his agents to take the hike.

Mere administrative matters took 80% of agents' time, with translations, report writing and the arbitrary deadlines set by the Security and Criminal Divisions crippling Mat and the San Juan office. Mat met with the island's bank presidents and explained his dilemma. Except for investigations of bank fraud and embezzlement, the local police accepted responsibility for investigating bank robberies until the major terrorism cases were under control or FBIHQ provided additional resources. Mat just could not allow himself to permit the PPR to handle bank fraud and embezzlement matters. The bank presidents wrote individual appeals supporting Mat to the director. In response, FBIHQ demanded still more reports.

Mat wrote to FBIHQ that the San Juan Division planned to place less emphasis on other cases, as terrorism was now their number-one priority. In the 1970s, the FBI had ten other nationwide priorities listed above terrorism in which they applied resources to fit priorities. The FBI prioritized changes annually, based on political factors, crime trends, media coverage, and so forth, but expected field offices to burn and record "manpower" hours according to its national priorities. FBIHQ tasked field offices with calculating work force hours consistent with FBI priorities to justify continued government funding.

Mat requested that FBIHQ rank terrorism as San Juan's number-one priority. This request did not sit well with management. The bureau chose not to confront, discuss, debate, question, or even answer Mat, which was FBIHQ's way of showing a SAC who was in charge. Mat expected a response, as his office needed resources to handle investigative leads that required attention, funds, and support. During follow-up calls, San Juan's well-documented requests came up missing at FBIHQ, leaving San Juan to twist in the wind.

Assistant Director Colwell told Mat that San Juan would receive the computers he had requested in about eight years, after FBIHQ handled the request from the Springfield, Illinois Division. But San Juan needed those computers *pronto.* In frustration, Mat met with the admiral at Roosevelt Roads Naval Base, who had been a congressional liaison in DC. The machine-gun murders of his personnel by terrorists caused the admiral much anger and concern. Mat and the admiral both shared a responsibility to stop the attacks and punish the perpetrators for killing two service members and wounding ten others, which included four women. Neither relished participating in another Purple Heart Ceremony. Mat advised the admiral of his resource problems. The admiral located surplus state-of-the-art Central Intelligence Agency (CIA) computers—the kind of technology that FBIHQ reported would not be available to San Juan for another eight years. The admiral had the computers flown in and set up within days.

Mat then requested personnel to input case data from the four Major Cases. Colwell stated that such resources were unavailable. Mat learned from a friend that Colwell had said maliciously, "Let's see him man those computers now that he has got them." With a few computer-savvy agents and support personnel in the San Juan office, local agents rose to the challenge and input the case data. Agents pulled double and triple duty, answered phones with one hand and input data on the computers with the other, while still attending to other assignments. It was not a very efficient or effective process. Agents had a hard time keeping up with the information flowing in so quickly. With the intensity of the terrorist bombings escalating, over 150 that year, the San Juan Division was forever playing catch-up. However, the office did not lack *esprit de corps.* Mat often shed a tear of pride over his personnel's hard work. It was remarkable what they accomplished with so little.

When the United States Ship (USS) Pensacola made a port call in San Juan, despite Mat's warnings, terrorists machine-gunned four Navy crew members on the street, killing one and injuring three. Mat was first on the scene. The PPR trampled all over the unprotected crime scene, but in spite of police, FBI agents found enough evidence to identify the multiple weapons used. The admiral's computer contribution and the data input proved invaluable. San Juan agents identified a known terrorist as responsible for the shootings.

The POCO investigation into the PPR, an organization composed of 11,000 police officers across the island, took a toll on the office in a much different manner than a mere lack of personnel and resources. The Puerto Rican police represented a flourishing organized criminal enterprise that made the Mafia look like kindergarteners. It was common knowledge that the PPR executed "contract" killings at $7,000 a hit, which included thirty days of surveillance beforehand. Part of the package deal involved bribing the local judges so there would be no complications.

In response to the FBI investigation, the PPR launched a counterattack of threats and intimidation against the FBI office and against Mat. Mat had to send his sons back to the mainland out of concern for their safety. The police set up cameras outside Mat's home and placed him under surveillance. Mat had his home swept for suspected wiretaps. Because of the threats by the Fuerzas Armadas de Liberación Nacional (FALN) terrorist organization and the island's police, Mat often toted a sawed-off shotgun and parked his car inside the governor's courtyard so it could not be bombed. The nuns across the street at the convent thought Mat carried a guitar in his guitar case. Since he needed every agent he could get, Mat asked the director to remove his personal bodyguards and assign them to the ongoing investigations.

Because of Major Case POCO, the PPR wanted Mat out of Puerto Rico, dead or alive. Meanwhile, Mat received information that San Juan field office employee Yvonne Shaffer had provided FBI information to unauthorized individuals. An uncomfortable SA Alex Nogueiras told Mat that he had something terrible to report. Mat called in his ASAC and secretary to hear Alex, who had just received the information from an informant that Mat's girlfriend, Yvonne, had passed information to the Socialist Party. Mat reported the tip to FBIHQ and told Alex to pursue the source. Assistant FBI Director Colwell called Mat and told him that Director Webster wanted him to stop dating Yvonne.

Mat obeyed Webster's orders. Webster stated in a later deposition that, while he had seen documents to that effect, he did not make such a request.

Office of Professional Responsibility (OPR) Chief David Flanders informed Mat that someone from FBIHQ would visit San Juan to handle the investigation of the allegation against Yvonne and promised to keep it all "in house." In April of 1981, the San Juan field office learned from a PPR informant that the PPR had instructed the informant to make the allegation in retaliation for the FBI's investigation of the Police of Puerto Rico. Mat passed this information without hesitation to FBIHQ.

Yvonne Shaffer did not want to remain on the island and cause any additional problems for Mat. When a position opened in the Legal Attaché Office in Mexico City, she requested transfer and appeared to be the selectee. The bureau summoned her to Washington under the pretext of an interview for that position; instead, they hooked her up to a polygraph machine and interrogated her for four weeks. FBIHQ denied her access to an attorney and subjected her to interrogation techniques more excessive than any they would dare to inflict on a suspect. Yvonne resigned from the FBI and Mat, without the consent of Director Webster, dated her until they married on July 31, 1981. After that, inspectors brought hell down on Mat and the San Juan office.

Prior to the San Juan inspection of December 1981, Mat knew he had problems; the bureau refused to send the resources he had requested for the Major Cases. The director himself visited San Juan for two days. Mat managed to speak to him, and, between the director's tennis games and sightseeing, he had altogether about three hours to explain the San Juan field office's efforts to battle the terrorists: putting them on the defensive, creating difficulty in placing more bombs, and catching them in the act. San Juan proved a safe enough place for the director to visit, but Webster left a telling sign for Mat. The stone-faced director refused to comment on the office's actions, provided no feedback and seemed disinterested. Mat had also given a presentation at the annual SAC conference where he sensed some at FBIHQ were envious of the major investigative cases in San Juan.

During the lead-up to the San Juan field office inspection, resources continued to dwindle. The inspection staff audits field offices every two years to identify misappropriations and compliance issues in investigative programs. Investigators also identify deficiencies. Terry Dinan headed the inspection. Dinan told Mat that they had planned no reviews of POCO and the other Major Cases since FBIHQ supervised and monitored those cases; however, the plan was to inspect "everything else." Mat, who had served on the inspection staff and participated in over twenty-five inspections, told Dinan that "everything else" amounted to less than 20% of their workload, as POCO and other Major Case bombings absorbed over three-quarters of the San Juan Field Office's resources. Mat was also puzzled since the inspection manual of rules and regulations states that the inspection staff looks into "all matters." Mat told the inspectors up front, "This is a setup. There is a contract on my office, and you plan on taking me out."

The pressure of events had spread the San Juan Division so thin that the inspectors did not have to look far to find problems. The Major Cases required the office to spend minimal time on several cases with set deadlines, such as applicant cases and civil rights matters. The inspectors—without surprise—found numerous weaknesses. Mat advised his field supervisors of his suspicions of a setup and instructed them to keep their eyes and ears open. One San Juan agent heard a scheming inspector's aide, John Guido, bragging in the bullpen, "We are going to nail these turkeys' hides to the wall." Mat confronted Guido and Dinan and sought to correct matters, but his efforts did no good.

All issues that were "written up" were unsubstantial hits. The inspectors found numerous clerical issues, such as missed serialized and chronologically filed mail. They found a few cases still open when a supervisor had marked the case for closure. The inspectors registered the administrative problems in San Juan as "serious," although serious violations meant instances of wrongful arrests, money or drugs lost, loss of controlled property, or misspent appropriations. San Juan had none of these. The inspection continued to freewheel downhill, and none of the investigators hid or denied they had a predetermined agenda. The inspection reported the deficiencies and "nailed to the wall" was Mat's hide, just as the frenzied John Guido promised.

Several months after the December inspection, Assistant Director Colwell called Mat to advise him of his demotion and transfer to Los Angeles but ordered him to report to Washington on his way to LA. Mat could recall no SAC, GS-16 (Senior Executive Service) who had ever received a demotion to Senior Administrative Assistant Special Agent in Charge. Colwell told Mat that this transfer was not a demotion. In large offices such as New York, Chicago, San Francisco, Los Angeles, and Miami, Senior Administrative ASACs often acted as the number-two man with other ASACs serving under them. Headquarters justified Mat's transfer to Los Angeles because of his supposed "administrative weaknesses," and there in Los Angeles, the SAC, Richard T. Bretzing, would help recondition Mat and remedy his weaknesses. After speaking with Bretzing, however, Mat did not believe that the intention was to help him or resurrect his career since the inspectors reported him as both ineffective and inefficient.

No welcome wagon showed up on Mat's first day as Bretzing's Senior ASAC. Mat told Bretzing that he already knew most LA field office employees from his previous assignment there; he felt he could be of great assistance, and his Spanish-speaking abilities would help the office. He knew about the upcoming 1984 Olympic Games. Mat had overseen the successful Pan American Games held in San Juan with no security issues. Bretzing, with a scowling expression, pointed to Mat's office and told him, "You belong behind that desk over there." He added that he understood that Mat was in LA as a special token representative of Hispanics. These comments incensed Mat, as both a special agent of the FBI and as a Mexican-American. Mat told Bretzing that, when he arrived in San Juan, he had noticed agents polarized and that he wanted such behavior stopped; his attitude would be no different in LA. He would not tolerate racism.

Bretzing informed him that he did not know why the bureau had sent Mat to LA. He had not asked for Mat. Bretzing chastised Mat, stating that he did not know and did not care to learn the nature of

Mat's problems. Observing the repeated phone calls between Bretzing and the director, Mat opined that neither of them preached temperance and that they planned to bushwhack him. Mat knew that the Administrative ASAC had responsibility for all resources, allocation of workers, personnel matters, case oversight and the expenditure of money. But Bretzing enlightened Mat as to his authority regarding such matters, telling Mat, "I am the agent in charge here and you are not."

Bretzing placed Mat "in charge" of the new FBI garage under construction to house bureau cars (Bucars), evidence, electronic technicians, and equipment, although the General Services Administration (GSA) had direct responsibility for the construction management, and Mat had no effective control over construction. Bretzing then complained about the garage's non-completion and consequent construction delays. A delay in the contract for the Motorola radios and construction of the required radio towers somehow became Mat's fault. John Hall, a former FBIHQ supervisor, had direct responsibility for the Motorola project, yet Bretzing pulled him off to work on the Olympic Games.

Within two months, Bretzing told Mat he was failing to meet expectations, although he identified no particular issue or incident to justify this. From the start, Bretzing omitted Mat from all of the strategy sessions, management meetings and the working lunches that Bretzing held with the other ASACs. Senior subordinates worked cases around Mat without his knowledge. Mat heard of the John DeLorean case through other agents. Mat saw Bretzing in his office with other agents, then noticed $6 million in cash on the table delivered by the San Francisco Special Weapons and Tactics (SWAT) team. Bretzing told Mat to count the money and go to the scene of the investigation, although Bretzing refused to brief Mat on the details. When Mat asked questions about the assignment, Bretzing told him that the other agents would fill in the details.

Bretzing excluded Mat from the 1984 Olympics and told Mat to stay out, despite his experience with the Pan American games in San Juan and his good contacts with the LAPD. On another occasion, Bretzing filed a formal report criticizing Mat for appearing without a suit and tie at a kidnapping payoff stakeout in West Covina. Meanwhile, ASAC Jim Nelson also showed up at an investigation without a suit, and, although Bretzing knew this, he did not write up Nelson. On another occasion, an undercover agent from another office later informed Mat that LA had deployed over one hundred agents to Palm Springs, California, to assist in an investigation. Neither Bretzing nor any other field office manager ever informed Mat, the person assigned responsibility for personnel of ongoing investigations.

Bretzing left the division without informing Mat, although, in his position, the chain of command required such notice. Mat learned from the SAC's secretary or the other ASACs that some of Bretzing's absences involved attendance at various Mormon Church events. Bretzing delegated responsibility to his other ASACs, but not to Mat. While Bretzing was on annual leave, Mat heard over the radio that a gunman had seized the Spanish Consulate and had taken hostages. The FBI had jurisdiction. He called the office and found Bretzing away on vacation in South Carolina. Mat telephoned Bretzing to take the lead, but Bretzing put Mat's subordinate, ASAC Christensen, a fellow Mormon, in charge. Mat, as the number-two man, did not agree but had to concede. Bretzing had promoted Christensen from supervisor to Los Angeles ASAC.

SA Rudy Valadez arrived on the scene at the consulate and set up a command post for negotiations while the FBI SWAT team and Christensen remained blocks away. No agents protected or contained the consulate's exits and entrances, and Rudy encountered a United Parcel Service (UPS) employee attempting to deliver a package at the front entrance. Rudy initiated hostage negotiations, established rapport with the hostage-taker, and obtained a promise from him that he would surrender his weapon and the hostages if certain reasonable arrangements took place within the next two hours.

When ASAC Christensen and an LAPD commander arrived, the commander requested a briefing. Christensen ordered Rudy to do so and the two left the room. While Rudy briefed the commander, the waiting LAPD SWAT and negotiating team, on another floor of the building, disconnected the consulate telephone without consultation with the FBI, took command of the negotiations and delayed the resolution that Rudy had advanced. This interference infuriated Rudy and Mat. Christensen received no admonishment while both Bretzing and Christensen danced around FBIHQ's subsequent inquiry.

The occupational nurse assigned to the Los Angeles office informed Mat that some serious problems existed; agents were 'walking wounded' on duty, which represented an alarming occupational hazard. She began by describing Richard W. Miller, a Mormon agent who had one of the worst reputations as an agent in the Los Angeles office, as being a fool for neglecting his duties and for his repeated failings. She complained about his obesity and wondered why management refused to make an issue about his total disregard for his responsibilities.

Mat reviewed Miller's personnel file and found his work substandard. Miller sold Amway products from the trunk of a bureau car, once left his office keys dangling in the lock of an FBI satellite office, attempted to convert prisoners to Mormonism while on the job, was in debt, and acted like a fool at work. Mat called Miller into his office and told him he had two choices: either face insubordination charges if he could not get in gear with his cases and lose some weight, or Mat would be happy to assist him in petitioning for medical disability retirement.

Bretzing told Mat, despite Mat's objections, to leave Miller alone and let ASAC Christensen handle it. Mat filed several reports about Miller, but both the bureau and Bretzing buried Mat's reports and recommendations. Bretzing protected Miller, provided him with counseling based on Mormon religious concepts, and kept Miller on the FBI payroll. Dr. David Soskis, an FBI contract employee, told Mat not to speak with Miller about his issues.

Not long afterwards, with Mat in El Paso, the verdict disgraced the FBI when a jury found Miller guilty of espionage for providing secret information to a Soviet Russian Secret Police (KGB) agent. Miller was the very first FBI agent ever charged as a traitor to his country. Miller's attorney subpoenaed both agent John Hunt and Mat to testify that Mat had attempted to fire Miller before he became a spy, and therefore the FBI was aware that Miller had serious problems. Mat sought legal counsel from the FBI prior to his testimony. They told him to rely on the guidance of the federal judge and Robert Bonner, the US Attorney. Mat was not in court to help Miller but to tell the truth.

Mat wanted Miller in jail because he was both an embarrassment to the FBI and a traitor. Mat testified as to what he saw in Miller's personnel file, the conversations he had with Miller, the recommendations he had made, the reports he had written, the conversations regarding Miller between Mat and Bretzing, and the instructions Mat received from Bretzing. Bretzing took the stand, testifying that Mat never spoke to him about Miller, nor did Mat ever provide him with any reports. Bretzing accused Mat of perjury. Although Miller went to prison, Bretzing initiated a criminal investigation into Mat's testimony, unbeknownst to Mat.

Bretzing kept copious notes on Mat, documenting his activities and hoping he could get rid of him. Bretzing considered Mat's transfer to LA to be a personal affront by FBIHQ. FBIHQ did not give Bretzing that prerogative, which made it uncomfortable for Bretzing to have a number-two man he did not want. Bretzing told Mat that he intended to give him a bad performance appraisal and that he should just accept a demotion. Mat felt the coercion to accept a lesser position to receive a decent evaluation.

Bretzing helped Mat draft a communication in which Mat volunteered to step down from his position. The bureau told Mat to write another letter, since Bretzing could not transfer him within the Los Angeles office. Bretzing told Mat he would transfer Mat to the Legal Attaché (Legat) Mexico position. FBIHQ again told Bretzing he did not have the authority. Bretzing told Mat that if he asked for a demotion and transfer in writing, then he would give him an overall successful rating. Mat agreed, so Bretzing gave him the fully successful rating. But then Mat spoke with Rudy Valadez, who convinced Mat to back out of the deal. Mat rescinded his verbal request for demotion. Furious, Bretzing snarled, "You have snookered me as I have never been snookered before."

Bretzing then flew to FBIHQ and, upon his return, called Mat into his office to inform him of his transfer to Christensen's criminal ASAC assignment and office, with Christensen to the administrative ASAC position with FBIHQ concurrence. Bretzing then announced to the twenty-six supervisors that Mat had accepted the criminal ASAC position. This was a calculated humiliation to Mat and to his secretary, Aileen Ikegami. Aileen did not want to lose any money or grade level, so retention of her pay grade forced Aileen to follow Mat, as no other ASAC held Mat's rank. Now Christensen, the number-two man in the office, occupied a lower pay grade than Mat.

Later, John Otto, the FBI's number-two man, told Mat of pending orders to transfer him to El Paso as an ASAC, but not as a punitive action or in retaliation of his EEO complaints. Mat left Bretzing's wrath and retaliation with a successful performance appraisal that coincided with his own appraisal of Bretzing's management style in EEO complaints. Mat proceeded to El Paso while Miller the spy continued working the streets of LA under the supervision of Bretzing.

2

Enforcement by the "Mattress Police"

Mat Perez filed separate EEO complaints against Richard Bretzing, Special Agent in Charge of the Los Angeles Field office of the FBI, and against FBI Director Webster. In each of his complaints, the FBI EEO office saw nothing, the DOJ EEO office heard nothing, and the EEOC refused to give it any thought. That negligence left Mat with a bad taste in his mouth and the odor of corruption. Although beaten, Mat stood up for the principles of his organization. He loved the credo of the FBI: Fidelity, Bravery, and Integrity. He now saw that others had manipulated the concept of fidelity away from its true significance to support a misappropriated individual monopoly of power. Bravery had slipped away, and integrity often faltered in a bureaucratic morass.

Mat now recognized all of this as the Equal Employment Opportunity Commission dismissed away his complaints one by one. The EEOC is an agency created to curtail abuses against designated groups that receive legal protection. The EEOC provides an avenue in which to seek redress for perceived abuses. The government wrote into law protections for complainants, those supporting the complainants, and those counselors investigating the facts of the alleged discrimination. When Bretzing and Webster limited Mat's opportunities and tried to render him impotent, the government had in place measures to ensure fairness toward the members of protected groups. America believed that people—no matter their race, ethnicity, or family background—could prove themselves capable, given sufficient opportunity. However, the EEOC, often lampooned as the "Mattress Police," in effect accomplished nothing and instead allowed the bureau to act with impunity.

The EEOC "Mattress Police," an organization funded by the US Government, assures American workers of their right to fairness in the workplace. When someone tears off the mattress tag that states, "Do not remove under penalty of law," no one ever shows up. The corollary is that, when someone in management discriminates against a subordinate, the EEOC sends a person corralled by a myriad of restrictions to conduct an inquiry or investigation. When EEO counselors trust and follow their EEO training and adhere to the letter of the law, it can often end their careers or damage them, as witnessed by those who assisted in Mat's EEO filings. Melvin Jeter, head of the EEO office at FBIHQ, derailed the process with his arbitrary decisions to curtail investigative interviews, and the EEO's effectiveness was bankrupt.

The ineptitude of the EEOC and the arrogance, belligerence, and underhandedness of FBI management forced Mat to file a civil case against the FBI in the federal court of El Paso. Mat's lawsuit raised questions of how an agency that shines in so many areas can falter in such an important area of responsibility. The FBI, the premier law enforcement agency in the United States, broke the law. EEO complaints have action deadlines requiring results within 180 days, but, in 1988, Mat's complaints, after years of delay, came to fruition, not through the EEO process established by law but through federal courts. Overall, Mat filed ten EEO complaints, one after another, between 1984 and 1986, each alleging discrimination based on national origin and religion, and blatant retaliation against Mat. One of his counselors resigned from the FBI because of reprisals. The EEOC failed in its responsibility to both recognize and remedy discrimination against Mat. The EEOC failed to protect Mat's witnesses from retaliation and contaminated the minds of counselors assigned to carry out EEO duties.

Arnie Gerardo, Gilbert Mireles, and Leo Gonzales served as EEO counselors for Mat's complaints. Rudy Valadez, German Zuniga and several other FBI agents assisted Mat with the lawsuit. Non-Hispanics who supported Mat's lawsuit also felt the wrath of retaliation from the bureau, as concern for justice was absent from FBI management. Arnie Gerardo, a well-educated professional who held two master's degrees and was working on his PhD, and Gil Mireles, with a list of accomplishments and honors, saw their careers destroyed because they met with Mat and attempted to follow EEO procedure. While a few Anglos helped Hispanics, the EEOC allowed discrimination to continue, never bothering to acknowledge the credibility of the personnel involved or recognizing their success stories as struggling immigrants of a protected class of national origin who now faced abuse by the agency charged with enforcing those laws.

One illustrative story is that of Arnie Gerardo. His father, Juan Gerardo, worked the fields in the US but returned to Sinaloa, Mexico, during the Great Depression. There his wife, Sara Rojas-Gerardo, gave birth to Arnie. The family, with five small children in tow, returned to the US where Juan took a job in a shutter factory. Juan held down two jobs that provided the two-bedroom, one-bath home that put a roof over the family's head, put food on the table and clothes on their backs. Juan knew hard work was his avenue to make it in life. During the family's first two Christmases in the United States, they celebrated with donated gifts, thanks to one of their neighbors who provided information about the Gerardo family to the Salvation Army.

Juan first worked as a custodian, then received a promotion and became a carpenter for a school, and he picked up side jobs from a local contractor who admired his skillful work. Sara did not have money to spend on luxuries; the only wine they drank was at church. She respected her husband's work ethic and accomplishments but pushed all of her children to concentrate on education. Her work, volunteerism, faith, and prayers paid off, and she was proud when Arnie graduated from college—the first member of his family to do so. Bob Sorenson, his baseball coach, helped Arnie win a scholarship. Sports helped Arnie to both stay out of trouble and make friends, but he pursued his education at the determined insistence of his mother. That education, his family values, a strong work ethic, and a commitment to faith helped Arnie get into the FBI.

Arnie handled several ancillary duties at the FBI Academy in Quantico, Virginia. He received a call one evening from Mat, who sought counseling on a possible Equal Employment Opportunity complaint. Arnie taught classes on EEO and trained counselors. Arnie once met Mat in LA but did not know him well. Mat had just received a fully successful rating but had also received orders downgrading him to a GS-15 position. Arnie listened as Mat, distraught, frustrated and confused, talked for hours. Mat wanted to send the supporting documentation even before Arnie agreed to become his counselor; Arnie warned Mat that if he became Mat's counselor he would have to terminate that role if Mat pursued the issue through court. Mat agreed and sent the documents.

Arnie received the disorganized assortment of documents, notes, file copies, and typewritten evidence. He reviewed the documents on his own time and took two weeks to organize the complaint. Arnie also ran it past a friend at Quantico; both concurred that the issues justified a complaint. Arnie then returned the complaint form to Mat with his name as Mat's counselor. Arnie had trust in regulations, believed in what he taught, and had faith that right would prevail. He did not know that someone had a detour in store for him and that volunteering to serve as an EEO counselor would soon short-circuit his rising career.

Another counselor involved in Mat's complaint was Gilbert Mireles, one of the eight children of Eloy and Eliser Mireles. Gilbert was a San Antonio agent who thought his FBI career was well on track. Gilbert's parents had a sixth-grade education, worked wagon trains herding cattle, and raised goats. They met about twenty miles beyond Hondo, New Mexico, in what is now the ghost town of Arabela. Eloy, as an adopted son, understood that he had to prove his worth to his adoptive family and to everyone else as well. This he did through hard work. Eloy worked from sunrise to sundown as a foreman at George Hibbard's feedlot. Hibbard knew that some locals treated Hispanics as second-class citizens, but he advised those ranchers that they had better treat his man Eloy right.

Eloy had privileges other Hispanics did not. Known as a horseman and a crack shot who also knew how to handle a lasso, Eloy set out on special weekends to participate in rodeos, more often than not taking home first prize and winning the pot. That money went to Eliser to buy food and pay bills. Two fifty-pound bags of beans, a sack of potatoes, a couple dozen eggs and a bag of flour were the weekly staples for their family of ten. On rare occasions, the family shared the luxury of eating a watermelon, which they devoured down to the rind. Toward Gil's junior year in high school, Hibbard gave Eloy a raise, and so they could afford what they called "round steak," a three-pound hunk of bologna to add to the *frijoles.* At Christmas time the children found the biggest tumbleweed they could and painted it green, then decorated it to serve as their Christmas tree. Under the tumbleweed lay wrapped gifts—the expected new pair of socks or underwear.

With Eloy obligated to spend all day at work, Eliser awoke first to prepare breakfast. Once the kids were off to school, she would work the fields all day, pausing only when the children returned from school, to prepare dinner and help them with homework. She was always the last to bed at night. The Mireles family often went without meat for reasons other than their lack of money. All of the kids in the neighborhood knew that Eliser could never refuse them a plate of food. Every now and then, Eloy brought a horse back to the neighborhood and gave all the kids horseback rides while Eliser provided snacks.

Gil served as an altar boy at Immaculate Conception Catholic Church from age five until he was twenty-three. Father Flannigan, the parish priest, made Gil the church accountant, since he had great faith and trust in Gil's honesty. The community called Gil *El Padrecito* (the little priest), and most thought that he would one day become a priest himself. When Gil and his brothers and sisters could sit in a saddle or hold a pitchfork, they helped contribute to the family. Hibbard noticed how Eloy's entire family pitched in with everything from routine duties to rounding up cattle during blizzards. Hibbard knew Gil was a good student, so Hibbard set aside a portion of Eloy's pay so Gil could attend college. Gilbert's world had a twenty-mile radius; a big adventure was when his high school team played a game two hundred miles away.

As the first and only member of his family to graduate from college, Gil wanted to give up, but he remembered the words of his father: "Do things right the first time so you don't have to do it again." Once attending college, he knew he just could not disappoint his family. His father never told Gil, but he told everyone else his proudest day was the day of Gil's college graduation. When other agents in the Albuquerque office told Gil that he would never qualify to become an agent, the persistence and support of FBI Agent Nichols helped make him into an agent. Gil's parents showed no outward emotion when Gil told them that the FBI had offered him a job as an agent. The FBI was an organization that fell beyond their elementary school education and twenty-mile compass; they had not a clue what the FBI did, and did not know the location of Virginia, where Gil would spend three months at the FBI Academy.

Gil earned a solid reputation, commendations and many honors; he did not seek honors as an EEO counselor. Trained in EEO, FBIHQ ordered him to travel to El Paso. There he met Mat Perez, an agent he did not know. Mat opened their first meeting by warning Gil of being an EEO counselor, "I am sorry about what is going to happen to your career; you are safe no more." Gil's association with Mat jolted Gil's career and reputation, and that is why he joined the class action lawsuit at its inception.

Mat's supporters in LA, among them Rudolph "Rudy" Valadez and Paul Magallanes, also fell from grace with the FBI. Rudy, one of three children, was a George Raft (the actor) look-alike, born in 1942 to migrant farm workers Adolph and Catalina "Katy" Valadez in Michigan. Rudy's birth certificate states his color is "Mexican." The Valadez home, with its one room, had a kitchen in the corner with a table, two chairs, and a pot-bellied wood stove—the sink was just outside the door, the outhouse some twenty feet away. Farms provided their food, hope their spiritual growth, and dreams their character. Katy's iron hand and whatever she could grasp with it instilled in Rudy, his sister Mary Ann and brother Ray the values, honor, and respect they carried with them into their adult lives, a strict code that forbid all misbehavior. Rudy's childhood environment offered him three choices in life: crime, the priesthood, or law enforcement. His mother vetoed the first option, girls the second, but the movies paved the way to an FBI career.

At a crime scene in Rudy's neighborhood in which a man had murdered his wife, Rudy saw the blood on the couch and a sandwich with one bite taken from it on a plate on an end table. He could forget the blood, but never forgot that sandwich, as his life to that point comprised earning and collecting pennies to buy food. From the window of his house, little Rudy witnessed a young car thief who stumbled and fell into his yard; as the boy struggled to rise, a pursuing police officer shot him in the back. He told the story in the back seat of a police car as the police, unaffected by the injustice he had witnessed, drove him around the neighborhood for several hours before returning him to his home with suggestions. Rudy picked potatoes, sold comic books, returned soda bottles, shined shoes, and did whatever other odd jobs came along to contribute to his family's finances. He was the first in his family to receive a college education and, with his diploma in hand, he joined the FBI, first as a support employee, then as an agent. SAC Bretzing considered Rudy's association with Mat to be a personal affront, as Bretzing demanded personal loyalty even while he launched attacks with disregard toward all who supported Mat.

One Hispanic Supervisory Special Agent (SSA) known as Paco assisted Mat with the lawsuit from FBIHQ. Paco was the fourth of eight children. His mother and father met on the southern side of Chicago, close to the Inland Steel Mill on Lake Michigan, where his father's work as a laborer provided the family income. Paco's father came to the US illegally from Michoacán, a Mexican state where the Catholic Church controlled education yet produced men like Miguel Hidalgo y Costilla, who led the Mexican War of Independence. With a third-grade education, Paco's father worked sixteen-hour double shifts at the mill. The family's two-bedroom, one-bath apartment had no hot water, no air conditioning and no heater but the gas furnace in the living room. His parents shared one bedroom, their eight children the other.

Paco's father walked to work in snowstorms, determined to get there while the children at home played, leaving their handprints on the half-inch of frost that formed different silhouettes on the inside of the windows. Dad's paycheck covered the rent, oil for the furnace, and a sack of potatoes to boot. Vacations were a dream, as Paco's extended family all lived in Mexico. When the steel mill went out on strike, Paco's father joined colleagues who traveled north to the farms of Michigan as migrant workers. Paco's father used a false name at work. When he first came to America, he and a friend applied for jobs together. The friend identified the two as brothers to their prospective boss and provided his surname. Following this cue, Paco's father assumed his friend's surname. Once Paco's father became a US citizen, he reverted to his true name, but Paco and the rest of the family kept the family name they used growing up.

Paco's maternal ancestors came from Eastern Europe. Some have the ability to learn languages fast and in less than two years; Paco's mother spoke more fluent Spanish than some Mexicans. His mother took on odd jobs to pay the bills, but she loved caring for her children. Her intelligence and language skills often turned into pro bono work in which she argued work or business issues for her immigrant neighbors. Their rough neighborhood attracted troublemakers and none for miles around had a college degree, so she restricted her children to carefully chosen friends. Discipline first came with a sharp look, followed by a belt or wooden spoon. The children knew about any shortcomings by just a look from their parents. None of the children ever got into much trouble. Their parents served as their role models.

Paco's teachers never served as role models, as the teachers gave the Anglo kids all of the encouragement and attention. The apartment in which they lived, always either too cold or too hot, did not encourage studies; yet, their choices were work or education. Paco first worked at a bowling alley setting pins. He came home proud, showing off the two dollars in cash he had earned for a week's work. His dad told him he must give half of his pay to his mother. This angered and confused him, but after he gave his mother a dollar, he felt overcome by a tremendous feeling of satisfaction. He had become a man, contributing to his family. Paco continued to contribute to his family with each of the other jobs he worked.

After graduation from high school, jobs were still hard to find, even with a diploma. Somehow, he ended up working at the mill with his father, riding in the back of a pickup truck with a clear view of the real world. He saw grown men with their dirty, empty faces and filthy clothing drenched in sweat. He knew all about his father's work ethic but now realized the harsh truth behind those sixteen-hour days. He then understood the importance of education and after work went straight to the library. His parents expressed joy when he completed college, the first in his family to do so; when he became an FBI agent, they were ecstatic. Now here he was, joining the plaintiffs against the FBI. By assisting the attorneys and the statistician in preparing for the trial, he exposed his status as a class member to agents who now shunned him. He thought he had encountered harsh conditions growing up, but now he faced even harsher conditions within the hallowed halls of FBIHQ.

Bitterness manifested in field offices. German Zuniga, a street agent, is the eighth child of Ernesto and Beatrice Zuniga, a couple who emigrated from Mexico to Kansas City, and he did not testify at the trial. German learned from his father that, on their way north, they had first stopped in Texas and encountered so much discrimination that it disgusted him. Discrimination was much like the tasteless and often cold spaghetti served at every meal when he had worked for the railroad. Ernesto, the disciplinarian of the family, moved on to Kansas City, where he found a one-bath home for $2,000 in an area populated by other Mexican immigrants. No crime existed in this ghetto, as the community's elders handled disciplinary issues by reporting offensive activities to parents for individual parental remedy.

The immigrant parents loved that America's opportunities ensured an education for their children. *Posadas, fiestas, conjuntos, quinceañeras, bodas,* and *pan con leche,* all served absent discrimination, made for a happy life. In his senior year of college, with the military not even on his radar screen, the US Army drafted German—the only pre-med student drafted despite a 2-S exemption. In desperation, he took every test the Marine Corps gave and passed them all, even the pilot's exam. The Marines gave him a deferment to complete his degree and then shipped him to South Vietnam, not as a fighter pilot, but as a chopper pilot.

After the Vietnam War, German became a police officer and worked for Kansas City Police Department (KCPD) Chief Clarence Kelly. The KCPD received widespread recognition as one of the top law enforcement organizations in the nation when Chief Kelly became director of the FBI. As one of twenty KCPD officers with a college degree, German soon joined Kelly at the FBI. Later under Webster, after experiencing discriminatory treatment by law enforcement for the first time in his life, much like his father vowed never to eat cold spaghetti again, German vowed to address the discrimination he and others had suffered by joining in the class action lawsuit. In return, he faced ostracism from his coworkers.

Hispanic agents with similar upbringings permeated the FBI. Noticeable in many of the histories of the Hispanic agents and their families was the assistance of remarkable individual Anglo mentors. Compassionate and empathic, these Anglo mentors often helped Hispanics rise to the ultimate level of professionalism, preferring not to leave that responsibility to a government agency. Benevolent individual Anglo mentors provided proof that they loved their country and its people.

The EEOC and the DOJ paid no attention to the EEO complaints that came from the bureau. The chief of the FBI's EEO program treated complaints like the pageantry of a bullfight without the music, and much like the picador who rides into the ring on a blinkered horse to poke at and weaken the fierce bull. The EEO chief first sent his counselors and investigators in with a predetermined agenda that weakened the complaints; this readied them for the matador, who waved his red muleta in front of the complainants to confuse them further before any sacrificial kill skewered any hope of career advancement.

Mat's sacrificial kill came in the City of Angels. In October of 1983, Mat sought Arnie as his EEO Counselor while Arnie was at Quantico. Mat did not file in LA with the belief that this would delay the counterattack from the already snookered Bretzing. Still it seemed Bretzing smothered Mat. The unfurling revelations about the bureau's biggest embarrassment, the bumbling Soviet spy Richard W. Miller, created additional havoc for Mat, even though, as the ASAC in LA, Mat sought to fire Miller from the FBI long before he spied for the Russians.

With Bretzing's allegations that Mat had perjured himself and with Mat's transfer to El Paso, OPR Investigator Gary Hart instructed Mat to meet him in DC following an in-service training in Sterling, Virginia. The DOJ had already declined any criminal investigation concerning the charges of perjury against Mat. However, Hart and Mat could not meet because a winter snowstorm closed FBIHQ and because Mat fell ill. Mat called Hart and left a message saying that he would not make it to the interview and was instead returning to El Paso. Hart became incensed, assuming that Mat had lied to him. Hart then retaliated and, in violation of the law, obtained a grand jury subpoena in an administrative disciplinary matter. Hart claimed that Mat had perjured himself and was insubordinate when he claimed he could not reach Hart by telephone and did not appear for the interview. Mat did not learn that the FBI had initiated this administrative inquiry based on alleged criminal "perjury" and insubordination charges against him until four and a half years later, when he reviewed the court's discovery documents for the civil suit.

The FBI violated the law in obtaining a grand jury subpoena for an administrative inquiry, and the legal division chose not to initiate an inquiry into this violation. Although the Department of Justice had exonerated Mat of the charge, the FBI continued its witch-hunt, hoping Mat had violated FBI regulations. The real mystery was why the FBI initiated an administrative inquiry into Mat's actions instead of investigating Bretzing, the man who had counseled and protected Miller, the spy. For some strange reason Bretzing's actions appeared inconsequential to the investigative brass. Although Bretzing solicited a confession from Miller after FBIHQ had the goods on him, Bretzing had protected Miller prior to FBIHQ entering onto the scene.

Bretzing's protection of and favoritism toward white Mormon males in Los Angeles appeared obvious to Mat and several others who experienced this disparity. With Mat isolated from Bretzing's front office, several disgruntled agents decided it was time to question the leadership of the LA Division. Besides Rudy Valadez, other Hispanic agents in Los Angeles also filed EEO complaints against Bretzing. Paul Magallanes had his weapon confiscated, and Bretzing placed him on limited duty because he reported minor back pain—pain that two FBI doctors and his personal physician confirmed would not interfere with his work.

In September 1986, an FBIHQ polygraph examiner visited Los Angeles in search of a Spanish speaker interested in a position as a polygraph operator. This candidate would have to be willing to transfer to Miami or San Juan. Six Hispanic agents in LA applied. However, the job went to an Anglo Mormon. The head of FBIHQ polygraph unit, Jonny Wendt, and SAC Bretzing, both Mormon, had a say in the decision. Bretzing awarded the polygraph operator position for a Spanish-speaking agent that entailed a transfer to the East Coast to Chris Spilsbury, but kept him in LA instead of transferring him.

When Special Agent John Hoos made a statement supporting Mat's EEO complaint, Bretzing, in retaliation, placed John on a tickler file—a file used to remind Bretzing he had unfinished business with Hoos. One year to the day later, Bretzing removed John as the division's media representative and eventually transferred him to a squad he had told Bretzing he did not want to be on.

Mat's secretary, Aileen Ikegami, endorsed Mat's EEO complaint and verified what she had seen and experienced; in retaliation, Bretzing removed her from her position. Bretzing broadcasted the message to his subordinates, "Right or wrong, do not get in my way." For the varied cast of badge-carrying agents sworn to uphold the truth, remaining on the sidelines seemed the safest place for their wallets and their careers, with plausible deniability of the phrase, "Evil prevails when good men do nothing."

Mat, at this point relocated to El Paso, received repeated calls from agents in other field offices across the country. EEO had neglected to address a plethora of complaints by Hispanic agents. Despite the protected nature of EEO complaints, agents faced management pressure and retaliation. Contrary to regulations, the FBI did not protect the complainants from retaliation because upper management believed their supervisors were, without a doubt, the "best and the brightest." To attack the credibility of the complainants seemed easier than making difficult systemic changes.

Distressed, Hispanic agents from across the country related their stories to Mat's, who met with El Paso attorney Jose Angel Silva. Juan Briones, a former FBI agent, steered Jose to Mat. Jose Silva's family owned Silva's Grocery Store, a neighborhood institution in south El Paso and the family business that provided for the children. Jose left El Paso to study law at Harvard. After graduation, he moved back El Paso to share and apply his Harvard law training to combat injustice. Jose listened to Mat's account and suggested that the most effective remedy to such a systemic problem would be a class action lawsuit. However, such a lawsuit would cost money—money that Mat did not have. It would also take time, something else that was in short supply. However, identifying and organizing the prospective complainants made sense. Mat and all of the other Hispanic agents deserved equal justice and an advocate for justice. Mat recognized the advantage of having many complainants on his side. Mat and Jose discussed the obstacles they needed to overcome. Jose and Mat, both men of faith, believed that God is on the side of justice. The hand of God would help them in their struggle to prevail in court.

On January 15, 1987, in a federal court in El Paso, Mat, attorney Jose Silva and his staff filed a class action lawsuit, on behalf of Mat and all other similarly situated plaintiffs, charging the FBI with discrimination. The lawsuit requested a protective order and alleged institutionalized discrimination, an unfair promotion system, unjustifiable assignments based on ethnicity, lack of recognition and awards for contributions, unfair work assignments, and national origin harassment. A class action suit is a strong tool for justice but is difficult to attain, as it requires certification to meet a certain threshold. Jose and Mat were pleased to learn that El Paso was the site of battle to settle the lawsuit. Now they needed to organize and advise their troops.

Mat knew of a core group of agents with pending EEO complaints or with past complaints that had no finding of discrimination against the bureau. He called a meeting in Albuquerque with representatives from Los Angeles and El Paso—all of whom were under FBI scrutiny. The group filmed the meeting for nationwide distribution and for the benefit of those Hispanic agents stationed abroad, and they included details and elements of the lawsuit for the Hispanic agents. On May 30, 1987, Rudy and Paul from Los Angeles traveled to Albuquerque, and Leo Gonzales and Mat arrived from El Paso to meet with Albuquerque agents German Zuniga, Armand Lara, Rose Marie Hackney, Alfredo Romero, and Jim Garay at the home of former agent Hugo Rodriguez.

Hugo had left the bureau because of frustrations. The SAC had earlier removed Hugo from the "Palace Guard" and assigned him to work in foreign counterintelligence. The Foreign Counterintelligence (FCI) supervisor instructed Hugo to work on filling out his three-cards—cards used to administer the time spent on case files by classification—as the Albuquerque FCI squad had few FCI cases and little work. Hugo was unhappy being so unproductive, so he quit.

On his final day at work, the ASAC admonished Hugo for parking his personal car in the bureau parking lot. Hugo replied, "Let's treat each other like adults." The ASAC responded, "Listen, boy, you will do what I tell you." Name-calling led to pushing and shoving. Hugo backed off, knowing he was on his way out of the FBI that would see the scuffle the ASAC's way. The SAC and ASAC did not attend his going-away luncheon. Hugo understood it as a reflection of the general attitude of prejudice against Hispanic agents. Now Hugo was happy to join Silva's legal team and help Mat prepare to win the class action against the FBI.

The videotape that the group produced began with a written announcement: "The following material is a communication protected by attorney/client privilege, containing attorney work-product." Mat's attorney Jose Silva then advised viewers that Mat had filed a class action lawsuit in federal court in the district of El Paso. This protected videotape would one day be available to the FBI under the court's discovery procedure. There was no intent to hide the activity, and Jose warned the viewers that they faced the possibility of FBI retaliation. All involved knew how FBI management operated. They also suspected that the tape would reach FBI hands well before the discovery phase and that the curious FBI would disregard the posted notice of protected attorney/client privilege.

Jose outlined the allegations of discrimination in non-technical language and asked those willing to listen to the tape to submit a declaration of statement to his office before the deadline for certification. Individual agents then spoke. Hugo wore a paper bag over his head and stated that the FBI would no doubt identify the group on the tape. Mat spoke of incidents he had experienced and stated that the class action was for the younger agents, as he himself was nearing retirement. Jim Garay spoke about how the Albuquerque office forbade Hispanic agents from speaking Spanish unless they received a specific task from the office that required Spanish. Garay also reported that the Management Assessment Program assessors downgraded John Navarrete's management assessment scores because he had an accent.

The LA agents spoke of the favoritism toward Mormons, the undeserved promotions of mediocre agents, and the disparate training. The Albuquerque agents reported that the color of their skin, their surnames, and their ability to speak Spanish imposed upon them the burdens of disparate assignments and stereotyping. When Mat arrived in El Paso, a city with a Hispanic majority, he told SAC Ron Hoverson that the office should request more Spanish-speaking agents. Hoverson then replied, "Who's going to speak to the Anglos?" Jose Silva ended the videotape by giving his office address and phone number.

One tape went to each division office with a Hispanic known to the core group. Most Hispanic agents knew each other from investigations, wiretaps, special assignments to other offices, or undercover duties. Friendship building is satisfying, but it is even more satisfying when there is trust. While there is no law against a third party providing attorney/client privileged information to the opposite party, it is unbecoming of an FBI agent to disrespect the doctrine of attorney/client privilege and sits similar to the legality of banks selling derivatives to their clients and then betting against them. Despite this, SA Ronald Orrantia allegedly provided a copy of the videotape to the San Diego FBI's SAC and ASAC. These two, Tom Kuker and Tom Hughes, now armed with privileged property, beat the drums, circled the wagons and intervened against Jose's discovery requests for personnel records. The unwarranted fear that Hispanic class action lawsuit participants, who all held top-secret clearances, might provide access to FBI files heightened the latent prejudice among non-plaintiff class members as they pictured their personnel files shared with criminals, communists, and terrorist groups.

With propagandized fear, impetuous bureau supporters created fanatics unwilling to question the cause of the lawsuit. Bigots stop asking questions to maintain the comfort of their status quo. It was much easier for bureau employees to mistrust the integrity and cause of their Hispanic coworkers. However, the paranoia did not stop there. The FBI also mistrusted US Federal Magistrate Janet Ruesch and US Federal Judge Lucius Bunton. While the Hispanic plaintiffs were powerless to stop the delusion, the judge and the magistrate were not powerless. They ordered that access to FBI files be provided and authorized Hispanic plaintiff class members to review those files to prepare for litigation.

Acting as privateers, the San Diego office shipped their pirated videotape to its captain. FBIHQ now had knowledge of the grounds of the case and digested the booty despite its clear label of attorney/client privilege. FBI badges made it right. Set in their ways and in their minds, the lawsuit provided them no time for self-examination, no time to step back to review the evidence of right and wrong, time to "batten down the hatches," take a stand, mount a counterattack and defend the citadel of the bureau at all costs. Forget the issues. Forget who was embarrassing the bureau. Forget the truth, and instead walk Hispanics down the plank; label them untrustworthy and disloyal interlopers—and stick a sword to their cause.

Hispanic agents with top-secret clearances and much experience arrived in Albuquerque on administrative leave to assist in reviewing files. Some of those agents had security clearances beyond top secret, as some were the principal security officers in their field division. The FBI assigned rookies—first office agents—to watch over these suspected disloyal agents to ensure that no one removed documents from the secure warehouse patrolled inside and out by armed guards. The structure of security turned upside down. There was far less concern about the outside consultants hired by the FBI to assist with the bureau's side of the lawsuit. The Hispanic agents encountered ostracism first-hand and knew there was more to come. Meanwhile, Hispanic agents discovered disturbing inconsistencies in their personnel files.

Career board meetings, personnel records, transfer assignments, temporary duty assignments, day agent work years (DAWY), disciplinary matters, inspection reports, and much more were provided by the bureau, although the tidal wave of information inundated both the attorneys and the plaintiff class members. Jose, Tony, and Hugo hired Dr. Gary LaFree, a statistician and professor at the University of New Mexico in Albuquerque. Gary, Jose, Tony, and Hugo secured the appropriate clearances to review FBI files. None of them or any other agents removed documents from the warehouse.

Restrictions applied to some computer records that only FBIHQ could process, so the plaintiffs assembled a team of Hispanic supervisory special agents from FBIHQ with years of hands-on experience in internal management processes. Hispanic agents proved discrimination by matching experience with documentation. This was not the kind of discrimination that involved hate, lynching, cross burnings, and vandalism, which the FBI believed essential to discrimination. Instead, this was common occurrence discrimination, a form of discrimination overlooked by the FBI. Hispanic agents prepared the facts of discrimination based on fundamental justice and workplace issues.

Justice has different meanings to different people. Not all Hispanic agents joined the lawsuit. Some did not care for Mat, some had specific personal or financial issues and some were neutral or wanted to play both sides. Unwavering fidelity to the FBI clouded the vision of some occluding fidelity to the rule of law, much like the dysfunction that leads to unreported abuses by family members, educators, religious leaders, and business management. Job insecurity and fear of retaliation were major factors that effected various agents' decisions not to join in, just as those factors also weighed on the minds of those who joined the class action. Mat was pleased that 310 other agents joined him, but somewhat disappointed that others whom he knew did not sign on.

Mat fought for his employees in San Juan; still, a substantial percentage of Puerto Rican agents chose not join the lawsuit. Another surprise was that Willis Walton, a close Hispanic friend of Mat, chose not to become a plaintiff class member. Mat and Walton worked undercover together, spent personal time together as family friends, and experienced discrimination together. Mat would have had Walton's back on any assignment or personal issue, but their friendship proved to be a one-way street. Other agents were happy Walton stayed away, since he had demonstrated conduct unbecoming of an FBI manager in having an affair with a subordinate's wife, yet the FBI kept him on. Plaintiff class members preferred not to have such agents representing their cause. Plaintiff class members suspected that many would choose not to join, as job security played on the minds of many agents. It is often hard to recognize *El Diablo* when he has one hand on your shoulder and the other in your pocket.

Money is always an issue for plaintiffs and their attorneys. It takes large sums of money to take depositions, answer the motions, analyze the evidence and argue the case. Antonio "Tony" Silva, one of Jose's partners at Silva and Silva, wanted no part of the lawsuit, as he feared for his life. He excelled as an expert in civil rights class action suits, but he did not want to get involved with litigation against a vengeful FBI. He also knew there would be delays and expenses—expenses difficult for a law office to handle and difficult for the individual Hispanic agents as well.

Agents made what contributions they could; they sold lapel pins designed by German Zuniga. They scheduled barbeques, *carnitas* dinners, *menudo* breakfasts, and held fundraisers in various cities with speakers, musicians and artists. Business people were reluctant to become involved for fear the FBI would target their businesses, and soliciting help in a battle with the FBI proved to be a difficult task. Politicians provided lip service but hesitated with any active support. Linda Ronstadt refused a benefit concert, even though she had family in law enforcement. To cap it all off, the Mexican American Legal

Defense and Education Fund (MALDEF), an agency founded to represent Hispanics with legal issues, refused to get involved, to the wonder and disbelief of the attorneys and the 311 agents.

Congressman Esteban Torres of California heard about the agents' hardships. Although he feared retaliation by the FBI, he knew he had to stand up for their rights. He drafted several communications to the FBI Director to facilitate the litigation process. Small donations arrived covertly from various groups who sought to maintain their anonymity. The League of United Latin American Citizens Council Four of San Antonio provided public reinforcement by making connections and spreading support. Little Joe and the Latinaires performed benefit concerts in both San Antonio and Dallas. Joe Sanchez and the Southern Grocers of California were the most generous with their donations. Attorney and Professor Lawrence Tribe of Harvard agreed to assist, if needed, on an appeal. The altruism in the testimony of FBI personnel John Hoos, Raymond Yelchak, Aileen Ikegami, and Joe Yablonsky validated the purpose of the lawsuit: a better FBI.

Hate plays a part in discrimination, but Hispanic agents did not have to prove hate, just unfair practices. A necessary part of law enforcement is ensuring the trust of your fellow agents. Trust came by sharing stories of humor to counterbalance the stresses of the job. FBI agents love what they do...and they share their stories with colleagues whether in carpools, at meals, while working out, on the firing range, when working wires or in bullpens. *No Left Turns* is a book that tells the stories of humorous activities of FBI agents and managers who find themselves in everyday situations, such as the fact that FBI Director J. Edgar Hoover did not like his drivers to make left turns. The top three executive directors had nicknames, "the Hulk, the Bulk, and the Sulk," with two based on personality and one on weight. The stories continued to accrue as Hispanic agents experienced and observed so-called "burro (donkey) moments," nicknaming the bureau *El Burro.* Many stories were of favoritism, unfairness, and broken policy.

Educated Hispanic agents who contributed much to the FBI took the strategy of collecting documents that verified the stories of both Anglo agents and agents of color who received special favors, stories of injustices, and anecdotes of mismanagement. Documented evidence became part of their testimony. The shared stories between Hispanics and non-plaintiff class members halted once the class action began, but it did not stop early enough to protect the "good ol' boys" in FBI management. Much like the legends of the Ark of the Covenant, which held important documents that ensured victory to the possessor, plaintiff class members carried this collection of documents as evidence into the courtroom to break down walls of discrimination within the FBI.

3

The First Day of Trial

For the plaintiff class members, justice seemed a long way off from the time they filed the class action lawsuit as their patience exhausted. The Hispanic agents were eager to put the trial behind them, but not until they had done their best and had their day in court. Big Brother's FBI deep pocket—the taxpayer money appropriated from investigative programs—proved capable of stalling and obstructing discovery requests to meet "the needs of the bureau" and prevent embarrassment. These delaying tactics hit the Hispanic agents and their attorneys right in the pocketbook, yet helped them gain opportunities to review discovered documents and analyze data, necessities for victory.

The bureau always seemed to have its way in court, and the senses of privilege and entitlement, and their mentality of winning at all costs, caused stress for the DOJ attorneys and even for the bureau itself because of the time limits imposed by the court. Although the FBI was able to afford all of the expenses, manufacture repeated delays, and drag out and appeal all requests by the plaintiffs and by the court, in the final analysis, they could not afford to be embarrassed. Embarrassing the Hispanic agents, who allegedly embarrassed the bureau, became an FBI management obsession, and they convinced many non-plaintiff class members to shun plaintiff class members. The abuse of hidden administrative practices caused management to lose its focus on disproving discrimination. The bureau wanted to embalm and stiffen silence into the plaintiffs, bury the case to its depths and return to doing as it pleased with the so-called needs of the bureau. Department of Justice attorneys Felix Baxter, Anne Gulyassy, Alan Ferber, Lainie Simon, and Sheridan Black led the charge for the FBI.

Anxiety was intense among the 311 plaintiff class members. No matter how wary, no matter how tired, no matter the money, no matter the time, there was now no turning back for the Hispanic agents and their attorneys. When the first day of the trial arrived, it was time to put anxiety to rest, set emotions aside, clear minds, reenergize, and prepare to win.

The preparatory phase entailed eighteen months of stress on both sides; the sense of being outcasts grew after the initial filing in January of 1987. Additional incidents, obstacles, and pressures piled up, right up to the nerve-wracking opening of the trial itself in August of 1988. Supervisors made it difficult for agents to testify, colleagues second-guessed Hispanic agents, and there was pressure to take sides. Long-time partners and friends created distance with harsh words, what had been coexistence and complacency developed into outright animosity, and latent discrimination and disparate treatment became overt. It was a different bureau.

It was trial time. The 311 agents wanted a quick decision in their favor, as the FBI was rendering faulty internal decisions. With the courtroom half-full of DOJ and FBI attorneys, the odds favored the defendants as the plaintiffs had only two attorneys, Antonio "Tony" V. Silva and Hugo Rodriguez, to examine the plaintiffs and defendants.

Judge Lucius Bunton also wanted to conclude the trial quickly. This was a high profile case, and he was the man on the spot. The judge had a long history and a good relationship with the FBI and its agents. He also respected Judge Sessions, the Texas judge appointed to replace FBI Director Webster. Discrimination may have occurred on Director Webster's watch, but if Judge Bunton rendered a finding of discrimination, then the obligation to fix the problem would land on his friend Bill Sessions. Judge Bunton respected the experience of Hispanic special agents of the FBI, and he recognized that a decision neither for nor against the FBI would be in harmony with his feelings;

a fair decision would require a dissection of the facts and the Wisdom of Solomon.

When Judge Bunton entered the courtroom, everyone stood as he recognized those before the bar and those in the gallery. The widespread publicity and vital importance of the trial brought many to the courtroom. Much like wedding guests in a church seated on either side of the aisle for either groom or bride, on the right facing the court were those on the government payroll, including a slew of Department of Justice attorneys, FBI attorneys, their assistants, retired FBI agents, and allied reporters.

On the left were the plaintiff class members waiting to testify, their two attorneys, and several family members and concerned citizens supporting the Hispanic agents. Murmured comments from those sitting on the right included, "We're going to kick your ass, Mat," "They have no business here," "You're embarrassing the bureau," "We are going to kick ass and take names," "You don't know who you are dealing with," and "You are going to lose." The comments witnessed inside the courtroom were less harsh than the ones muttered outside the courthouse.

Even before the trial began, the attorneys argued, and accusations flew back and forth. While there would be no gunfights, the settlement would be *mano a mano* in Judge Bunton's courtroom.

In his opening statement, Hugo Rodriguez declared:

> The FBI can go across this world and they can find a spy. They can find someone who has assassinated a judge. They can find bank robbers. They can find terrorists. They can find kidnappers. Oddly enough, the FBI cannot find, nor is it interested in finding within its own house, the cancer—discrimination. The clear message to the American public was "do as I say, not as I do." We will investigate others. We will imprison others. We will require, says the Department of Justice, for private industry and other agencies to do certain things, but not do it to our own.
>
> You will hear testimony from the defendants that no complaint of discrimination brought by any Hispanic has ever been upheld internally within the FBI. Three hundred and

eleven people lie? We think not. Ironically they are no longer the investigators, nor the perpetrator of the crime, they are the victims—victims who are second-class citizens in their own house, victims who their employer has now identified as being disloyal and being less dedicated because they are here before this court trying to redress the wrongs brought against them. Three hundred and eleven of them cannot be wrong.

Their most difficult decision to date has not been whether they throw their life on the line to help protect someone, whether they risk their lives, whether they try to prevent a crime. Without reservation, every one of them said to participate and stand up in El Paso and tell the truth, why Goliath intimidates them. The FBI is an awesome force. It has intimidated presidents and it has intimidated senators; it has intimidated judges. Worst of all, it intimidates their own.

We must ask why Hispanic FBI agents are willing to risk their careers to come before this court, and the answer is simple. They believe in the truth and they love the FBI. They are not here to challenge the FBI. They are here to make the FBI a better place for them and their children.

Your Honor, when I was trying to explain this case to some people who are not as familiar with the law as this court, I had a very difficult time. The only thing I could think of was the National Football League—something simple I could talk to a jock about, the NFL. That powerful force so many people in this country are proud of, that they look to for enjoyment and entertainment, discussed every Sunday and every Monday in every coffee shop in America. The FBI is like the NFL, three initials. Not too long ago there was a big controversy in the NFL, and that controversy was, can a black be a quarterback of a Super Bowl team? People know that some [of the] best players in the NFL are blacks. They carry the ball. My agents investigate cases. They throw the passes. They go on undercover assignments. They catch the ball. They go on dangerous assignments. They are the blockers. They do not get promoted. Can Hispanic

FBI agents be the quarterback of a Super Bowl team? No one thought a black could do it until Doug Williams did it last year and did it well, and took the Washington NFL team to the championship. What happened after Doug Williams took them to the championship? Did he get the notoriety, the attention, and the endorsements that laud all before him? The answer is no. Every Super Bowl quarterback prior to him received more recognition, more remuneration than did Doug Williams.

What happens to those Hispanics that get to the highest level of the FBI? You will hear testimony [that] they do not receive the same recognition or support of others. However, the irony is if they can block, if they can pass, and if they can catch, why can they not coach the team? Why isn't there a black head football coach in the NFL? Why aren't there more Hispanic Special Agents in Charge? I know what the public perceives. Blacks aren't qualified, they know nothing about football, they can't lead, and they are not as experienced.

Their employer, the institution, the FBI, is not above the law. You will listen to testimony from Hispanics that they are not promoted in equal numbers. How they are disciplined harsher, given assignments that are more dangerous. They do the majority of the undercover work. They do not receive the recognition, do not get the endorsements. You will hear not only Hispanic FBI agents, but also non-Hispanics tell this court the same thing. You will hear it from present non-Hispanic FBI agents and former non-Hispanic FBI agents. The tragedy of it is that you will also hear from those that tried to help these Hispanic FBI agents, who have stood up and told the truth either through the complaint process or in court, and how they have been retaliated by the dragon against them for them standing up and telling the truth. This permeates not only Hispanics, but throughout the entire system.

The FBI will have one simple defense, Your Honor: needs of the FBI. To the FBI, needs of the FBI is the magic carpet that sweeps them across all personnel actions and allows them to do pretextually what violates the law. You will hear 'needs of the bureau' repeatedly. And what is 'needs of the bureau'? An arbitrary and capriciously enforced doctrine by whoever decides that something needs to be accomplished. But it violates Title VII, it violates the laws of this nation and the needs of the bureau are not paramount to the rights of these Hispanic FBI agents.

You will witness testimony that Hispanic agents are discriminated against in promotions. You will hear testimony and statistical evidence they are discriminated against in being overrepresented in undercover assignments. You will witness testimony and receive evidence they are discriminated against in assignments away from their home. You will listen to testimony and they will tell you they are discriminated against in their geographical assignments, the substantive work assignments they are given by the FBI, in transfer and in all other personnel areas. This has been a very difficult row for them to hoe during these last eighteen months. However, I told every one of them it is only the beginning. We are here to make the FBI a better place. The FBI is not above the law. These people enjoy the same rights and privileges as any other citizen of this country. Thank you, Your Honor.

Government attorney Alan Ferber provided the opening statement for the DOJ and the FBI. In his statement, he conceded that the FBI is not above the law. He stated that they would produce the facts, and how the law applies to the facts is what was important. Ferber stated that the plaintiffs' disparate impact claim, which alleged that the FBI's policies on promotions, transfers, assignments and discipline were discriminatory in operation against Hispanic special agents, was untrue. He held that the disparate treatment claim required proof of intentionality and discriminatory motives; he also denied that Mat Perez was a victim of anti-Hispanic bias perpetrated by various bureau officials. He claimed that Mat's career suffered because of the consequences of his actions. In the government's statistical analysis, no disparate impact showed up, and Hispanics fared as well or even better than non-Hispanics in the challenged areas.

There was, Ferber said, no logical coherence to the plaintiffs' claims of systemic discrimination. Some plaintiff class members believed an assignment to San Juan to be a hardship, while others sought assignment there. Ferber claimed that the bureau officials who dealt with Mat Perez were not and never had been racially prejudiced, nor did they ever act in reprisal.

The bureau's motivations, Ferber claimed, came from nothing more than a desire to promote efficiency and advance needs of the bureau in accomplishing its job. The FBI recognized and acted upon Mat's job-related skills and weaknesses. Ferber maintained that there was no evidence that anyone acted against Mat because of his ethnicity. He held that there was no evidence of discrimination or anti-Hispanic bias that played any part in personal decisions or actions. The evidence, he insisted, would instead show some persons accused of being anti-Hispanic but who had married Hispanics or adopted Mexican children, or who had selected a Hispanic as their closest associate to perform their church-related responsibilities.

Ferber claimed,

> Now, even if plaintiffs were to make out a prima facie case of discrimination, the law does provide that a defendant can rebut such claim by showing a business necessity for the policies or practices in question. The evidence will show, in a nutshell, the bureau must be able to utilize each agent's talents and abilities, including the ability to speak Spanish, or operate successfully in certain undercover assignments, in the accomplishment of the bureau's law enforcement commission.

The FBI's law enforcement responsibility requires using agents with Hispanic backgrounds. "The defendants' statistical analysis will prove with precision and clarity that Hispanics as a class are not assigned, transferred, promoted or disciplined unfairly in comparison to non-Hispanic agents, and [the story of] Mat Perez will demonstrate a series of job-related, not race-related, problems. Plaintiffs will be shown, Your Honor, to have failed to carry their burden of proof."

Ferber's response for the FBI was as predicted by plaintiff class members and their attorneys; all actions of the FBI were justifiable by the so-called "needs of the bureau." In every violation of policy, regulation, or law, the bureau would claim an exemption for "the needs of the bureau," a magical phrase with the power to allow stepping on, over or through anything found to be obstructing the way. This time it would be up to the Federal Court to decide if the FBI was above the law, entitled to remove the blindfold from the eyes of Lady Justice and wear her colors on their collective foreheads like some form of gangster justice.

David Rarity, Jr., the personnel officer for the FBI and the lead hitter representing the FBI as defendants, faced four hours of questions from Hugo Rodriguez, the attorney for the team of Mat Perez and the plaintiffs. The FBI underestimated Hugo, who was a former FBI agent and had learned how to play FBI tactics.

Rarity knew all about policy as the personnel officer for the FBI. He had been responsible for much of the implementation and promulgation of the personnel practices established for the FBI through the Department of Justice and the Office of Personnel Management (OPM). Rarity looked like an FBI agent straight out of central casting: a square-jawed, good-looking, and well-dressed young man who represented the bureau well in appearance, knowledge, experience, and culture. Rarity was a Senior Executive Service (SES) employee who rose through the ranks of the FBI and who would no doubt impress the judge, the DOJ attorneys, the media, and the courtroom spectators.

A Rhode Islander with successful Ku Klux Klan and civil rights investigations under his belt, Rarity would without a doubt tell the truth, but in English, as he confessed that he had forgotten the Serbo-Croatian language training he had received from the bureau. He could recall signing no contractual agreement stating that his training required the actual utilization of his language training, a policy in effect—at least for Hispanic agents—at the time of his testimony. His testimony revealed that the bureau's return on its investment of two transfers and a year of language school training ended without

Rarity becoming competent enough to serve as a linguist on even one Serbo-Croatian Title III (T-III) wiretap. Under the Federal Wiretap Act, the FBI often lacked the linguists needed to overhear real-time surveillance of all kinds of electronic communications.

As the career board secretary, a non-voting ombudsman for those who sought career advancement, Rarity knew all about the available and qualified agents who wished to move up into management positions. With his position and diverse experience, Rarity's testimony educated the court on the special nomenclature and language of the FBI. He answered the questions according to his experience and expertise. He had done nothing wrong, except for the mindless support of procedures and decisions already made by his superiors.

If Rarity had ever stood up against a single injustice during a career board meeting, he did not mention it. If he had ever stood up for a single administrative issue raised by agents, he never mentioned that either. Considering the trial, if Rarity introduced even one example of an injustice he had seen resolved, the team he represented might have become discouraged. His knowledge, and his candid and direct responses, helped the judge to understand the basic cultural structure and operating procedures of the FBI.

At Headquarters, beneath the director of the FBI, serve three executive assistant directors, besides another ten assistant directors of each of the divisions, the deputies under each of them, and then the section chiefs and the unit chiefs who manage supervisors and support staff. In the field are assistant directors, special agents in charge, assistant special agents in charge, and supervisors. Rarity worked for the administrative division, where careers foster or fail based on information received from other divisions.

Those who participate in the Career Development Program (CDP) begin as relief supervisors, except for those who are fast-tracked to FBIHQ. A relief supervisor is a position in which an agent stands in for a supervisor. Any training as a relief is ad hoc as it deals with opening, assigning, and closing cases, or what the bureau termed "referred upon completion" (RUC), an acronym for the closure of an investigative lead that originated in another field office.

Rarity's testimony that a relief supervisor was not a part of management, with supervisory levels beginning as GS-14, contradicted the FBI expert statistician's statement that Hispanic agents often served in management as relief supervisors. One of two career boards selects the agent depending on the grade considered. During Rarity's tenure as secretary of the career board, he could recall no one ever selected as a manager whom the SAC did not recommend, although he left the possibility open.

He also did not recall a single case in which an agent recommended by the career board did not receive the position for which the agent had applied, stating, "All appeals are over" once the career board selects an agent. Although the career board can overrule an assistant director's recommendation for the management program, Rarity did not provide the court with a single example of such happening.

Rarity admitted he did not apply for every supervisory position he had obtained and testified that some management promotions occurred without a bidding process in the selection. "When the director or the career board makes a decision that they want you from point A to point B, you go. When they have a documented need and say, 'we want this person over here,' that is the end. It must be that way. The director of the FBI decides." Rarity could not imagine it was possible that these exceptions affected Hispanics, so in his mind there was nothing wrong with making such exceptions.

The objective criteria utilized by the career board in its selection of FBI managers took the shotgun approach and included everything they could get their hands on, from personnel files, individuals' background checks, related experience or lack thereof for the position, awards, the SAC or Section's input, performance appraisals, language competency, specialties, etc. The FBI did not use a more objective point system such as the one used by the Drug Enforcement Administration (DEA). Rarity neglected to mention that the deciding division often supplied a list of all of the supposed attributes of the candidates and even prepared a matrix chart for the career board. No one from the bureau testified as to why some criteria was absent from some matrices or why sometimes even the names of applicants went missing.

Rarity testified about the Management Assessment Program (MAP), both MAP I and MAP II, which are the programs that evaluate candidates for FBI supervisory and executive positions. "I would have to think that the way in which MAP is validated everyone has an equal chance, in the way it was designed; MAP was designed not by the FBI, but an outside consultant." Rarity added that very few people go through the MAP processes without contingencies to work off. Rarity acknowledged that, somehow, some agents with lower MAP scores received promotions over other agents with higher scores.

"The needs of the bureau" is a philosophical concept never pondered by the likes of Aristotle or Socrates, but the concept became a virtual Bureau Bible that channeled the Manual of Administrative and Operational Procedures (MAOP) and the Manual of Investigative Operations and Guidelines (MIOG). No documentation encodes the meaning of the "needs of the bureau." However, Rarity testified, "When we all signed on as special agents, we signed the agreement that we would accept the needs of the bureau."

Rarity was also in charge of the Transfer Unit, which made TDY assignments, and he gave as examples of the "needs of the bureau" the riots at the federal prisons in Atlanta and New Orleans. When asked if Hispanic FBI agents served TDY there, he questioningly answered, "Must have been," as if he were perhaps unsure. However, when asked if Hispanic FBI agents comprised the majority of the TDY in Atlanta, he responded, "I would have to say so, because the majority of the subjects were Hispanic and wanted to speak in the Hispanic language. So it wouldn't have done no good to send me there." This was a surprising and unexpected statement from Rarity, as FBI agents expect success wherever they are—an attitude inculcated during training. He added, "One might as well not even go into parts of Arlington, Virginia, if one does not speak Vietnamese." Just making such a statement expressed Rarity's limited experience, the kind of limitations that led to the pigeonholing of Hispanic agents.

Rarity, as the agent in charge of overseeing administrative leave, claimed not to know if the FBI initiated administrative inquiries into plaintiff class members for their utilization of leave for participation in the lawsuit. However, when asked if anyone contacted him from LA concerning utilization of annual leave to participate in the litigation, he answered, "Are you talking about Paul Magallanes?" Rarity had advised Paul that participation in the lawsuit meant he was "skating on thin ice."

When the bureau confiscates a special agent's weapon, it is usually due to a doctor's certification that the medication the agent is taking could impair his or her judgment and that person should not carry a weapon. To take away a special agent's weapon is tantamount to telling the agent he is no longer a special agent; it is a very serious step. Management can make the same move if there is a serious psychological problem. The FBI removes a special agent's gun under those two specific circumstances. Paul Magallanes, a class member, had his weapon confiscated because he reported a back injury. However, his personal physician and two FBI doctors all stated Paul suffered no impairment. This left the impression on the court that the exigent circumstance in removing Paul's weapon was the FBI's diagnosis that he was a member of the plaintiff class.

Rarity testified that the FBI could never compel foreign language speaking agents not hired under the FBI language program to accept language-based assignments or transfers, and the FBI could force no agent to take a language test if they did not come under that specific program or if they qualified under another program. Rarity confirmed SA Lorena Sierra's transfer orders to Chicago. In her case, there was a caveat on her orders, which stated that SA Sierra was an accountant. There was no indication of any kind that she was a Spanish speaker, other than perhaps an assumption based on her appearance and last name. Rarity proclaimed it would be ludicrous to put agents on a Title III if they had not volunteered or demonstrated proficiency in a foreign language. However, such ludicrous behavior showed up in records as the FBI forced agents with Hispanic surnames to take language qualification tests and serve in the language program.

Rarity testified that, when the FBI hires persons with special abilities to speak a foreign language, those recruits sign a contractual agreement to utilize that language during their tenure in the FBI. Those in the position of being fast-tracked—the attorneys, accountants, and scientists—never sign such a contractual agreement. He knew of no one who was fast-tracked because of linguistic ability. When an attorney, accountant, or scientist steps down from a supervisory position, the FBI does not then require them to continue to utilize their specialty. However, language specialists must continue in their specialty because the bureau considers it a critical need to protect the bureau's investment in foreign language speakers.

Some field offices lost agents due to the low pay that they received from the FBI. The FBI ranked fiftieth in salary level, far below California's state and local law enforcement agencies, and because of this, some divisions received locality pay. Rarity testified that he did not see how anyone could consider the San Juan Division to be a hardship office, although he had never visited San Juan. To him, the FBI needed to staff it, with either English or Spanish speakers.

Assignment to San Juan could not be considered a hardship, even when one's family developed island fever, even when a spouse or an entire family did not speak the language, even when the house where the family lived had to have bureau-supplied burglar alarms and burglar bars on the windows, even if the children had to be picked up by US military buses and bused to school on a US military base, or even with agents forced to work twelve-plus hour shifts with agents who wanted out. It was much more convenient for the bureau to force a solution and then to hide behind the "needs of the bureau." Even native Puerto Rican agents who grew up there wanted out because of the island's miserable working conditions.

Rarity, who became familiar with the San Juan transfer policy during the trial, testified that anyone serving in San Juan did a minimum four-year tour of duty. An additional fifth year, he testified, almost guaranteed that person would then get to go to their office of preference. Director Webster approved the policy change in October of 1987 based on input from San Juan's SAC James C. Esposito. Mat Perez, the lead plaintiff, first suggested such a change when he served as SAC eight years before, in 1979. Mat also asked for more agents because of the number of terrorism cases and the long list of Major Cases in San

Juan. The FBI dragged its collective feet and neglected to make the changes that Mat recommended.

Rarity recognized that the FBI promoted agents who were the subjects of an administrative inquiry. FBI agents with prior military service have due process outside the agency through the Merit System Protection Board (MSPB) while non-veterans do not. Non-veterans are entitled to due process, whereby they can respond to their accuser and an internal administrative review with no appellate process because the FBI is an Excepted Service agency. The FBI is Excepted Service for personnel hiring and personnel actions, meaning the director of the FBI has the final say on personnel hiring and actions for all non-former military employees. Some Hispanic class members and other agents relied on the MSPB.

Rarity, who was in excellent physical condition and who remained on the stand for four hours, at one point became antagonistic and maintained that he had never heard the term "PT," used for Physical Training, a term most agents—if they had never heard of it—learned at the academy. The FBI allows each agent three paid hours a week to maintain their physical fitness throughout their career.

Rarity did know the definition of the FBI term "Rabbi": "that there was a hook that somebody got where they were because they knew somebody," but he responded that he did not know of such a system within the FBI. As in the movie *A Few Good Men,* in which the term "code red" existed but was never explained in manuals and was not on the books, it seemed illogical that Rarity knew the definition for a slang term but maintained that such a reality did not exist in the FBI, as if descriptive words appeared before real life. The reality Rarity described had to exist for someone to apply the term "Rabbi." A more logical answer might have been to explain that the "Rabbi system" may have occurred in the distant past, but Rarity did not choose that route.

Rarity himself claimed to have been the victim of discrimination during his time in Bogalusa, Louisiana, and he said that he had suffered physically, mentally, and verbally. He said that it was not because of his Rhode Island Yankee accent, but because he was an FBI agent. There was the barber who shaved half of his head then closed up shop.

He was also the target of a cross burning, and his wife was verbally abused in a beauty parlor. Hispanic agents comprised over four hundred of the approximate nine thousand agents who worked at the bureau, and Rarity described the most critical need facing the FBI was the need for Spanish speakers. He testified that the FBI wrote only fair policy. Rarity claimed he understood policy and regulations.

Rarity believed that the FBI applied policy equally to everyone and that the 311 Hispanic agents had just perceived discrimination when it did not exist. All 311 Hispanic agents who claimed discrimination—physically, mentally and emotionally—worked under the same fair policy as everyone else. He said that the 311 Hispanic agents would have to prove to him just how the FBI had discriminated against them. The lawsuit proceeded to do just that. As with the discriminatory experiences encountered by Rarity in Bogalusa, Hispanic agents likened discrimination to their employer shaving off half of their careers, burning a cross on the front lawn of their desires and verbally abusing those they loved.

FBI officials had neglected to explain to the DOJ their internal FBI MAP policy, "a 2 with a hook is better than a 4," meaning connected friends with lower scores received promotions over those with higher scores. The "hook," the "Rabbi," and "fiefdoms," had life.

4

Armand A. Lara

Armand A. Lara, a special agent with the FBI, entered on duty under the foreign language program on June 21, 1971, testing in Spanish as a 3+ out of a possible 5 rating. When Armand applied to the FBI, an agent in the Seattle Division told Armand that someone at FBIHQ had inquired about whether he "looked too Mexican." Judge Bunton expressed complete surprise, questioning aloud what looking "too Mexican" meant. The Seattle agent told the caller from FBIHQ that Armand looked like a Mexican movie actor, which seemed to have somewhat relieved the concern of FBIHQ. Though—continuing along those lines—Armand might have looked like Pancho, the sidekick of the "Cisco Kid." From that point on, the FBI would have two problems: an agent who "looked too Mexican" and an agent with an ongoing weight problem.

Armand also sensed discrimination at his first assignment in El Paso. The SAC and ASAC told him that Julian De La Rosa, from the FBIHQ EEO office, anticipated attending the League of United Latin American Citizens (LULAC) convention in El Paso. The SAC asked Armand to accompany De La Rosa to the convention since De la Rosa did not speak Spanish. The SAC added that he felt the other two Hispanic agents in the office, Frank Castro and Armando Guerra, were "too dark-skinned" to represent the FBI at a LULAC function. LULAC is an organization that promotes civic activities and Hispanic civil rights and advocates on specific political and economic issues. After the LULAC convention, the SAC instructed the two Hispanic agents with the "too-dark skin" to go undercover and masquerade as plumbers, so that they would look even more like Mexicans, and surprise a fugitive.

SAC Donald Sullivan disapproved of the civic activities of Armand's wife in the establishment of the Women Against Rape Crisis Center in El Paso. The SAC discussed Armand's wife's activities with Armand, and even opened an illegal and unauthorized sub-file in Armand's personnel file on his wife and her activities. This was in direct violation of the Attorney General's Guidelines. The SAC even summoned Armand's wife to his office. Armand learned through the discovery phase of the lawsuit that the sub-file on Mrs. Lara's activities, established in 1974, negatively affected management decisions on his career. For the previous fourteen years, the file of FBI surveillance and his wife's recorded activities had dogged Armand, all because Mrs. Lara had helped to open a rape crisis center.

Faced with pressure at the office and seeing little chance for promotion, Armand transferred from El Paso to San Juan, Puerto Rico, where transfers came to anyone foolish enough to raise their hand, even if they spoke no Spanish. After a month and a half assigned to a squad, working several cases, and locating a home in San Juan, Armand found out that the FBI now wanted to transfer him to Aguadilla, Puerto Rico. Aguadilla is a small town on the forsaken northwestern end of the island. Again, Armand did not discover the reason for this transfer until the discovery phase of the lawsuit, when he learned that the FBI wanted to isolate him because of his wife's involvement in civic activities. The FBI took exception to the fact that Armand's wife reverted to using her maiden name to maintain her professional identity.

Exiled to Aguadilla for the next five and a half years, Armand's marriage crumbled. After serving out his five-year tour, he requested a transfer to Albuquerque and ended up at the Gallup, New Mexico Resident Agency, which the FBI considered a hardship office because of the overall living conditions. Armand saw no need for a Spanish speaker in Gallup and believed his transfer to be a continuation of his exile for his now ex-wife's activities as a civic activist.

In Albuquerque, he became a relief supervisor and traveled to two dozen TDY assignments on what Hispanics nicknamed the "Taco Circuit," which had a minimum duration of 30 days and at times a maximum of 150 days, and none of which ever had non-Hispanic Spanish speakers assigned to the Title IIIs. During his TDY assignments, his Gallup cases went unaddressed; their completions fell behind and had to wait his return. The recurring TDY assignments hurt his chances for promotion. Along with working his cases and those of others, Armand was the SWAT team leader and trained the FBI Albuquerque Division SWAT team and various Police Department SWAT teams. Armand served as the fugitive coordinator and as an applicant interviewer.

Armand often heard racist slurs and jokes concerning Hispanics at the office and even at luncheons that non-FBI personnel attended. Armand filed no complaints, as he believed any such filing would be the kiss of death for his career. Armand applied for nine management positions but had no success. Armand was unaware that "wearing a bad jacket"—the sub-file jacket on his ex-wife—held him back, not his lack of experience. "Wearing a bad jacket" is a slang term meaning one is marked or labeled without one's knowledge.

ASAC Leroy Teitsworth told Armand of an administrative inquiry that accused him of selling arms to the Contra Rebels in Nicaragua and kept him from a promotion. Armand had no knowledge that he was under investigation for something he had never done. Armand allegedly sold guns to the Contras with Hugo Rodriguez, the attorney questioning him. The alleged file did not appear during discovery, nor was he ever interviewed. The allegation seemed more of a pretext to prevent him from receiving promotions, but he now worried about retaliation for his alleged participation. Agents under administrative inquiry sometimes received promotions, but not Armand.

Attorney Sheridan Black, representing the DOJ, asked Armand if he was familiar with all of the qualifications of each agent who had applied for the same promotions for which he had applied. He was not. For the DOJ, that implied Armand could not prove discrimination.

However, the other side of that argument was that Black could not prove the agents who received the promotions were more qualified than Armand. Armand knew Teitsworth and other agents had fast-tracked to positions such as ASACs, but Armand seemed stuck in mud. The FBI did not justify Armand's assignment as a Spanish speaker to Gallup. Armand theorized that if he had not been a class member, had not worn a sub-file jacket, had not been the subject of a phantom administrative inquiry, and had not had a wife who participated in civic activities, perhaps he could have been a "good ol' boy" and received promotions the old-fashioned way.

SAC Sullivan signed off on Armand's performance appraisals and rated him as excellent, which implied to the DOJ that Sullivan had no anti-Hispanic bias. Following that line of argument to its logical conclusion, it meant that someone with an anti-Hispanic bias would be consistently anti-Hispanic, and a thief would naturally steal everything within reach rather than capitalizing on an opportunity.

Both Sullivan and ASAC Thomas D. Westfall suggested to Armand that a transfer out of El Paso might be advisable. The DOJ suggested that the El Paso FBI office wanted to ensure his wife's activities would not harm the FBI's relationship with the police department, since they had to interact with the EPPD. Armand read from an exhibit that stated,

> SAC has previously counseled Special Agent Lara to the effect this office interposes no objections to the legitimate civic activities of his spouse and desires only that she pursue her civic interests in a dignified, diplomatic, and discrete manner. SAC does not feel those adjectives would characterize her current activities. However, it would not appear that further counseling would be productive.

An objective reading implied that the Lara family was not only hardheaded, but that Mrs. Lara's activities in the service of the community appeared undignified, undiplomatic and indiscrete—the kinds of actions that justify sending an illegal sub-file on to the San Juan's field office and FBIHQ.

Sullivan testified that, while he never visited San Juan, he recommended Armand be sent there as his work proved independent of review. The sub-file stemmed from the actions of Armand's wife in founding a rape crisis center. Sullivan said at first the rape crisis center seemed a wholesome endeavor, but it led to a confrontation when the EPPD refused to provide investigative reports to the center due to privacy regulations. However, El Paso Police Department Chief Robert Minnie provided written testimony that the activities of Armand's wife never interfered at all with FBI-EPPD relations. Sullivan's initials appeared on all documents that dealt with the sessions he held with Armand and with his wife.

On cross-examination, Sullivan testified that newspaper articles about the relationship between the crisis center and the EPPD led him to believe there was somewhat of a dispute or disagreement, but he did not remember and did not identify a specific reason for such a confrontation even after reviewing the newspaper articles and the FBI's sub-file on Mrs. Lara. Sullivan stated that he notified FBIHQ because he had an ongoing responsibility for the maintenance of good relations with the EPPD, not because he wanted to get rid of Armand. Sullivan claimed he could not remember the details of the counseling sessions, but read from one exhibit, "The above is for the information of the bureau. It may be significant that following the SAC's contact with SA Lara on August 1st, '74, by memo dated August 2nd, '74, he changed his office of preference to San Juan."

The upshot was that Sullivan, the head of the El Paso office and Armand's reviewing official, opened an illegal sub-file on Armand's wife. This was despite the fact that, in his words, Mrs. Lara's "wholesome endeavor" did not interfere with FBI relations, the activities of Armand's wife did not affect Armand's work, and the chief of police believed relations with the FBI were good. Sullivan's assumptions about Mrs. Lara that resulted in his opening a sub-file in violation of guidelines were unjustified.

5

Julian Frank Perez

Julian "Jay" Perez graduated with a Bachelor of Science in accounting from St. Joseph's College in Indiana and a Master of Business Administration (MBA) from Bernard Baruch College, Graduate School of Business, at the City University of New York (CUNY). After graduation, he joined the US Army, and after that he spent three and a half years as an Internal Revenue Service (IRS) Agent auditing complicated income tax returns. He became an FBI agent on November 4, 1968, under the modified program, which considered his three years of professional experience.

Jay's first assignment was in Philadelphia, where he worked white collar and organized crime and assisted non-Spanish speaking agents, work for which he received no credit. He faced the same situation in New York where he worked gambling investigations and cultivated ghetto informants. He later became the criminal informant coordinator for the entire New York Division, worked the graveyard shift and completed translations, in addition to conducting light undercover operations. Jay received a MAP level 4 rating, rated exceptional in terms of management aptitude and ability with no contingencies. He received a promotion to supervisor of the white-collar crime squad.

Jay applied for the Grade-15 (GS-15) program manager position for white-collar crime. The agent vacating the position was a GS-15 who both supervised GS-14s and relieved the ASAC and SAC. While in New York, Richard Bretzing, an executive unpopular with Hispanic agents in Los Angeles, promoted Jay because of his high MAP scores, experience as an accountant, and outstanding performance appraisals. However, Bretzing also downgraded Jay's GS-15 position to a GS-14 position and, in consequence, Jay did not receive the pay to which he should have been entitled, while all of the Anglo program managers with similar responsibilities kept both their GS-15 ratings and pay grades.

Jay left New York for the FBI Academy as administrator of the MAP I and MAP II programs—programs designed to evaluate an agent's management aptitudes. He traveled and taught police officials the "Theory of Administration of Assessment Centers," a three-credit-hour, college-level course sanctioned and sponsored by the University of Virginia. MAP served as an arm of the career board for the FBI. Prior to 1974, first-line supervisors—middle and senior management staff—recommended and selected agents for promotion. No systematic or detailed analysis of the skills and competencies required for any specific position existed. Career boards reviewed personnel files, evaluated recommendations and interviewed candidates; there were no written tests. Often times, promotion materialized by directive in what was a "We want you, welcome to the club" selection process.

In 1973, this process changed in a dramatic fashion when Clarence Kelly, the Chief of the Kansas City Police Department, became the director of the FBI. Among the many innovative changes he implemented in the bureau was an imperative for review boards and programs to identify and train managers to achieve heightened performance. In 1974, Kelly ordered the establishment of an assessment center to address these issues. The assessment center made promotions competitive, more objective and systematic. As the process was job-specific, a candidate could have a high level of confidence in the results. The FBI was now better able to defend its promotion system process if a candidate were ever to contest the results.

The fundamental task of the assessment center was to identify the strengths and weaknesses of potential managers. The process identifies which knowledge, skills, and leadership qualities are required for a given supervisory position. These attributes, known as "dimensions," are necessary for successful performance. Typical dimensions include leadership, written communication, planning, organization, interpersonal sensitivity, oral communication, decisiveness, control of personnel and effective delegation.

The testing process requires timed situational exercises designed to simulate real-life situations and problems that the candidate will encounter on the job. Trained assessors consider the candidates' responses and make written notes to justify their conclusions. In each exercise, assessors identify the various dimensions under evaluation, then classify and score them on a scale of 1 to 5. A score of level 3 or higher is passing. A score of anything less than 3 reflects a deficiency in the measured dimension. A low score requires candidates to undertake developmental training to remedy the deficiency before consideration for further advancement. As the assessor responsible for the review of candidate scores, Jay recalled no one ever receiving an overall score of level 5, as the assessors contend that no one is perfect. The assessment center administrator reviews the entire range of performance ratings, which candidates have a right to contest. MAP does its utmost to minimize subjectivity and to create trust.

It was still common, however, to find a promotion given to an individual whose work record had fewer tangible accomplishments when compared to other candidates. Agents described this familiar "good ol' boy" connection with the in-house FBI saying, "a 2 with a hook is worth more than a 4." It was still too easy for a senior manager or for the career board to favor a candidate with a little creative rationalization or favoritism, which all too often trumped an objective score. Jay discovered that there were several managers who lacked faith in an objective selection process and instead manifested a pack mentality in which those who were "in" enjoyed protection and benefits and tossed aside those who were "out." Identifying "integrity" as the most important leadership trait, Jay maintained that a leader with integrity would earn the trust of his employees, and those employees would then do all they could to ensure recognition of that organization and leader as the best, since integrity ensured everyone's success.

Assisting non-Spanish speaking agents with their cases took time away from Jay's cases. Jay completed Spanish-language interviews, did the paperwork, and then both he and the case agent appeared on the FD-302, the official FBI report form used for trials. However, once the case concluded, Jay received no statistical credit. Failure to assist another agent is not something a dedicated agent wants or is willing to do. However, there is obvious and blatant unfairness when management refuses to credit vital assistance provided to another agent.

Jay testified,

> For an individual to be successful as an FBI agent, there are two things that are very important. One is the individual statistical accomplishments and the other is an administrative profile. From an evaluated agent adjudged as a good investigator, management looks at his statistical accomplishments, developed informants, [and] cases initiated and carried through to conclusion with arrests and successful prosecution obtained. Those are the statistical accomplishments. Administrative profile would be exposure to management. They have to know of the decisions that an agent can make, not only in investigations, but also in administrative things as a relief supervisor acting as a supervisor. Getting involved in discussions with other supervisors and ASACs so they can see just how well you can perform. Then they know who you are and remember your name. As a relief supervisor, you would have access to, or opportunity to call, FBI Headquarters and talk with bureau supervisors and bureau managers. Then your name becomes known, an administrative profile.

The assignments given to Spanish-speaking agents created a clear liability regarding promotion. An agent may initiate investigations and have them progress, and then management would assign the agent to a Title III or undercover operation, which required the agent to be away for several months. Supervisors then reassigned the "good" cases assigned to the Hispanic agent now on TDY, leaving them only the less important cases. The new case agent then received the honors, awards and credit that should rightfully have gone to the Hispanic undercover agent or Title III contributor. Many times, non-Spanish speaking agents depended on the Hispanic undercover operative, the Title III listeners, etcetera, relaying their results to obtain a successful prosecution. The non-Spanish speaking case agents received the kudos, the administrative profile and the credit, and the Hispanic agent moved on to another undercover operation or another Title III to cover the "needs of the bureau."

On one memorable occasion, the New York career board stated that, although Jay had high MAP scores, good performance ratings, an MBA and all of the requisite experience, they felt that Jay lacked leadership qualities and was not an aggressive enough agent. They did not keep these thoughts to themselves but sent this assessment off to their superiors at FBIHQ. Incorrect information in a personnel file is bad enough, but forwarding bad information to FBIHQ made it nothing short of evil. Jay believed that an EEO complaint would only add additional undue pressure for him and his family. Even though he had all of the right credentials, he testified, "It seems that I have to be better, I have to be more than mediocre, and I have to be outstanding as opposed to other non-Hispanic groups."

As a supervisor, Jay once received a directive from FBIHQ that listed agents with Hispanic surnames and informed each of them that they could not opt out of taking an upcoming Spanish language oral proficiency exam. Judge Bunton recalled Rarity's testimony that the FBI never forced agents under the modified program to participate in another program. At this point in the trial, the judge took over the questioning and discovered that the Spanish exam took all of about fifteen minutes. On this examination, there was no one to verify if Jay was the person who took the exam. Jay had the ability to translate from Spanish to English but required a dictionary to do so. The bureau never provided Jay with the results of the exam. It was through discovery that Jay learned that he had received a 3+ rating—a rating he thought was much higher than his actual ability, as he would have felt uncomfortable teaching a professional course or conducting a hostile interview in Spanish, both of which would require quick responses and exchanges of information.

Jay considered his assignments in various undercover roles as Hispanic criminal characters as "an offer you could not refuse." Jay testified, "Management will look at you as an agent who is not really dedicated to his trade, not aggressive, and not reliable. That will reflect on their opinion, and I am convinced it will reflect on their judgment in your career." Supervisors who assigned agents to undercover roles asked for Hispanic agents not because of their need for Spanish speakers, but because they "looked Hispanic." Jay believed that there was a common chain of thought in the bureau that Hispanic agents looked more like criminals or could pass themselves off as criminals than non-Hispanic FBI agents. Jay stated of his Irish supervisor, "Apparently Hispanics had more of a criminal look about them than anybody else. My mother doesn't agree with that."

On cross-examination, Jay acknowledged that the FBI had the authority to reduce a GS-15 position to a GS-14 position, adding that, while he earned GS-14 pay, the GS-15 responsibilities did not go away. The judge noted the inconsistency in language testing Hispanic agents who came in under the modified program and the fact that Jay received GS-14 pay for GS-15 duties, and that the FBI often undermined MAP scores, selecting instead their chosen candidates.

6

Felipe Frocht

Felipe Frocht first came to the United States from Uruguay as a foreign exchange student at age sixteen. In 1968, he entered the US Military Academy at West Point, New York, graduated with an engineering degree, and then served five years in the United States Army as a captain commanding an aero squadron. He joined the FBI in October 1977 under the language program—though he thought he entered under the modified program because of his military experience. He served first in Phoenix and then with the San Francisco Division.

Spanish language speakers have normal investigative duties, as well as numerous added assignments for special interviews, wiretaps, undercover investigations, and TDY assignments. When they are not traveling, they assist in interviews and translations and accomplish related paperwork for the agents who do not have translation capability. In contrast to non-Spanish speaking agents, Spanish speakers always work longer hours, carry a heavier workload, and have assignments that are more unpleasant. Spanish speakers are utility agents rather than case agents; the bureau's attitude seemed to be, "You are a Spanish speaker. We can use you for whatever we want, whenever we want, for as long as we want because that is what serves the needs of the bureau." That attitude did not apply to Anglo Spanish speakers.

Supervisors and field agents alike made discriminatory comments to Felipe, asking, "Where is your green card?" or "Why don't you speak English?" and told him, "You should not even be an agent." He saw numerous derogatory cartoons and comments posted in FBI offices. He never filed a complaint though, as he feared additional browbeating and intimidation.

Felipe worked field investigations in Spanish, used his Spanish language skills during SWAT operations, and worked numerous Spanish language "specials" throughout the country; except for the usual three weeks of annual leave and a few days off here and there, life was just one continuous work assignment for him. He used his Spanish language abilities half the time, often putting in twelve-hour shifts. When assigned to English-speaking Title IIIs, he learned that, to his surprise, agents worked eight-hour shifts because there were plenty of English speakers in the FBI. While Felipe's assignments were in seedy areas and rattrap hotels, non-Spanish speaking agents received assignments in which they benefitted from reimbursement for ski lift tickets and accommodations in nice condominiums.

Felipe tested at a 4+ rating in Spanish and sought a foreign assignment in a Legat position, but instead he found access to such assignments limited. He testified,

> My supervisor told me that any significant cases I had would be reassigned and cases that were not worth anything would wait until I returned. Therefore, I end up with lower quality cases and lower statistics. When time for the next special comes around, they will say, "you do not have significant cases, so you are the one to go TDY," creating a separation from [your] family, friends, supervisors, and observation of your work. Letters of commendation or thank you letters given to agents for serving on a wiretap are not even considered for promotions to a supervisory level.

Felipe's supervisor, William Edmond Smith, lowered his performance rating for informant development because he was away on TDY for five consecutive months. On one occasion, Smith instructed him not to "open" two informants he developed until right before an upcoming inspection. Felipe testified that, "this was so that when I opened these particular informants, it would show a response to a memorandum he made saying that we do not have enough informants, and we show that we are responding to his superior management and leadership skills."

For three years, Felipe worked an undercover assignment that had not gone to trial. He took the position because of both peer and managerial pressure. He knew of no agent who ever said "no" to an undercover assignment. Contrary to bureau regulations, Felipe received no training to work an undercover assignment, nor was he ever evaluated psychologically or monitored as to his physical or emotional stability. He received no reentry assistance upon completion of the assignment. Felipe complained about this to Supervisor Joe Chiaramonte and ASAC John Giaquinto. He completed no psychological debriefing because, once FBIHQ determined the operation was ending, management reassigned him to Chicago to work a wiretap.

On two occasions Felipe requested in writing that he be removed from the Spanish language program based on an FBIHQ memo that stated if a person had participated in the program for five years, that person could request removal from the program. However, management denied his requests. Felipe submitted a memorandum stating that he no longer wished to participate in the Career Development Program since his wife had also become a special agent. Although a fellow agent relinquished his selection for in-service training at Quantico so Felipe could visit his wife during the time she was in new agents' training, the division sent another agent instead.

Felipe is fluent in Spanish, French and English, although his English needed improvement, according to some Anglo agents. The FBI administered his French and Spanish tests by telephone. Felipe feared reprisal for his testimony because the FBI puts the thumb on those who challenge it. As retaliation, he noticed more assignments to wiretaps and additional harassment from his peers. His supervisors told him things like, "I hope you know what you're doing," and "I hope you guys burn." Felipe, a plaintiff class member, told his supervisor he wanted to reenter the Career Development Program. The supervisor, William Smith, told Felipe he would not support his request.

On cross-examination, Felipe confirmed his belief. His transfer to San Jose, California, as a Spanish speaker was not justified as he performed mere clerical work while assigned there, was the office janitor, and conducted technical training that required little Spanish. After four months in San Jose, he put in a request for transfer to San Francisco.

7

Alba Lorena Sierra

Lorena entered the bureau on September 23, 1986. She qualified to be an FBI Special Agent under the accounting program and earned her degree from California State University. After completion of training at Quantico, she transferred to the Chicago Division. The class action lawsuit marked the first time she had ever testified in court.

On the third day of training at Quantico, her counselors Hugh McMenamin and Rita Hopkins requested she resign. They told her that she just did not fit into the mold of an FBI agent and that the FBI was not the right place for her. They encouraged her to rethink her options. Although her counselors never told her they were discouraging her because she was Hispanic, she knew this to be the case when she added up and analyzed the ethnic comments they had made to her. Lorena thought diversity would benefit the bureau, instead of everyone looking the same. She passed all of the requisite academic exams during her training. She also passed all of the physical exams and all of the firearms marksmanship training.

Lorena did not understand what "mold" they expected her to fit into or how to stop the harassment. She had no intent to harm the bureau environment or create any discomfort for anyone. She appealed to her classmates for help, as they all knew what she was going through. Her classmates supported her, but management insisted she cut her hair, look more like the pictures in *Vogue* magazine, tone down her style of dress and appear more conservative. Contemptuous FBI supervisors, mindless of the law, were the first to tell Lorena that her appearance contaminated their conservative FBI mold.

She testified, "I was hired and they needed me because of my ethnicity, but at the same time they wanted to tone me down and mold me into what an FBI agent should look like." The judge interrupted her testimony, stating he did not know what "tone down" meant. He said, "I have a red nose, you know, and I try to tone it down. Is it something, makeup, or what are we talking about?" She stated she did not understand what they expected her to do. Among the suggestions she received were to cut her long dark hair and to style it differently. She went to an Anglo classmate to ask for fashion advice, took it, and made changes. However, this was still not good enough; counselors told her she just looked "too ethnic."

After twelve weeks of academic training and completion of physical fitness tests, agents in training are encouraged to remain active and to participate in sports and activities. Lorena received transfer orders to San Diego. The weekend before graduation, however, she and her classmates went on a class ski trip approved by the counselors. While skiing, Lorena injured her knee. The counselors told her not to worry; she could hobble across the stage on crutches. Everything would be fine, they said. Then, management blocked her from the graduation ceremonies and informed her that she would have to be "recycled." Recycling occurs during training when, due to events beyond their control, agents cannot complete the course, so the bureau gives them the option of returning later to do so. Although Lorena had already passed all of her marksmanship, physical and academic exams prior to the last week and had no exams at all scheduled during the final week, this decision kept her from graduating with the other agents in her training class.

Prior to all new agents' training at Quantico, officials swear in trainees as FBI agents on the first day they report for class, so Lorena was already an agent when she injured her leg. She even went ahead and sat through the last week of class—a week dedicated to lectures without exams or drills. She did not understand the reasoning behind recycling her, but accepted she must return and re-do the last week of new agent classes before she could receive her credentials as an agent. In the interim, the FBI reassigned her to Los Angeles, the same city in which she had applied to become an agent. In LA, management assigned her to handle questions and complaints from the public. This is an agent position in which she maintained her GS-10 rating. However, two weeks later, SAC Richard Bretzing transferred Lorena and made her a switchboard operator, downgrading her to a GS-4. At this point Judge Bunton interrupted her testimony and stated, "That is awfully good stuff, Ms. Sierra."

Two months later, FBIHQ notified her that they had canceled her assignment to San Diego. In the meantime, LA assigned two non-Hispanic, "recycled" female agents from the academy to handle applicant matters. At the same time that the FBI deemed Spanish translations critical and the LA drug squads and foreign counterintelligence squads needed translators, SAC Bretzing kept Lorena answering the telephone at a GS-4 position. This not only shortchanged the bureau, but also caused Lorena to lose $11,000 in pay. Management requested that Lorena sign a memo stating that she could not function as an agent because of her injury and that she consented to take an assignment as a switchboard operator to continue employment. Lorena needed the job. If the bureau would lead to work as an FBI agent, she figured she had to do what they said.

When she returned to Quantico to complete the missing week, her counselor informed her that she would have to repeat nine weeks of training. They forced her to retake all of her exams. Jim Greenleaf, the assistant director in charge of training, was the supervisor who had given Lorena the memorandum that stated that she was to return to finish the final week of training; however, now both Greenleaf and the Los Angles Division had decided it would be necessary for her to redo nine weeks. Lorena repeated all nine weeks of training, and once again passed all of her exams, but agents still harassed her for her appearance that did not fit the FBI mold.

During the first seven weeks of Lorena's second trip through training, her unit chief, Richard Hildreth, scolded her for being out of shape, even though she passed all physical tests. The maximum number of points an FBI agent can receive on the physical fitness test is fifty. The average number of points for the women in her class fell between seventeen and twenty. Lorena earned twenty-six points. Hildreth told her that he planned to make it difficult for her, as he felt she should resign and because, as he told her, he did not appreciate her presence. Lorena, tenacious in her determination, would not resign, as she had now completed training twice and knew she had accomplished as much, or more than, other agents.

Despite the pressure from both her counselor, David Miller, and from Hildreth to resign, Lorena overcame the adversity. She completed fifteen weeks of training, plus an additional nine weeks. During the last week of her second training, Hildreth told Lorena that, thanks to his close and careful supervision, she had improved enough to justify her graduation, even though the previous week he had still wanted to fire her. Once out of Quantico, Lorena hoped the harassment to be over.

Lorena's first assignment was the Chicago field office. In Chicago, she became part of what agents called the "Taco Circuit" for Spanish-speaking wires and assignments assisting other agents with Spanish language, instead of applying her accounting capabilities. Through discovery, Lorena found in her file a memorandum from Hildreth to her new supervisor Elaine Smith, warning Smith that Lorena was "worthless as an agent." When the DOJ objected to disclosing this information in court, the judge responded, "The letter speaks for itself."

Hildreth, who had told her upfront that he would do everything in his power to fire her, now requested that her new supervisor monitor, assess, and counsel her on her appearance. After passing all of the exact same exams given to other agents at Quantico, Hildreth now denied her the opportunity to start fresh at her new office as all other agents are able to do. Quantico's "Agent Mold" tainted her appearance even before she arrived in Chicago. Lorena transferred to the Terrorist Squad under the no-nonsense Supervisor William Dyson. With no hazardous material of discriminatory animus toward her "ethnic" looks, Dyson, considering her ability, rated her performance as successful and detailed her self-motivation and her requirement of minimal supervision.

Ms. Gulyassy conducted the cross-examination and pointed out that Lorena's assignment in LA as a switchboard operator had benefited "the needs of the bureau" and that Hildreth's letter advised that, without close careful supervision, SA Sierra might not be a successful agent, and outlined specific steps to assist in helping Lorena in becoming successful. Lorena responded, "You are talking about putting me on the applicant squad under close supervision, to be assigned with a mature agent to assess my personal appearance, how to go about grooming myself and stuff like that."

On the eighth day of the trial, Gary A. Lisotto testified that Lorena Sierra, Linda Rary and Karen Badian were all employees of the FBI, who for one reason could not complete their new agent training at Quantico. In LA, since she was in a cast and on crutches, the office gave Lorena a sedentary position, first complaint duty, and then, since LA needed telephone operators, as an operator. When Rary and Badian arrived in LA, there was a major recruitment effort under way, so they worked applicants. Los Angeles also needed translators, but Lisotto claimed to be unaware of why Lorena did not work as a translator. He did not know if anyone counseled Rary or Badian on their appearance or encouraged them to leave the FBI.

Hugh J. McMenamin testified that Lorena Sierra was a marginal trainee in the areas of firearms, defensive tactics and practical problems, and that she had great difficulty in all three areas. He instructed her to improve her performance or management would force her to come before the New Agents Review Board to determine her suitability for the job.

During cross-examination, McMenamin read from a document he wrote during her first training session, "That upon recertification for strenuous physical activity by an orthopedist, SA Sierra returned to Quantico at the start of training week fifteen so that she might fulfill the final phase of firearms qualifications." He could not provide an answer as to why FBI management forced Lorena to repeat nine weeks of training when she returned.

Lydia Jechorek testified that Lorena was young, bright, somewhat immature, a loner, and appeared to be disinterested. On numerous occasions counselors had to ask Lorena to pull back her hair and remove her long earrings. They counseled her on the dangers of long fingernails and her style of dress. Jechorek testified that Lorena wore tops that accentuated her bust and tight, form-fitting pants. Jechorek advised Lorena to make sure her clothing was "professional."

Attorney Hugo coaxed the stern-looking Jechorek, asking, "Does the FBI want all its FBI women to look like you?" Jechorek made no response. In addressing Lorena's demotion from GS-10 to GS-4 telephone operator, Hugo asked Lorena, "Did you take the oath of office as a special agent on the first day on the job?" Lorena responded that yes, she had taken the FBI agents' oath of office when she first reported to Quantico.

8

Dr. Gary LaFree

On the second day of the trial, Dr. Gary LaFree testified that he received his bachelor's degree, master's degree and Ph.D. from Indiana University in 1973, 1975 and 1979, respectively. He taught as a professor at the University of New Mexico in the sociology department and in the law school. He served as the director of the New Mexico Criminal Justice Statistical Analysis Center. The plaintiffs hired him to examine statistical evidence of a disparity between Hispanics and non-Hispanics regarding promotions, assignments, transfers and disciplinary action within the FBI. Gary found several disparities. He submitted his report to the court in a document titled, "A Study of Promotions, Assignments, and Disciplinary Actions by the Federal Bureau of Investigation." He stated that he had experience testifying for both plaintiffs and defendants, and that he had accomplished work for the US government, employers, and individuals.

Gary had trouble obtaining a security clearance from the FBI, and the initial information given to him by the Personal Information Network System (PINS) included erroneous, disorganized and misleading data, all of which created delays in completing his research for trial. Many of the issues that the plaintiffs had asked him to review, the bureau excluded in the original PINS tapes. The bureau provided no information on undercover assignments, none on transfers, none on career boards, and none on MAP participation. Other information appeared to be erroneous, or at least difficult to interpret through computerization. The FBI produced records that indicated that some agents transferred to San Juan ten or twelve times—an impossible outcome. Requests for correct information came through a continuous process of discovery requests.

Security access made research difficult. FBI management told Gary to make notes on data at a warehouse in Albuquerque, in which the FBI forbade him to use a computer and disallowed him to remove any documents. Travel to Washington was expensive and difficult. The FBI denied him access to some FBI data systems. FBIHQ informed him that some data did not exist, yet he found a letter from Dr. Klemm, the FBI's consultant and expert witness, concerning the same machine-readable transfer data he sought. On his second trip to FBIHQ, which Gary labeled the "Bonanza trip," he had access to the career board, and the undercover and personal information he required.

Gary found a significant difference between Hispanics and non-Hispanics as to disparity in each grade, with few Hispanic agents in management positions. Hispanics represented 4.3% of the FBI's agent population. This meant that the statistical probability of Hispanic agents in Grades 15 through 18 should have numbered at about 40. The FBI was not even close to that number, as the proportion fell at .78, less than 1%. However, Gary found that a disproportionate number of Hispanic agents participated in MAP I and II—programs crucial to obtaining management-level positions. Hispanic agents received more administrative actions than non-Hispanic agents; 33.4% of all Hispanic special agents had served in San Juan, Puerto Rico, and that Hispanics accounted for 25% of all temporary duty assignments.

In reviewing Dr. Klemm's defendants report, Gary noted flaws wherein she had divided the sample comparisons into smaller units, which reduced the chance of finding a significant difference. Dr. Klemm's analysis also failed to deal with the current conditions of Hispanic agents in the FBI. Gary observed that Dr. Klemm's report did not include statistical tests of the differences between Hispanics and non-Hispanics regarding management and non-management positions.

Felix Baxter, amid cross-examination, asked Gary to address the potential issues behind the statistical disparity between Hispanics and non-Hispanics on promotions, task assignments, location assignments and disciplinary actions. Gary stated his purpose was not to explain why there were discrepancies or disparities between the groups, but to show that such disparities existed. None of the excuses offered by the FBI would have made any difference in the statistical data he obtained.

When management gave Gary bad information or told him that the data did not exist, he was fortunate to have a few Hispanic agents available to provide assistance. Gary said, "I assume volition has to do with the internal workings inside the individual's mind. I am comparing the differences between Hispanic and non-Hispanic in various aspects of the FBI organization, and disciplinary action and assignments."

On the sixth day of the trial, Dr. Rebecca Klemm, who received more than $200,000 in consulting fees from the FBI, testified that Hispanic agents advance in promotions at a much faster rate than non-Hispanics. At this point, Judge Bunton tried to clarify another part of her testimony and determine whether Dr. Klemm had identified Spanish-speaking agents with Anglo surnames, giving as examples two fictitious names such as a George Johnson or a George Jones, and if she had done any analysis on the number who had dropped out of the language program. She had not:

> THE COURT: The reason I would do that, I mean do you know whether George Johnson speaks English or Spanish? That is not a Hispanic name. I was raised in Marfa; we did not have a single person by the name of George Johnson or George Jones that could speak Spanish.
>
> KLEMM: I do not know about George Johnson or George Jones. There is a Eugene O'Leary, III, who is Hispanic; I have been surprised at some of the names actually.

Dr. Klemm, surprised that Hispanics sometimes had Anglo surnames, was not an expert qualified to testify on FBI policies and procedures. In his final analysis, Judge Bunton ruled that the statistics she had provided to the court were irrelevant. Attorney Tony Silva worked his way through a mountain of questions and demonstrated his expertise in cases dealing with statistical data much too onerously detailed to include in summary.

There was no higher FBI authority to "present on the record" than John D. Glover, who was the executive assistant director of the Administrative Services Division of the FBI. When the court referred to official charts or data provided by the FBI that contained obvious errors or that contradicted his testimony, Glover testified that he "assumed they were correct," "let's assume they are correct," or said that "maybe there were exceptions," but that they are "generally okay," and "could be correct."

Thousands of FBI agents arrive early and leave work late, skip lunch or a visit to the gym to prepare relevant documents and data for a trial. Agents in the courtroom were disheartened that Glover appeared satisfied that the FBI produced exhibits to a federal court with erroneous data and analysis that he "assumed to be correct"—this from the EAD in charge of administration and records. Good thing Glover was not in charge of the gun vault or armory.

Glover described the bureau's three-card system as an agent's personal capture of time in and out of the over two hundred classifications of investigative programs. Hugo asked Glover to fill out a three-card as a Hispanic working undercover on a drug case, bank robbery or white-collar crime case. After puzzling over the request for some time, he admitted he could not do it and told the court that the plaintiff attorney assumed that the FBI had no other record keeping system. When asked, Glover failed to provide guidance to any other form of record keeping that could record the requested data. Glover said it was conceivable that an agent might just write in "undercover assignment" on the three-card but admitted he had no knowledge of how this information would be captured at FBIHQ.

Glover, who claimed to be working on his Ph.D., did not find it at all strange or unusual that the FBI produced a statistical chart, which claimed to show that 4.3% of relief supervisors were Hispanic, which, in what was an incredible coincidence, was the exact percentage of Hispanics in the FBI. He also failed to explain why only 2.39% of Hispanics attended MAP. Glover testified that Hispanics and non-Hispanics in MAP did well but failed to advance equally.

Glover, who climbed the ladder quickly and had been made a SAC within thirteen years, testified that field supervisor service was a required prerequisite for Mat and anyone else to become a SAC, although he had never served as a field supervisor. He agreed with the Klemm report that supposedly proved Hispanics received promotions at a faster rate than their non-Hispanic counterparts, and then read twenty-two names of Anglo SACs who averaged fifteen years of service before being promoted to SACs.

Once the judge certified the lawsuit, the FBI promoted Julian De La Rosa, a Hispanic with twenty-five years of service who was not a plaintiff class member, to a SAC position. Now there were two Hispanic-surnamed SACs. The lawsuit also led to the immediate promotions of Gene O'Leary, Tony Riggio, and Leroy Teitsworth to Grade 15 positions, all non-class members now represented to the judge as Hispanics. Glover, as chairperson of the executive career board, testified that there were some positions yet unannounced where the career board made the selection, which he thought was fair.

Glover did not believe in the necessity that candidates for foreign assignments demonstrate fluent or near-fluent proficiency in the local language, since an FBI policy was in effect which stated that the minimal language proficiency was a level 3 rating. Hispanic agents were eligible for positions as English-speaking legal attaches, but there was no evidence of a Hispanic ever receiving such a post.

Glover testified that the FBI hired attorneys consistent with the needs of the organization and that they employed over one thousand attorneys, including three hundred actual attorney positions in the FBI and others who served in investigative capacities. Hugo questioned Glover:

> RODRIGUEZ: Assume we have two agents, agent A and agent B. Both of these individuals come under the diversified program. Agent A, without government expense, obtains a law degree. Agent B does nothing but grow up in a Spanish household with no enhancement of language. Can the FBI require agent A to do legal work in the FBI?
>
> GLOVER: No.

RODRIGUEZ: Can the FBI require agent B to use their Spanish-speaking ability for the FBI?

GLOVER: The minority program is within the modified program, so it is conceivable the answer is yes.

RODRIGUEZ: Do you see that as contradictory?

GLOVER: No, I do not.

Glover saw no difference in Anglo agents dropping out of the language program after three years, even those trained by the FBI. Since the Spanish language was a priority for the bureau, management forbade Hispanic agents to drop out.

On the seventh day of the trial, Executive Assistant Director John E. Otto agreed with Dr. Klemm's report that wiretap work counted in promoting supervisors. However, in reviewing the minutes of many career board meetings, he found no mention anywhere of wiretap work. Major Cases require a lot of timely attention. It was not customary to have more than a few major ongoing cases in an office, although it sometimes happened. Otto claimed that the FBI considered the four Major Cases in finding Mat and his staff of fifty-five agents with administrative deficiencies.

Mat returned to LA because Otto maintained that Mat needed assistance in administration and because Bretzing was an outstanding administrator able to assist him in working through his weaknesses. However, Otto failed to provide any instruction to Bretzing, and Bretzing testified that he had received no information on Mat's shortcomings or even been advised in advance of his transfer back to LA. Otto did not ask for or receive a report on any administrative training that Mat might have received or that Bretzing may have provided.

Otto was also willing to demote Mat from GS-16 to GS-14 in Houston, as Mat had failed to perform well at the Administrative ASAC level, but Otto said that it was not his role to remove Mat's Grade 16 for poor performance. He testified that there were nine SACs who never served as field supervisors, yet FBIHQ ruled that Mat must serve as a supervisor before receiving any consideration for further promotion.

Otto verified that he allowed SAC Dick Held to handpick all of the agents he wanted in San Juan, yet FBIHQ denied Mat the same opportunity. He threatened Mat with insubordination charges when he requested removal of a supervisor.

Otto testified that the FBI did not promote Mat to SAC El Paso because of a pending administrative matter of insubordination. He said he was unsure of the specifics but that Glover knew them. Hugo advised the court that, on the previous day, Glover testified that Otto would be the one with the information. A news reporter in the courtroom whispered that, while FBI field agents train to point and fire their weapons at the Firearms Range, management trains for finger pointing and buck-passing.

Otto could not identify a single Hispanic agent who had served on the career boards at headquarters, who was assigned to the DEA as an executive, or was in the English-speaking Legal Attaché Office. Yet, he knew Hispanics had joined the FBI as early as the 1960s.

Otto entered the FBI on October 12, 1964 and became a SAC within twelve years. Women had served as FBI agents for over sixteen years, but after all that time there were still no female SACs, ASACs, or section chiefs. Upon hearing this revelation, the judge quizzed Otto:

THE COURT: How many women are SACs?

OTTO: We have no women who are SACs. The first women came aboard the FBI in 1972, if I am not mistaken.

THE COURT: Sixteen years, you mean nobody has risen to SAC in sixteen years?

OTTO: We have some women close to that and will become SACs, yes.

THE COURT: The answer is none now?

OTTO: We do not have any now, no. There are no women SACs in the FBI, sir.

THE COURT: ASACs?

OTTO: We have no women ASACs either in the FBI.

THE COURT: Is there a quota or a cap on promotions for any minority group in the FBI?

OTTO: No, there is not.

THE COURT: Is there a quota to MAP?

OTTO: No.

THE COURT: MAP II?

OTTO: No. There are no quotas.

THE COURT: Assume a hundred go through MAP I. The list comes in to you. These hundred folks will attend. Is there any determination made of whether this hundred are women or blacks or Hispanics agents, [and] is there any attempt made to determine how many of these hundred are minorities?

OTTO: Not at the present time, no, sir. We are trying to recommend the best persons possible.

9

Edmundo L. Guevara

Ed Guevara, born in Ecuador, moved to the United States in 1954. He became a naturalized citizen, attended Hunter College in New York City and received a Bachelor of Arts in health, public education and physical education. He became a special agent on April 25, 1976, and after training returned to New York. In 1981, he received a master's degree in health education from Delphi University. His work experience in the FBI included fugitive apprehension work, foreign counterintelligence, bank robbery, and organized crime. He served as a staff investigator on the President's Commission on Organized Crime. Ed came into the FBI under the Spanish Language Program, receiving a level 3+ proficiency rating. He served as a defensive tactics instructor, hostage negotiator, and a SWAT team member. Ed applied for several supervisory positions, but management informed him that his FBI law enforcement experience, teaching experience, and master's degree were just not enough.

Ed applied for a two-year term position under Manny Gonzalez, Chief Investigator for the President's Commission, and became one of two investigators assigned to the President's Commission on Organized Crime. He worked as a supervisory staff investigator, GS-14 level, and supervised twelve to fifteen police officers and agents; he accomplished every related function in preparation for hearings, completed a region-by-region analysis of organized crime and compiled a report that went straight to the President of the United States.

Yet when Ed applied for the position of supervisor of the Garden City Resident Agency in New York, the New York Division selected Pasquale D'Amuro. D'Amuro had not even applied for the position, nor did he go before the New York career board. D'Amuro lived in New Jersey, and the New York Division created a "cause transfer" which allowed his family to move to Long Island and enable him to work in a supervisory position before the official selection process. This new position required work on property crimes, bank robbery, and fugitive matters, all of which Ed had.

ASAC Jules Bonavolonta told Ed that, as a consolation, he would receive the next desk for which he applied in New York. Ed later applied for the Luchese Organized Crime Supervisor Squad. Ed knew the Luchese family inside out, and he had cracked a very important related case that received lots of media attention. Instead, the position went to Dennis Weaver of Cincinnati, which was not a hotbed of organized crime. The secretary of the career board, Robin Montgomery, told Ed that he not only failed to get the position but that he was not even one of the top candidates.

Ed served as the principal relief supervisor under Dennis Weaver, a position that included a $700 cash award. However, Ed did not receive the financial award because of a dispute over a day-off. When Ed attempted to initiate an EEO complaint, the EEO coordinator, David Martinez, advised him as a friend that if he enjoyed working near his residence in Queens, he better not proceed and pursue his EEO complaint.

The FBI had a regular policy of transferring agents in their first office to a second office within a few years; however, sometimes agents remained longer in some large offices. The Pilot 44 Group program transferred first office agents who served for over ten years in New York to their office of preference. Because Ed belonged to that group, he received a transfer out of New York. Ed grew tired of the forced travel to other offices for Title IIIs, and tired of assisting non-Spanish speaking agents and doing all of their paperwork for them, and he had finally decided his Spanish-language abilities were a detriment to his career as they caused him to be away from his family for extended periods.

Under cross-examination, Mr. Baxter attempted to make the point that his Spanish had not been a detriment to Ed, even though he had received no promotions. Even as high-level officials at FBIHQ recognized Ed for his work, Ed feared reprisal. He reconfirmed that, despite the recognition of his accomplishments and experience, none of that recognition ever translated into a promotion.

10

Fernando E. Mata

Fernando E. Mata became a special agent of the FBI on August 14, 1972, and assignments in Chicago, Newark and Miami followed. He came to the United States from Cuba in 1961 and received a bachelor's degree in science in Emporia, Kansas, then went on to Washington Law School in Topeka to receive his law degree. He is a member of the Kansas Bar Association. The DOJ attempted to prevent Fernando from testifying as his complaint of discrimination involved classified material, and they could not declassify the proposed exhibits in order to complete his deposition.

Fernando served as an assistant legal adviser in the Newark office, where he taught criminal law to local law enforcement officers and other FBI agents. However, when he showed interest in a legal position at FBIHQ, management informed him that his name, a Cuban accent and his background would reflect badly on the FBI.

Between 1979 and 1985, while working out of the Miami office, Fernando served undercover on national security foreign counter-intelligence assignments that required extensive foreign travel with another principal US intelligence agency. In recognition of his work, he received the Attorney General's Award from the Department of Justice in 1983. This is the highest investigative award presented to an FBI agent. At no time did he ever receive any undercover training or psychological re-entry counseling. Fernando received several other commendations, incentive awards and letters of recommendation, none of which helped him to attain his goal of a supervisory position in the FBI Intelligence Division, which dealt with Latin American affairs, or a Cuban foreign counterintelligence supervisory position in the Miami office. Fernando testified that the FBI saw fit to promote both Anthony Amoroso and Lance Emory as past recipients of the Attorney General's Award, yet the FBI denied him a promotion.

The Attorney General's Award identified Fernando as an agent who worked "frequently in an atmosphere of substantial personal hazard." Fernando now realized that the atmosphere of substantial personal hazard was no harsher on the outside than on the inside.

Fernando participated in a fundraiser to support the class action lawsuit; a story appeared the next day in a Miami newspaper with the headline, "Hispanic FBI Agent Says Bureau Discriminates, Will Not Promote Him." William E. Wells, SAC Miami, called an all-agents conference in which he singled out Fernando by name. When Wells said that he wanted to see all of the Hispanic agents in his conference room after the meeting, the Anglo agents all applauded. After that, Fernando was ridiculed and ostracized.

In the meeting with the Hispanics, Wells declared that Fernando had embarrassed the bureau and set back recruiting efforts for the FBI. He stated that when someone carries FBI credentials they lose their First Amendment rights. Fernando spoke up,

> Mr. Wells, I disagree with you, there is something more precious at stake here than even being an FBI agent, which is being an American citizen. I am a citizen by choice, not because I was born here, and I became a citizen because I wanted to become a citizen. The Constitution of the United States is the most precious document that exists here, and you cannot take that away from me or from any FBI agent. I want to let you know of that First Amendment right and I respect you as a SAC in the Miami Division, but this is something that you cannot take away from me, or anybody in this room. Because that is what, above all, I as an FBI agent will uphold and will respect.

During cross-examination, Ms. Black mentioned that there was an insubordination charge pending against Fernando and that, at no time before that charge of disobeying orders in context of his foreign counterintelligence assignments, did Fernando ever make any claim of being under stress. Ms. Black maintained that during the Miami SAC's all-agents meeting, Wells had stated that he did not want the lawsuit to be divisive and that any complaints of discrimination needed internal handling. Fernando testified that Wells told him that he and Paul Magallanes had violated MAOP procedures and projected disciplinary action. Ms. Black, referring to Fernando's applications for various positions, stressed that Fernando did not know the specific qualifications of those candidates selected over him and therefore had no proof of discrimination.

Several days later, Ricardo Jose Melendez testified that he thought the all-agent meeting called by Wells was more about managerial techniques to prevent problems within the division and within the Miami community than about inaccurate information printed in the newspaper. During the initial meeting, Wells appeared angry, but Melendez did not recall Wells mentioning Fernando Mata by name, except when he read the newspaper article. On cross-examination, Melendez stated that, although he was not a class member and had experienced no discrimination, he respected agents like Ed Mireles and thought that the 311 class-member agents could be depended on to testify truthfully on issues of discrimination.

Arturo Rivera, a non-class member, testified that the office did not promote Fernando because the squad members did not support Fernando when he served as a relief supervisor. Under oath, he testified that he knew of no discrimination at all in the FBI, but admitted he had no reason to question the integrity or veracity of the Hispanic class members. He did not remember discussing issues of discrimination in Miami with his Hispanic agent friends.

11

Hector Jose Berrios

Hector Jose Berrios began his FBI career as a clerk. He entered the FBI under the modified program with professional work experience as a productive planner. He also took the Spanish Language exam prior to entering the bureau but did not pass. He holds a bachelor's degree in economics. During his career as an investigator, he worked criminal investigations and foreign and counterintelligence investigations. He received fifteen commendations and never received a performance rating lower than superior.

Hector applied for two separate supervisory positions; the first was a position at FBI headquarters as a foreign counterintelligence supervisor. The New York office career board recommended him, as did his supervisors from the intelligence division and the FBI Assistant Director of Intelligence. A non-Hispanic agent got the job instead. Hector also applied for a supervisory position in New York, and the assistant director of that division recommended him. That position also went to a non-Hispanic agent.

More than once the bureau ordered Hector to retake the Spanish-language examination. He sought counsel from his supervisor, Tom Harper; his ASAC, Kevin Donovan; and SAC Donald McGorty, and he discussed with each the bureau's insistence that he retake the Spanish exam. They all counseled against it. They told him that there were no regulations requiring him to do so and that FBIHQ had singled him out because of his Spanish surname. Hector took the exam because his SAC told him that one of the assistant directors of the FBI had informed the SAC that if Hector refused take the exam he would have Hector fired. This same SAC had earlier informed Hector that the FBI could not force him to take the test. Hector, who six years earlier had failed the exam, and had since engaged in no academic study or practice to enhance his language skills, now discovered that, to his surprise, he had passed the test with a 3 proficiency rating.

After the FBI compelled Hector to take the Spanish exam by threatening him with termination, and he had taken and passed it, management disciplined him for "conduct bordering on insubordination" because of his initial reluctance to take the exam. Hector learned through discovery that SAC McGorty, who had counseled him not to take the examination, had followed up by sending a communication to FBIHQ that recommended Hector's suspension for five days, that he serve ninety days of probation and receive a letter of censure.

On cross-examination by Ms. Simon, Hector testified that he worked undercover and on special assignments requiring use of the Spanish language both before and after passing the test. Hector dropped out of the career development program because of his frustration at not receiving promotions. Hector had felt more qualified than Thomas Harper, the candidate selected, because Hector had served as the acting squad supervisor, knew all the cases and the personnel, had rated the personnel, and served on that squad for two years. Harper was a Cuban-American with a Spanish rating of 4+ on his PINS data. Dodge Frederick from headquarters told Hector he was the only applicant, but the bureau decided to relist the opening and seek additional applicants, and then selected Harper instead of Hector.

John D. Glover testified that he had no recollection of disciplining Hector Berrios for his reluctance in taking the Spanish language exam. To his knowledge, FBI agents volunteer for language tests. An agent who enters under a language program as a prerequisite for his or her employment is required throughout their career to utilize that language. He was unaware that Hector had not come into the bureau under the language program. Glover testified that he saw no discrimination in requiring an agent to use their Spanish language skills, even if that person had not come into the bureau under the language program, and though they did not require agents to use their legal experience as attorneys if they had not entered under the attorney program.

On the eighth day of the trial, Margaret Gulotta, Field Operations Program Manager, Language Services Unit at FBIHQ, testified that she knew of no one who had the authority to force Hector to take the language exam, find him insubordinate, or suspend him for his reluctance to do so. She believed that forcing a person to take a test and then expecting that person to pass was not a good policy. She was unaware that, in 1986, Gordon McGinley, chief of the Language Services Unit, had told the SAC conference in San Francisco there was no need for additional Spanish speakers in the FBI.

Gulotta introduced a classified Department of Defense Language testing document, access to which the FBI had denied to plaintiff attorneys. Gulotta confirmed the government expert's report that claimed to have found that Hispanics worked only 5 of the 201 temporary duty (TDY) assignments in 1987. However, afterwards she read from a 1987 exhibit in which the first ten names of agents listed and assigned TDY more than twice were Hispanic. In doing so, she contradicted both the findings of the FBI "expert" and her confirmation and verification of those findings.

The FBI promulgated a policy that an agent could write a letter to his SAC and request removal from the language program after serving three years. Gulotta testified that she had not heard of one Hispanic whom the FBI removed from the language commitment. She added that all such actions revolved around "the needs of the bureau."

The Language Unit assumed, when testing telephonically, that the agent at the other end of the line taking the language test was the agent who they were supposed to test, but there was no failsafe method of verification and no requirement for the person taking the test to prove they were who they claimed to be.

12

John Navarrete

John Navarrete, born, raised and educated in El Paso, Texas, received a bachelor's degree in political science and a master's degree in education from the University of Texas at El Paso (UTEP). He became a schoolteacher, coach and an assistant principal for the Ysleta Independent School District prior to accepting a position with the FBI. He entered the bureau on October 6, 1969. In 1986, he transferred to FBI Headquarters in the Criminal Investigative Division, the Drug Section, assigned to combat Mexican drug traffickers.

John worked fifteen to twenty Title IIIs that ran for thirty days or more. If a Title III is productive, courts normally approve a thirty-day extension, which requires the absence of the agent from their other investigative duties for ninety days but sometimes longer. Hispanic agents assigned to T-IIIs find them burdensome because they have less of an opportunity to develop as supervisory special agents. John oversaw Title III investigations at FBIHQ. He believed it was unnecessary to have special agents staff Title IIIs.

SAC Jack Hinchcliffe approved John's attendance at MAP I as a supervisory slot would be available soon in San Juan. The MAP assessors determined his management potential was contingent upon development in the areas of judgment, leadership and tenacity. MAP assessors also documented that he spoke with a Hispanic accent. The notation of accents in personnel files in private industry would be unwarranted and a detriment to the person. Management never removed John's MAP contingencies or struck the note about his accent.

In January of 1978, when he returned to El Paso, Texas, John submitted a request to step down from the career development program because of the large amount of work involved in his current investigation of the assassination of a federal judge. When he later sought to return to the career development program, his supervisor informed him that he had MAP contingencies that would block him from receiving promotions. Yet John noticed that agents received promotions who never attended MAP. All the while, the bureau continued to promote supervisors with contingencies.

John worked in Puerto Rico as a supervisor in 1983 when San Juan needed to increase the office staff by thirty agents. When an office receives authorization to increase their resources by thirty agents, it is because the office is working major investigations. Non-Spanish-speaking Anglo agents signed up for Spanish language training at a cost of $16,000 per agent and then received transfer orders to San Juan, which entailed a two-year commitment instead of four.

Ms. Black, the DOJ attorney, pointed out that it was common for MAP attendees to have contingencies. While assigned to Newark, John met the director of the FBI and, through conversation and not a formal complaint, mentioned that he felt underutilized and unable to reach his full potential in Hackensack. Several days later, the SAC called John into his office and told him that the director's office wanted to know what an "American Indian" was doing in Hackensack. Afterwards John transferred to San Juan. John did not know which was worse: MAP assessors blacklisting him because of an alleged accent or the director of the FBI misidentifying his ethnicity.

13

John Paletti

John Paletti received a Bachelor of Arts in criminology from Brooklyn College. Prior to becoming an FBI agent, he was a New York Police Department (NYPD) officer for two years, a United States immigration officer for one year, and a US Customs officer for seven years. He experienced no discrimination as a police officer, immigrations officer or customs officer. John entered the FBI in 1986, assigned to the New Haven Division Hartford resident agency for two years. He worked organized crime, La Costra Nostra matters and the Macheteros, a Puerto Rican domestic terrorist group. At the time of the trial, John had thirteen cumulative years of professional law enforcement experience.

The first time John experienced discrimination was while working for the FBI. A promotion from GS-11 to GS-12 that was due in January of 1988 did not occur, in violation of federal regulations, because his supervisor discovered he was a member of the class action. Although his current appraisals were fully successful, the bureau held up his promotion. He requested a transfer to another squad but was unsuccessful, while other agents received transfers.

On cross-examination, Mr. Baxter advised John that an administrative inquiry against him prevented his promotion. John responded, "There was an administrative inquiry in 1987, but FBI regulations, as well as Federal General Regulations for Personnel, do not contain any provisions for holding back one's promotion based on an administrative inquiry." When he inquired about his pending promotion, Wanda Harrison in the FBI Pay and Position Management Unit informed him about "how Headquarters doesn't necessarily go by the FBI Administrative Manual; they have their own little set of guidelines."

14

Raymond M. Campos

Raymond "Ray" Campos, born in Las Vegas, New Mexico, attended the University of Utah on an athletic scholarship and graduated in 1967 with a BA in Spanish. He joined the Marine Corps, served for six and a half years as an instructor pilot and test pilot, stationed in South Vietnam. He received a promotion to Captain and served as operations officer of a squadron. Ray joined the FBI in 1973, served in San Francisco, at first working general criminal and foreign counter-intelligence matters. He transferred to Oakland, California, where he worked general property crimes.

Ray transferred to San Juan in 1977 and stayed for two years. There he worked civil rights matters, political corruption and property crimes. He served as the SWAT team coordinator for the office and coordinated the Pan American Games in 1979. Ray was the designated pilot for the office. He initiated the pilot program in San Juan. He transferred in 1979 to Phoenix, Arizona, working on the Organized Crime Squad. Ray worked on the Narcotics Squad as the Narcotics Coordinator, served as the Organized Crime Task Force Coordinator, and as the Special Operations Group Coordinator. Since joining the bureau, he earned over fifty letters of commendation that included within-grade promotions and monetary awards. He was proud to be an American, and both Hispanic and Mormon.

Ray submitted seven applications for advancement and suffered discrimination because he was a Spanish-speaking Hispanic agent. Of all of the agents selected for promotion in which he submitted applications, none were Hispanic. He entered into the FBI through the modified program because of his professional experience in the Marine Corps. He did not expect the FBI to force him to use his Spanish language abilities to the point of detriment. FBIHQ forced him to take the Spanish exam after becoming an FBI agent, and he passed with a level 4+ proficiency rating; he received transfer orders for San Juan. Ray expected reprisal for his testimony and involvement in the lawsuit. He often heard racial slurs and ethnic jokes directed at Hispanics. His ASAC questioned his involvement with the lawsuit.

On cross-examination, DOJ attorney Sheridan Black attempted to imply that, if Spanish and piloting were such detriments to his career, those skills would never have appeared listed in his applications. Ray countered that those assets never helped with promotions. He thought that a remark made by SAC Herbert Hawkins was discriminatory, and Hawkins became incensed when Ray told him so. Ray also thought that the remarks of ASAC Larry McCormick, which attempted to restrict his lawsuit participation by ordering him to return at once after testifying in court, attempted to deny him the opportunity to secure his rights. Black attempted to dismiss the anti-Hispanic and anti-Mormon slurs overheard by Ray as not serious because he did not hear such statements regularly throughout his FBI career.

On the seventh day of the trial, Larry J. McCormick, ASAC Phoenix Division, testified that he had learned that Raymond Campos had written a memo indicating his absence from the office for two weeks was because he was an exempted agent assisting the trial attorneys in the trial. He called FBIHQ and learned that Ray was not on the "approved" list, so he instructed Ray's supervisor to tell Ray that, upon completion of his testimony, he was to return to Phoenix. McCormick said that he took instruction from legal counsel in refusing to allow Ray to help plaintiff's counsel for two weeks.

The Marine Corps found it beneficial to promote Ray to Captain. The FBI found it beneficial to hire one of the few, one of the proud Marines because of his experience, yet promoting Ray was unreasonable. Although he earned over fifty commendations, it was not enough for him to receive a promotion within the FBI. Even though the FBI put food on his family's table, it was impossible for Ray to advise his son to assume his role into the FBI, because he did not want his son to become just another casualty of discrimination.

Promotions eluded Ray, although he had an excellent work record—a record unlike Victor Gonzalez, a non-class member, whom Mat promoted to supervisor in San Juan. Gonzalez did not feel Mat supported him enough. Gonzalez also testified on the seventh day of the lawsuit that he received his promotion to GS-15 following the filing of the lawsuit. He served as an ombudsman with four primary duties. He mentioned three of the four responsibilities of an ombudsman but could not remember the primary role. After squirming in the witness seat and experiencing a minute of stress and perspiration, the DOJ provided him with the answer: his principal responsibility was to handle questions raised by agents or support personnel in the field.

As an ombudsman and a native-born Puerto Rican agent, Gonzalez made none of the security changes that the San Juan agents requested. Instead, ombudsman Doug Ball made those changes. Unlike Ray, Gonzalez never once sat on a wire or worked undercover. Gonzalez testified that he had never seen or even heard of discrimination within the bureau but said he would encourage agents in career advancement "if I see potential."

15

Rogelio De La Garza

Rogelio De La Garza graduated from Pan American University in 1971 with a BA in accounting. He worked as an accountant for a year and then taught accounting at a business college for six months prior to joining the FBI in October of 1972. He entered the FBI under the Spanish Language program. His first assignment was in Chicago, Illinois, where he worked applicant and fugitive cases. Most fugitives were Spanish speakers. He then worked on the gambling squad, specializing in Puerto Rican Bolita cases, which were numbers rackets. He transferred to San Juan, Puerto Rico, for two years working all types of "reactive work": applicants, civil rights, bank robberies, extortions, and kidnappings. From San Juan, he transferred to Miami and worked accounting, terrorism, and foreign counterintelligence for six years before transferring to the San Antonio Division to work in the Laredo, Texas RA. He did not think he looked Hispanic, yet his work assignments all took him in that direction. He believed he suffered discrimination because of his numerous transfers, assignments, and lack of career development.

Rogelio received good ratings in most of his MAP elements, except in judgment and problem analysis. He requested help in working off the contingencies, but no one helped him. He left the Career Development Program (CDP) because of his involvement in an

FBI-DEA joint investigation that required uncompensated duties and, because this assignment was away from the office, it made it even more difficult for him to remove the contingencies. Rogelio later returned to the Career Development Program, as he desired advancement within the FBI. He felt he was much more qualified than another agent selected for a supervisory position in the McAllen RA.

Rogelio's wife received a degree from the University of Houston's Pharmacy School and held a pharmacy license from the Commonwealth of Puerto Rico but was unemployed, as on the island there were more applicants for pharmacy positions than there were jobs. Rogelio informed his SAC that Florida, California, New York, Hawaii, and the District of Columbia were the places that refused to reciprocate his wife's Puerto Rican pharmacist license. SAC Jack Hinchcliffe told him that he did not make phone calls to assist agents who served two-year assignments in San Juan, but that he would help if Rogelio would extend his assignment. Since he did not extend it, the FBI transferred Rogelio to Miami, Florida, a state in which his wife could not use her pharmacist's license. The SAC told Rogelio that his transfer from San Juan to Miami was to debrief former Cuban political prisoners, but when he arrived in Miami, the SAC there put him on the accounting squad instead. The FBI often used reassignment as a punitive measure against agents.

While in Miami, Rogelio filed an EEO complaint over the night supervisor position. The office announced a position requiring a Spanish speaker and other specific criteria. Rogelio met all the requirements. Instead, Miami awarded the position to a first office agent, even though he did not have the majority of skills that the position required. Rogelio reported that filing the EEO complaint hindered his career and that he also feared retaliation or being labeled a malcontent because of his testimony in the class action.

From Miami, Rogelio received transfer orders to San Antonio, his office of preference, but ended up instead in Laredo, Texas. If he refused the transfer, it would limit his chance of ever getting to San Antonio. ASAC De La Rosa told Rogelio that the transfer to the Laredo RA was due to his Spanish-speaking talents.

16

Aaron H. Sanchez

Aaron H. Sanchez graduated with a B.A. in education from Minnesota State University and worked for the Bureau of Indian Affairs and the Navajo tribe. After two years, he got a job at the US Agency for International Development (USAID) working in community development projects in various Latin American countries and with various US embassies on projects in rural areas and third-world cities. In 1975, he joined the bureau in San Diego, his first office. He later received a hardship transfer from San Diego to Denver and, in January of 1984, arrived in Los Angeles. Aaron received a QSI, a recognized quality step increase, due to his exceptional work, and this included the remuneration of a salary increase.

Aaron and six other Hispanic agents applied for a Spanish-speaking polygraph examiner position announced in the Los Angeles office, which SAC Bretzing awarded to Chris Spilsbury, a non-Hispanic. The Hispanic agents who applied met every prerequisite, and most sent memos or copies of previous applications for polygraph examiner positions, both English and Spanish. One FBIHQ exhibit dated two years previous showed the bureau sought more Spanish-speaking polygraph examiners; another exhibit showed Spilsbury did not even apply for the position.

Aaron learned that Spilsbury got the position when Spilsbury announced in the squad room that he was the selectee. Aaron and the others requested a meeting with ASAC Gary Lisotto, who called headquarters. FBIHQ confirmed Spilsbury as the best candidate because he spoke Spanish and once lived in Mexico. Of the Spanish test scores obtained, one Hispanic scored lower than Spilsbury, one equivalent and the other four all scored higher. All of the Hispanics had more investigative time in the bureau and handled larger caseloads than Spilsbury. The agents asked the FBI to repeat the selection process and grant individual interviews to all of the agents who applied for the position, just as FBIHQ provided Spilsbury with the opportunity to interview.

Lisotto told the agents that the matter was out of his hands even though, as the Administrative ASAC, it should have been his call. The agents sought a fair process.

The Hispanic agents informed Lisotto that they did not want to take the EEO route, but they preferred FBI guidelines be followed. Aaron testified,

> I suppose, Your Honor, that is one of the biggest reasons, but that was the straw that broke the back as to why I'm here. Somehow I was very angry that an organization I have given twenty-two years suddenly looks upon me as a nonentity, as a person good enough to work Title IIIs, to do undercover work, to work informants, but being considered for anything more than a street agent I am not.

SAC Richard Bretzing and Spilsbury were both Mormons. Spilsbury's wife gave piano lessons to Bretzing's children. The original request for the position of polygraph examiner required a transfer to either Miami or San Juan, but Spilsbury was not required to leave Los Angeles. Spilsbury told Aaron he had no interest in the job and would not apply, as he did not want to go to either Miami or to San Juan. When Aaron later asked him where he would be transferred, Spilsbury responded, "No, that has all been changed; I don't have to go anywhere, I will be a polygraph examiner right here in the Los Angeles Division." The lead polygraph examiner in the Los Angeles

Division, Donald Finley, told Aaron that Los Angeles did not need another polygrapher. Aaron also spoke with Paul Minor of the Polygraph Unit, and Minor told him he was not in favor of an additional polygraph examiner in Los Angeles either.

Aaron believed that drug-related crimes were the most dangerous to agents in the bureau and the closest to the dangers that police officers face. When criminals kidnapped an informant who spoke only Spanish, there was a lack of guidance, as the surveillance team could not follow and endangered operations.

Aaron also confirmed that the LA office allowed Karen Badian and Linda Sue Rary, the "recycled" non-Hispanic agents, to work as agents and receive agent pay while the office demoted Lorena Sierra and forced her to work as a telephone operator. Aaron verified that filing an EEO complaint was something that you just did not do, as it embarrassed the bureau and always came back to haunt you.

On cross-examination, Ms. Simon maintained that all assignments are dangerous to all agents: blacks, Anglos and Hispanics. Aaron pointed out that the major difference is the language problem involved in working undercover, as the agents listening in do not always understand the action on the street and have to rely on someone else to interpret. Title IIIs are also different because of language, as they require a translation besides the standard analysis, and the translation must be good enough to stand up in court.

John Giaquinto testified later, on the eighth day of the trial, that in 1986 there was an interest in adding more Spanish-speaking polygraph examiners. Two of the forty-three field polygraph examiners were Spanish speakers. Their workload had increased, and this placed a heavy burden on the two examiners. Giaquinto testified that the FBI needed four polygraphers in Florida and San Juan. He received a call from Jim Nelson, ASAC Los Angeles, notifying him that the LA office recommended Chris Spilsbury for a polygrapher position but that he was to remain in LA.

On cross-examination, Giaquinto read from an exhibit whereby he identified six Hispanics who had more time and experience than Spilsbury and five Hispanics who had a superior Spanish-speaking rating than Spilsbury. However, Giaquinto selected none of those agents. He also stated that he did not know if the children of Victor Bazan, Paul Magallanes, Aaron Sanchez, Alanna Lavelle, Henry "Hank" Tenorio and Rudy Valadez ever took piano lessons from Mrs. Spilsbury or if those agents were Mormon.

The FBI never filled the four positions for Spanish-speaking polygraphers. Giaquinto testified that the unit supervisors made the final decision and that no one ever consulted with Bretzing about the choice.

Hugo quizzed Giaquinto about why he had earlier told Special Agent John Holford, in response to an official EEO complaint filed by the Hispanic agents, that Spilsbury was selected because he spoke at a level 5 Spanish speaker who was born and raised in Mexico, as he now testified that Spilsbury spoke as a 3+ Spanish speaker. Giaquinto claimed that he never told Holford that Spilsbury was a level 5 Spanish speaker, adding that agents make mistakes on reports used for adjudication. One can understand that close, careful listening is critical in an interview and that, while mistakes happen, changing a rating to a 5 in a final report when a trained FBI investigator hears 3+ from someone the likes of Giaquinto, is improbable. Giaquinto appeared to place his own personal importance above the FBI, which called the FBI's credibility into question. Giaquinto, like Glover, did not leave the FBI's reputation for the accuracy of their reports in good standing, as it was easier to throw the underlings under the bus.

17

Rudolph (Rudy) Valadez

Rudy Valadez, assigned to the Los Angeles Division, entered the FBI in May of 1967 as a clerk. He obtained a B.A. in justice and law from the American University School of Public Affairs in Washington, DC. Rudy wanted to be an FBI agent, so he took all of the tests offered for the position and passed everything but the Spanish language test, which he bombed. He entered special agent service under the modified program for professional experience with assignments to Pittsburg, Houston and San Antonio before heading to Los Angeles. About a year and a half after becoming an agent, the bureau retested him on his Spanish language ability, and he passed, much to his detriment, he later said. He had taken no academic or remedial courses in between the time he failed the initial exam and when he passed the second. He enjoyed doing counterintelligence and counterterrorism work.

Rudy worked fifteen "Taco Circuit" Title III wiretaps in field divisions around the country, including San Juan, some of which utilized non-agent personnel. He received incentive awards and high performance appraisals. When he received a fully successful rating, his supervisor indicated that it was attributable to his many temporary duty assignments outside of the division. Rudy knew all about the FBI promotional protocol. Rudy served as principal relief and acting supervisor on various counterintelligence squads, which served as a prerequisite for advancement. He requested MAP in-service testing but to no avail. He testified that the LA career board had a list of relief supervisors with noted qualifications for MAP training/evaluation for supervisory positions. The board would rate the candidates, narrow it down to the top three and then select the top candidate. Rudy's position in the rankings went up and down but never rose to the top.

Over the years, Rudy applied for two dozen supervisory positions, but never received a promotion. He submitted applications for advancement beginning in 1981. He applied for positions in the Intelligence Division, supervisory desks in field offices, staff counselor positions, jobs with the Terrorist Division, positions as assistant legal attaché and assignments in a Resident Agency. Rudy testified,

> They told me that I was too expert and my expertise was needed in the Los Angeles Division Headquarters. A month later, they sent an inexperienced agent to that RA. Later my ASAC told me, "We will send you to the Santa Ana RA to work narcotics." I told him I did not want to go to the RA to work narcotics. He told me, "If push comes to shove, you will go over there on the needs of the bureau." I said, "with all due respect, if push comes to shove, we will go to court on this one."

Rudy filed two EEO complaints. The first alleged discrimination based on religion, age, national origin and race, because he applied for a polygraph examiner's position in the Los Angeles Division and the individual selected was an Anglo Mormon agent with far less experience. The selection was secret and the LA office did not even consider the Hispanic agents who applied. His second EEO complaint stemmed from SAC Richard Bretzing telling Rudy he qualified to be a supervisor but to expect no promotion to supervisor until he changed his attitude toward management. Bretzing expected loyalty to Bretzing first, rather than loyalty to the FBI or its principles.

Ms. Gulyassy, on cross-examination, brought out Rudy's incentive awards as a relief supervisor, as an investigator, and as an informant developer, and asked, "Isn't it possible that some of the characteristics that make you a good investigator, a respected and valuable special agent in the field, might not transfer as well to a management position?" This possibility could have applied to any person selected.

Rudy led raids against dangerous people. Agents came to him for advice on administrative matters. He studied the manuals of rules and regulations and foreign counter intelligence guidelines to manage his and other agents' cases responsibly. As relief supervisor and acting supervisor, he managed entire squads besides his cases. The career board reported, "It was believed that SA Valadez realized he had a demanding type of personality with little tolerance for dissension, but that he was willing to modify his personality if necessary in order to get the job done." This was news to Rudy. The career board had put him in a box that made him difficult to promote. He felt insulted when the DOJ patronized him by saying in some selections that he was the third-rated candidate, as if placing was an honor.

Rudy referred to Bretzing's discrimination as sophisticated and animated; by animus he controlled the career board in LA and the management in-service training. Supervisor Gary Auer did not believe Rudy worked hard enough to earn a management position when Rudy served under him on the Russian squad, yet Auer told Rudy earlier that he considered him as qualified as a supervisor. Rudy did not need to speak Russian to manage the Russian Squad. Few, if any, Soviet counterintelligence supervisors spoke Russian.

Further, no inspector or any manager ever found any fault with his work during any field inspection or when Rudy was relieving or acting as a supervisor. His performance appraisals were superior and exceptional, he received letters of commendation, he received several awards, and during his eighteen years with the FBI, his work experience was expansive. Despite twenty-two applications, none resulted in promotion. The bureau put Rudy in a real-life *Catch-22*.

On day seven of the trial, Melvin L. Jeter, head of the FBI EEO program, proved a hostile witness and another example of management's lack of professionalism. Jeter rejected Rudy's EEO complaints as he had with so many others. He authorized EEO counselors to travel outside of their division but refused to allow Leo Gonzales, Arnie Gerardo, or Gil Mireles to travel for Mat's complaints. Jeter restricted the witnesses whom they could interview and removed them as Mat's counselors.

Jeter removed Leo Gonzales, EEO counselor in the El Paso office, as Jeter claimed there was a conflict of interest, and he did not think Leo could be objective. Jeter made a snap determination that Leo was not acting as an EEO counselor but an EEO advocate. Leo and Mat Perez both named Jeter as a discriminating official in their EEO complaints. Jeter stated, "...helping Mr. Perez and his litany of allegations has not been one of the most favored things."

Agents filed 216 formal EEO complaints against the FBI during the previous ten-year span. Jeter claimed not to know of any Hispanic who had a successful outcome from their EEO complaint. The FBI did not settle any of the EEO complaints filed by Mat Perez, yet the FBI settled a select few with non-Hispanics, though Jeter could offer no examples. Jeter replaced agent EEO counselors with support employees and felt it was proper to send a GS-4 support employee to question a GS-17 SAC on EEO personnel policies. Jeter chose not to sit on the FBI career board since he maintained that all of the "members are well aware of the law."

The EEO office never once conducted studies to determine whether the promotional processes, FBI training programs, assignments, MAP, or commendations and incentives were fair to Hispanics and other minorities. Yet, Jeter stated that there was no discrimination against Hispanics during the period between January 1978 and December 1987. Jeter would claim eight different times he had "no idea" when Hugo questioned him of his assignment as the EEO officer, such as the following:

> RODRIGUEZ: What do you do to ensure each employee is advised why they did not receive a position according to this Supervisor's Handbook?
>
> JETER: I would have no idea why an individual did or did not receive a job, unless they made it known.
>
> RODRIGUEZ: Thank you, Mr. Jeter. Now only blacks are the EEO officers in the FBI; is that correct?

JETER: There is only one EEO officer, and I happen to be black and I am proud of it.

RODRIGUEZ: Good. And the individual prior to you, Mr. Jeter?

JETER: A fellow by the name of William Crawford.

RODRIGUEZ: What is his race, Mr. Jeter?

JETER: I believe black.

RODRIGUEZ: You believe he was black? You don't know?

JETER: I have no idea.

Agent Jack Garcia filed an EEO complaint because of harassment over his weight. When Jeter was asked about his personal weight problem, he bantered, "I'm not overweight. It is not my weight I have a problem with; it is my height."

Jeter replaced William Crawford, a black agent who ran the EEO program. Under oath, Jeter testified that he knew Crawford but had no idea if Crawford was black. The court would soon find the FBI's EEO program to be morally bankrupt.

18

Hector Luis Lugo

Hector Lugo, born and raised in New York City, received a Bachelor of Science degree in marketing and management from Fordham University and his law degree from Hofstra Law School. He served as a law clerk for a circuit court judge in New York for two years, and eight years before the trial he entered the bureau as a special agent under the legal program. He did not speak Spanish. The bureau rated his Spanish as X, that is, as someone who has no Spanish language ability. He served in the Albany, Houston and New York offices; he did intelligence work and investigated white-collar crimes. He worked as the applicant recruiter for the New York FBI office and recruited Hispanics for special agent, translator and support positions. Hector traveled throughout New York City and around the country, visited colleges, law schools and conventions and discussed career opportunities in the FBI with an emphasis on recruiting Hispanics.

Hector opined that the FBI should base promotions on background, experience and other factors besides seniority. He applied for supervisor at FBIHQ, a job with responsibilities including recruitment and intelligence operations in Latin American countries. He did not receive that position, although Supervisor Tom Harper told him he was the most qualified person for the job. Hector testified to his determination to expose discrimination, which had occurred in the past and was still present in the FBI.

Hector did not file an EEO complaint when he did not receive the position because he "found it a waste of time and the bureau very intimidating, and pretty much indoctrinated agents not to make waves, not to cause trouble. If things happen, it happens for a reason for the needs of the bureau. I did not."

19

Martin Regalado

Martin Regalado entered the bureau six years before the trial. He attended Amherst College on a full academic scholarship. Awarded a fellowship to study law and one of the college's annual memorial prizes, he attended the University of California at Berkeley's Boalt Hall School of Law and received a full academic scholarship. He served as associate editor of the California Law Review and was on the Appellate Advocacy Board. He passed the California bar exam and practiced law for about a year and a half before joining the bureau.

Martin worked in the San Francisco Division on the bank robbery squad, investigated thefts from interstate shipments, and assisted another agent who worked a Major Case. He transferred to the Oklahoma City Division and worked organized crime, narcotics, applicants, and white-collar crime. He then transferred to the San Juan Division, assigned to the Puerto Rican Terrorist Squad for three years before heading to the West Covina Resident Agency out of the Los Angeles Division. In reviewing his file, Martin discovered he had qualified for the FBI under three programs: law, the modified program, and the minority program. Martin relied on his dictionary when he studied Spanish. At the direction of the FBI, he took the Spanish test although he believed he could not function proficiently, and he received a rating of 2+.

Martin believed that for five of his six years with the FBI, he served as an Anglo agent's personal assistant. While in San Francisco and the Oakland Resident Agency, he had no real cases assigned to him—all he did was help other agents. In the Oklahoma City Division, he did not receive assigned cases with any prosecutable potential until assigned to the white-collar crimes squad. Even then, special assignments and TDYs hampered his investigative efforts. The average Anglo FBI agent had more investigative experience because, unlike Hispanic agents, they remained in their assignments. Assignment on thirty, sixty or ninety-day specials took him away from his work; management reassigned his good cases with convictions credited to the replacement agents. Other cases went unattended until he returned from TDY. Then the basis of his evaluation was on statistical accomplishments. Martin's ethnic background had everything to do with the selection of his TDY assignments, as he was not proficient in Spanish.

Martin recalled the times that he applied for almost a dozen training in-services, but the FBI selected others with less experience and fewer years of service. After his arrival in San Juan, Martin voiced his concern to SAC Esposito that the length of the tour in San Juan was discriminatory. He believed that this complaint led management to deny him training opportunities. He asked his supervisor Ronald Iden, ASAC Harry Brandon and Esposito for an informant development in-service, but they denied it and his performance appraisal in that element suffered. The policy of affording all agents with a transfer to a top twelve office (the twelve largest offices of the FBI) at the end of two years in the bureau did not occur in his case as he transferred to San Juan and was marooned there for an additional three years. Martin recounted, "So after five years in the bureau I was in the same position of facing transfer to a top twelve office that Anglos would have been after two years in the bureau." Martin recalled that supervisors told him that taking the Spanish test would not affect future transfers.

When Martin applied for a position in the Legal Division, he was unsure of the qualifications of the selectee. He testified, "But I venture to say whoever was selected was not a Law Review graduate of a top ten law school, or did not have my academic or professional background."

Martin also sent a request to publish an article to William Baker, the Assistant Director of the Public Affairs Office. The article, titled, "The FBI: Does it Discriminate Against Hispanic Agents?" examined the disparity in the treatment of Hispanic and Anglo agents. In the article Martin noted that Hispanics are subject to special assignments more often, that a tour of duty in Puerto Rico is compulsory for Hispanic agents whereas Anglo agents never have to worry about it, that the opportunity for career advancement for Hispanics in the bureau is limited, that the Hispanic agents are treated differently, that the FBI refuses to acknowledge that any such problems exist, and finally, that a lawsuit was inevitable. In the attached memo, he offered the FBI ten days to respond before publication. The standard procedure is to take a proposed article up the chain of command and submit the request to the SAC, who would then forward it on to FBIHQ. Martin had every right to pen such an article and to publish it. Esposito took particular offense at Martin's narrow timeframe. Martin assumed that their lack of response indicated approval of his request.

Esposito testified that Martin disapproved of the San Juan transfer policy, which had changed from a two-year to a four-year minimum. Martin filed a Freedom of Information Act request with the bureau, and a year and a half later he received several documents, including the inspection report on the San Juan Division in 1982. Using these documents, he reached several conclusions:

> First, the most obvious conclusion that I or anyone else reached in reading that report was that the report attempted to blame the plaintiff in this lawsuit, Mat Perez, for all of the problems that were in San Juan. The bureau was attempting to make him a scapegoat for all the problems affecting San Juan. It was unfair because, according to documents I received, many of those problems existed long before Mat Perez arrived in San Juan and continues to exist even to this date.

Martin wanted to join three of his new agent class members at FBIHQ legal counsel. Now that he had provided testimony and sat opposite legal counsel and Beth Dixler, one of his class members, Martin believed that his chances for career advancement in the bureau were nil. His entire experience with the FBI caused Martin to conclude that there was clear and obvious discrimination.

20

Maria Villaruel

Maria Villaruel, born in Mexico, came to the US at age eight. Raised in Detroit, Michigan, she attended Wayne State University and earned a bachelor's degree in English and Spanish. She also obtained a secondary teaching degree as well as a law degree from Wayne State University Law School. Maria came into the FBI through the law and language programs, became an agent in January of 1981 through the Detroit office, and returned to Detroit for a month before going on a special assignment to Miami for five months. She transferred to San Juan, Puerto Rico, for five years and then went on to the Tampa office.

Maria testified that TDY assignments were discriminatory toward Hispanic agents. Detroit received a communication requesting a Spanish speaker for an undercover operation codenamed "Bancoshares," which involved organized crime and narcotics. As it developed, Maria did not use her Spanish ability at all but instead covered leads for the case agent. Her main duty amounted to counting drug money for the money laundering case. The judge joshed her, asking if the FBI wanted her to count in English or Spanish.

In January of 1985, she went to Quantico for three weeks to train as a legal advisor. Once certified as a legal advisor, that agent then assists the principal legal advisor in the office with legal training for fellow agents, handles administrative claims, and reviews complaints and affidavits for other agents. The job includes anything related to legal issues besides the normal investigative duties. In the field, there is a principal legal advisor in each office and several legal advisors who assist. Maria attended the three-week legal in-service, which included privacy act training and a forfeiture and seizure in-service, all in preparation to become a legal advisor in the field. While in San Juan, she served as the legal advisor. When she transferred from San Juan to Tampa, SAC Esposito acknowledged her experience and interest in working as a legal advisor in a communication to FBIHQ. Four months before the trial, the SAC named Vicki Johnson, a first office agent with less than three years of experience, the principal legal advisor for the Tampa division. Tampa then sent Johnson to the in-service training that Maria had completed years prior.

Maria testified that the Office Services Manager (OSM) in Tampa was successful in a discrimination case against SAC Robert Butler. The SAC indicated to the OSM that she did not receive a promotion because she was Hispanic, was too emotional and could not handle the responsibilities of an OSM. Maria felt her participation in the class action lawsuit would blackball her, as she had already heard comments that she was a troublemaker and a malcontent.

On cross-examination, Maria pointed out that, in San Juan, non-Spanish speakers served as the case agents and Spanish speakers worked for them. The case agent gets credit for the case's completion and success; meanwhile, the Hispanic agents were out on the street working in the off-sites, were sent to wires, worked undercover, and pulled double duty. Maria acknowledged that the bureau had granted her a transfer request; however, there was no monetary benefit or promotion tied to the request. The DOJ felt compelled to impeach her testimony by pointing out that FBIHQ Legal Division had a Hispanic agent on staff, Derrick DeHolm, with not exactly a Hispanic surname.

There was a funny exchange between the judge and Maria when Maria spoke about the difficulties of working in San Juan and how this precluded one from voting in a presidential election. Her husband, a US Marshal of Puerto Rican descent, also wanted out of San Juan.

THE COURT: You are married to a United States Marshal?

VILLARUEL: Yes, sir. Your Honor, it is so bad.

THE COURT: We are still talking about Puerto Rico now, we are not talking about the Marshal, okay?

Judge Bunton also asked her about the pronunciation of her name with the double *l's*, which together sound like the letter *y*. Maria said, "I am not sure, Your Honor. I would like to think it was a continuation of Pancho Villa."

Robert V. Butler testified that he and Maria spoke when he needed to replace the principal legal advisor in the Tampa Division. Maria told him that she planned to marry and settle down, and she had expressed interest in working on a drug squad. He replaced the PLA on February 8, 1988, with Vicki Johnson, who had volunteered for the position. He chose Johnson as a first office agent with the idea that, if she transferred out in about a year, Maria would be in position to take over the PLA slot, and he planned to consider Maria for the PLA position the next time it became available. Maria never complained to him, and she later became a relief supervisor in the Tampa office.

On cross-examination, Butler identified Arlene Vargas as the OSM who had filed an EEO complaint alleging that Butler had discriminated against her and in which she prevailed. Butler explained the finding was that, while he had explained why he had not selected Arlene, there were no stated reasons given as to why he had selected the other individual. Hugo reminded Butler that he had earlier testified that he had groomed Vicki Johnson, considering her in the short term so that Maria could be the next PLA. Butler, devoid of any progressive promotional plans for Maria, responded that it was his thought process at the time, but that things could always change.

21

Ernesto Patino

Ernesto Patino, born in Juarez, Mexico and educated in El Paso, Texas, received his music education degree from the University of Texas at El Paso. He served as a school teacher prior to joining the FBI. He entered the FBI under the modified program and, while an agent, he took the Spanish language test. His first office assignment was Miami, then San Antonio, then San Juan, before transferring back to the Miami Division. He had been a special agent for the FBI for seventeen years at the time of the trial. He had extensive experience in foreign counterintelligence, handled Major Cases, and received numerous incentive awards and high performance evaluations throughout his career. He participated in the career development program for five years. Ernie thought, without a doubt, that the bureau was an institution that discriminated against persons of Hispanic background.

Ernie applied, to no avail, for five assistant legal attaché (ALAT) positions in Spanish-speaking cities such as Bogotá, Panama City and Mexico City. He believed, as did many associates, that agents belonging to the Mormon faith monopolized FBI posts in Latin America. Ernie, who was bilingual and bicultural, noted repeated examples of people who could not communicate in the Spanish language receiving preference for legal attaché assignments and language training through the Berlitz Institute. In the capacity of an ALAT or Legat, one of the duties of an agent is to meet high-ranking government officials and law enforcement counterparts in the government; therefore, it is imperative that language skills be top notch so that agents can converse fluently. As an institution, the FBI ignored this element. The bureau asserted that FBIHQ experience was a requirement for Legat positions, but this was a rule that the FBI contravened many times.

Ernie dropped out of the CDP program because the bureau passed him over for promotions. The bureau also initiated an administrative inquiry against him, which destroyed his faith in the FBI and left him blackballed by headquarters. Ernie consented to a polygraph, the findings of which exonerated him; however, he still felt stigmatized. The FBI revoked his security clearances while under investigation and put him on the drug squad. All of his assignments related to his Spanish language ability. He pointed out that, even when he worked the Cuban exile community, he could not pass himself off as a Cuban because of his accent. Ernie described the pervasive FBI misperception that stereotypes all Hispanics as a homogenous group. He was certain he would never become a supervisor or a Legat because of his participation in the class action.

On cross-examination, Ms. Simon pointed out that Ernie had dropped out of the career development program and, to become a Legat, agents had to be in that program. Ernie said that his Spanish language credentials and record of accomplishments ought to have been more than enough to obtain a Legat position. In reference to his long-term undercover assignments outside of the United States and the temporary revocation of his security clearance, Ernie knew that in itself was not discriminatory as he had accepted the assignment, but the way the FBI handled the administrative inquiry was discriminatory.

Ms. Simon mentioned that Ernie listed his office of preference (OP) as Miami in 1976, and there he was in Miami in 1977. She asked Ernie, "And 1976 is before 1977, is it not?" The judge shook his head and answered for Ernie, "Yes, it sure was." Ernie, and the judge as well, thought that the DOJ should not have wasted time questioning whether Ernie was in his OP, but should have instead concentrated on Ernie's allegations of systemic discrimination.

22

Samuel Carlos Martinez

Sam Martinez received a Bachelor of Business Administration with a major in accounting from the University of Texas at El Paso (UTEP). He joined the FBI in 1973 and served in San Francisco, Chicago, Denver, FBIHQ, Mexico City, Los Angeles and then FBIHQ again. In 1973, the FBI placed an emphasis on recruiting lawyers, accountants, Spanish speakers, members of minority groups and female agents. The FBI recruited Sam as an accountant, but he entered the bureau under the Spanish language program as his recruiter informed him that there was no need to take the accounting exam. With twelve years of service, Sam went to Mexico to coordinate the kidnapping investigation of DEA Agent Enrique "Kiki" Camarena and coordinate all FBI work within the central and northwest territories of Mexico.

When Sam arrived as an assistant legal attaché (ALAT) in Mexico City, all of the other agents were Mormons. A Legat office liaises with foreign judicial agencies, which have interests in developing and resolving FBI cases that extend beyond US borders, and assists foreign governments with their judicial interests and training. Legat offices are also responsible for cooperating with the established agencies at the US Embassy or Consulates.

The FBI has no operational investigative authority outside of the US but makes investigative requests to foreign entities to retrieve data and information to support FBI cases. Without authority to investigate, FBI agents are still responsible for keeping their eyes and ears open for any information that benefits the United States government.

In the United States, agents recruit, develop, and work with informants. In foreign assignments, the FBI is nonoperational and in some countries, the FBI obtains "assets" to develop and organize information before presenting an official government request. For instance, a field office might send information about the location of a fugitive, an asset would verify the information and then the Legat office would send a request to the foreign government to apprehend the fugitive.

Informants and assets receive payments from the US government for their services and expenses. People with information call or come to the embassy to provide information. The term walk-in refers to a situation in which a person comes to an office and provides information. After Sam described to the court what a walk-in was, Judge Bunton said, "A walk-in is kind of like a walk-on in the NFL and may or may not be cut. He may come back again, become part of the team or he may just move right on."

After arriving in Mexico, Sam received a call from a foreign national in which the information seemed too important and confidential to discuss over the phone. This person walked in and talked all day, providing information that seemed unbelievable and incredible. Sam told the walk-in to return in three days to review a written report to ensure Sam understood the information to be correct.

When Sam went over the report, the walk-in added and changed information before the final teletype went to FBIHQ, DEA and the US Embassy. Sam asked the Legat if they should send the walk-in to an FBI field office where he could be an informant, but the Legat told Sam to just turn the walk-in over to the DEA.

Sam informed DEA Mexico of the availability of this walk-in. The DEA had many major investigations besides the much more significant Kiki Camarena kidnapping. The walk-in was hiding in a hotel. The only contact he had was with Sam and with a Mexican customs officer who had been the walk-in's long-time friend. After a prolonged time span and financial strains for the walk-in, Sam told the Legat that the FBI had gained a substantive case from the walk-in's information and that the source deserved a one-time payment, even though they were turning him over to DEA. The Legat told Sam to let the DEA handle it.

By this time, the nervous walk-in repeatedly contacted Sam, and Legat support personnel believed the calls to be extreme. The Legat and the walk-in had met at the US Embassy several times before while meeting with Sam. The walk-in provided additional information during debriefings. He was in a unique position to assist the FBI and other offices with drug investigations.

With the Legat denying funds for the walk-in, who feared being in public, and the DEA otherwise too occupied to take over, Sam advised the walk-in to leave Mexico. The walk-in had no cash but had two weapons, a .357 Magnum and an AR-15, which he could sell for money to finance his departure from the country. Sam contacted a Mexican security firm authorized to own the AR-15 and confirmed the interest in the weapons. The walk-in gave the weapons to Sam. The next day the Legat saw the AR-15 in the trunk of the bureau car, and Sam informed him of the transaction. Legat John Walser instructed Sam to remove the weapon from the car quickly. Sam delivered the weapons that evening, collected the money and delivered the money to the walk-in the next day. At that point, the walk-in left the country.

About a year later, in August of 1986, as Sam was leaving the Legat office to catch a flight with the acting ambassador, the military attaché, and the head of the DEA in Mexico, the Legat asked Sam if he was selling guns to informants. Sam responded he was not. On arrival in Guadalajara, Sam called the Legat on a secure line and told him that the allegation of selling weapons to informants came from misinformation regarding the walk-in's weapons. Walser received the information from the head of the DEA in Mexico, Ed Heath, who heard it third-hand from a customs officer at the embassy.

Walser, as the Legat, seemed puzzled about what to do with this information. Sam told him to send the information to FBIHQ to avoid any more misstatements and that it would be best that the FBI hear the information first from within rather than from an outside agency.

Walser often said that one had to "CYA," cover your ass, while waving one arm across his backside. Walser's mantra returned.

The Legat showed Sam the airtel (an FBI internal communication) dated September 24, 1986, which Walser sent a month after their initial conversation. It surprised Sam because other than their first conversation, Walser never discussed the incident before he prepared the report. It contained many factual errors on details and omission of his prior knowledge of the AR-15 he saw in the car a year earlier.

Sam pointed out errors in Walser's report. The airtel further stated that Sam was dealing with an informant, that he paid for the walk-in's hotel and meals, that he lacked judgment in his actions, that he had been reprimanded, that he had violated Mexican laws and that Acting Ambassador Morris Busby wanted him out of Mexico, all of which were false. Sam asked the Legat to correct the airtel. He refused.

In November of 1986, the Legat and Sam went to FBIHQ to provide signed statements regarding the incident. Sam learned that the Legat had badmouthed him, declared that Sam had used poor judgment and could not think straight, that Sam was incapable of writing in either English or Spanish, that he was "a loose cannon" conducting arrests when Legats are supposed to be non-operational in foreign countries, and that he did not deserve supervisory duties. This information went up the ladder to Executive Assistant Director Oliver B. Revell, who had the authority to remove Sam from Mexico.

In January of 1987, Walser told Sam that the Administrative Services Division had overruled Revell and that Sam could probably remain in Mexico until his two-year contract expired. Sam asked Walser to show him where his paperwork was substandard, where he signed off on poorly written documents, when he lacked judgment and so forth. Walser told Sam that he could work with him, adding that office assistant Irma Macias and ALAT Roger Toronto approved of Sam's work performance and paperwork.

Sam then told Walser that he had contacted an experienced attorney and judge in Mexico, a former Mexican Ambassador to Spain. Sam gave the judge the facts regarding the gun sale and transfer matter, posing them as a hypothetical situation with no names given. He asked the judge to render a hypothetical legal opinion based on Mexican law. The judge opined that there was no violation of Mexican law and that it was more in line with the law to remove the weapons from the custody of an individual in a case in which it was unknown if that individual had the authority to possess an AR-15. Walser exploded, fuming, "I can beat him on that, and I know the law because I grew up with it!" Walser demonstrated that he did not really intend to work with Sam.

Working together became even more difficult over the next three months as Walser refused to correct the facts. He leveled additional accusations against Sam, even when there was no viable connection at all. Kathleen Horne, a Mormon support employee, told Sam not to judge other Mormons by the actions of Walser, saying, "Sammy, he treats me bad because he thinks I'm stupid, but he doesn't treat me as bad as he treats you." Another support employee, Luis Rodriquez, told Sam, "I never thought I would see it or I never thought I would say it, but that man hates you and I think he is jealous of your work." Irma Macias, a support employee, told Sam, "He is out to get you on everything, even when you are not involved in anything." Lynn Vissers, the Legat's secretary, told Sam she knew Walser discriminated against him. Sam told Ann Arnold, a loyal FBI employee who had retired, that he might call her as a witness since he had filed an EEO complaint. Ann responded, "It's about time. There is only so much that a man should take for the sake of his dignity."

Sam sought EEO counseling on January 1, 1987, because of harassment, intimidation and denial of an extension of his tour in Mexico. He filed an EEO complaint through Leo Gonzales in El Paso, Texas, requesting anonymity to avoid further harassment. He did not seek EEO counseling in Mexico because the agents were Mormon friends of Walser. Mel Jeter, the EEO Unit Chief, told Sam not to have any contact with Leo Gonzales and that he would handle the EEO case. Jeter then followed up by mailing Walser the EEO complaint. Walser told Sam, "I can beat you on this!" and then listed the allegations one by one.

There was no resolution of the EEO complaint when the class action trial began. An EEO investigator, Rick Copeland, told John Navarrete, a witness in the EEO complaint, that John could only provide information on what he knew concerning the denial of extension to Mexico but no further information about discrimination. Limiting investigations was Jeter's way of resolving the EEO complaint in favor of the FBI. Sam knew of no Hispanic agent who had succeeded in the EEO process. He thought that Jeter, although a member of a minority group, played an important role in the FBI's systemic discrimination. Sam attended Director Webster's deposition on the lawsuit and testified, "I feel that discrimination is systemic and when former Director Webster states in his deposition that individual discrimination does exist in the bureau but he did not feel it was institutional, I can sort of agree with that. However, if the institution is not doing anything about individual discrimination, then it is institutional and systemic discrimination."

On March 9, 1987, over a year and a half after the gun sale incident, Sam received a notice accusing him of criminal activity, lack of candor and insubordination. The document stated that Sam had ten days to respond and thirty days advance written notice before any final consideration to his response. Despite the ten days to respond, the FBI advertised Sam's position in Mexico on March 12, 1987, and followed up with another teletype that sent him to FBIHQ for an indefinite period. Walser now claimed that Sam requested to leave Mexico, contrary to statements in his EEO complaint.

Sam told Walser he was upset about the criminal charges, and the charges of insubordination and lack of candor surprised him. Sam requested an FBI polygraph test because he had no other way of resolving the allegation of insubordination and lack of candor, as the FBI took management's word over that of a subordinate. Tom Kirk from the Office of Professional Responsibility (OPR) told Sam that some statements of fact differed in his and Walser's statements. Kirk told him that there was no need to seek a polygraph, as his action might result in only an oral reprimand or even a letter of censure. The OPR and the Office of Liaison and International Affairs (OLIA) denied Sam's request for a polygraph exam.

Sam paid a retired FBI polygrapher for an exam and there was no finding of insubordination to Walser's requests or any lack of candor found on Sam's part. Additionally, the polygraph showed Sam was truthful concerning allegations against Walser. After Sam told Walser of the results, Walser sent a memorandum to FBIHQ advising that there was probably no insubordination by Sam and that the lack of candor occurred in exigent circumstances, since Sam was leaving to catch a private flight with the acting ambassador. No one at FBIHQ paid any attention to either Walser's memo or the polygraph results.

Dr. David Soskis, who was on retainer for the FBI and knew the specifics of the gun sale matter, told Sam that, if he had not acted to remove the source from Mexico, it could have created more problems for the FBI and would have resulted in harm to the source. Over a year passed when the walk-in, who now worked for the DEA and Customs, mentioned that Sam had helped him out by locating buyers for the weapons. That action turned on its head, which led to misinformation that Sam sold machine guns to informants.

On a Monday morning, when Sam returned from an out-of-town trip, fellow agent Roger Toronto instructed him to write down all information concerning a security violation that occurred over the weekend in which a Marine guard found classified documents in Walser's desk. Sam gave the report to Toronto and advised him that he did not appreciate the insinuation of complicity. Toronto told Sam, "Well that's what it looks like; Walser couldn't have done it as he was out of town."

Legat Walser had written a memorandum to FBIHQ, indicating that he could not have committed the security violation as he was out of town and it looked like Sam was trying to frame him. Sam went to the regional security office and obtained a previous security violation where the Embassy found Sam responsible, showing that on his ninth day of travel Marine guards found classified documents behind the radiator in his office. He took the report to Toronto to show that he accepted the responsibility of the security violation and did not claim he could not be responsible. Sam told Toronto, "I didn't blame you fucking Mormons when I was out of town for two weeks and got my security violation."

It was already too late. OPR ordered Sam to FBIHQ for an indefinite period to investigate the security allegation, re-fingerprinted and palm printed him, and isolated him from his family. The investigation found Walser responsible for the security violation, to which he finally admitted, but FBIHQ did not allow Sam to return to his assignment in Mexico. Sam knew the bureau was out to retaliate against him because of his EEO complaint. Retaliation in the bureau operated much like an undocumented "contract" or "hit" without a paper trail.

Back at FBIHQ, agents kept away from Sam as if he were a pariah; his family was marooned in a foreign country with no bureau consideration as to their safety or well-being. Sam asked to speak to EAD Buck Revell, but Revell forced him to wait for over a month. Sam told Revell that he would have made the same decision and removed an agent from Mexico if he received no other information but such a collection of misinformation. He asked Revell to separate the people from the issues and to look at the conflicting documentation sent by the Legat before he made a final decision. Ending the meeting, Revell lied by saying he had not yet decided.

On a document that recommended censure dated six months earlier, Revell's initials appeared. In his handwriting, Revell also added a reduction in grade and one year of probation. The day following Sam's meeting with Revell, Sam received the official notification that the FBI was demoting him with orders to Los Angeles. The demotion letter provided an opportunity to appeal through an oral interview with EAD John Glover before he rendered a final decision. Sam sent several requests to Glover, asking for an oral review to appeal the demotion, but Glover denied his requests. Glover would in no way go against Buck Revell.

Sam sent Glover a letter recalling that, when they first met, Glover spoke of having an open door policy. Now with the door closed, Sam's alternative to addressing the lies that led to the unjust demotion was to make a presentation outside the bureau before the Merit System Protection Board (MSPB).

In the interim, Sam asked for any office, just not LA, as the SAC in LA was a Mormon who engendered numerous complaints by other Hispanics, and Sam was confident that Bretzing would retaliate against him. Sam requested a temporary assignment to the Washington Field Office (WFO) as he was appealing the demotion and had an active EEO case. Martin V. Hale, the deputy of the Office of Liaison and International Affairs (OLIA), told Sam that he would have to take a voluntary reduction in grade for WFO. Sam told Hale that supervisor Frank Quijada and ASAC Leroy Teitsworth of Albuquerque had asked him to transfer there. Hale told Sam that he would not get what he wanted. Sam responded that he would not work in any FBI field office with a charge on his record of involvement in criminal activity.

His service as a US military veteran entitled Sam to take issues before the Merit System Protection Board. He had a copy of the polygraph results, the legal brief by a Mexican judge, a timeline of events and FBI documents to present. Irving Kator, his attorney, called him two days before the hearing to tell him that the FBI declined to pursue the hearing and would settle with a warning. Kator cautioned Sam not to ask for too much or the FBI might find another way to get at him. The MSPB reinstated Sam as a GS-14 with a substantive desk at FBIHQ and awarded him back pay and attorney's fees. However, Sam did not feel exonerated, as the misinformation remained in his personnel file and he had incurred additional expenses, so he kept the EEO case active.

Based on Sam's EEO complaint, the FBI opened an administrative inquiry on Walser. Martin Hale told Walser of the inquiry and together the two prepared a response, something that Hale said was normal—somehow though, that assistance was always missing when Sam faced allegations. Hale wanted Sam to change his allegations so that Walser could get a new position and a transfer. Sam said, "He asked me to change some wording which I told him that, by changing my affidavit, I was making it into a milquetoast affidavit so that Walser could be transferred, as SAC Richard Schwein had informed me. What you want to do for one agent, you neglected to do for another."

Then Sam role-played dumb, acting as if he did not understand the changes Hale wanted. Hale then, in his own handwriting, changed Sam's affidavit. Sam initialed the changes made by Hale. Hale testified in court five days after Sam, denying that he had asked Sam to change the allegations or made any changes, yet Sam kept photocopies of the changes made in Hale's handwriting.

During the cross-examination of Sam, Mr. Ferber brought out that, until the problem with Walser, Sam had good appraisals, a clean record, a good entry interview, commendations, worked successful cases, served as a relief supervisor, and that he had received a promotion on his first application for a promotion. Mr. Ferber maintained there was no discrimination. Sam responded that a person's character diminishes if he makes a big deal about minor skirmishes, but that he had been a victim of other incidents of discrimination.

Walser adopted Hispanic children, lived in Mexico, and had Hispanic relatives. Yet, as Sam testified,

> In the Book of Mormon, there are quotes saying Lamanites, whom Mormons associate as having dark skin as Hispanics, are cursed with dark skin and are described as "dark and loathsome." There are people in the Mormon Church who believe certain parts of their theology. A belief exists that if you are a Lamanite and convert to the Mormon religion, you become "white and delightsome" in the hereafter, and Walser has said Hispanics cannot do anything right and sends reports to FBIHQ that Hispanics are "inherently corrupt." That is discrimination with a Mormon bias.

When asked if EAD Revell had anti-Hispanic biases, Sam responded that he gave Revell every opportunity to verify documents and statements and every opportunity to seek the truth and investigate, but Revell instead acted upon the discriminatory information and biases of Walser. Sam added, "I did not want him to close the door on me, so yes I do believe that Revell was culpable in discriminating." Revell had no reason to state that he had not decided on Sam's demotion, a statement that Revell knew to be false.

John M. Walser testified that the DEA SAC advised him that Sam sold a machine gun in Mexico and claimed that Sam did not consult with him before he engaged in transferring the guns. Following the EEO complaint and on his way out of Mexico, Walser gave Sam an unacceptable performance appraisal. Sam informed him that regulations required granting him time to work through an unacceptable rating. Walser then changed the rating to minimally acceptable and stated, "There were about fourteen instances of administrative insubordination, which borders on administrative insubordination where he disregarded my instructions." According to Walser, Sam's last appraisal had nothing to do with the EEO complaint, although he informed the court that he gave Sam a fully successful rating and recommended Sam for MAP I prior to the EEO complaint. Sam contested the minimally acceptable rating, and it did not stand.

Walser said that the head of the EEO office sent him a copy of the EEO complaint after March 9, 1987, which was the day Sam had advised Walser of the complaint. On March 20, 1987, Walser sent a communication to FBIHQ stating that Sam did not want to extend his stay in Mexico City as an ALAT. Walser claimed that, although he read the EEO complaint, he did not know that the EEO complaint requested that Sam remain in Mexico.

Walser testified that he did not know that Sam had taken and passed a polygraph examination denying Walser's charges. He also did not remember sending the March 18, 1987 communication after Sam had told him that he was taking a polygraph to deny any allegations of insubordination and lack of candor. Walser sent FBIHQ the communication stating that his original accusations against Sam may have not been as recollected and that he supposed Sam had followed his instructions.

Tony Silva asked Walser to review the exhibit regarding Sam's polygraph examination results, showing that the allegations made by Walser were false and that the allegations made by Sam against Walser were true. Walser, taking his time, said he saw no reference to it being a polygraph examination; frustrated, a DOJ attorney stated that the document spoke for itself. Walser's charges alleging insubordination, lack of candor, and unfitness for supervisory assignments came after Sam filed his EEO complaint.

Walser testified that he showed no Mormon favoritism. He said that when Irma Macias and Kathleen Horne had applied for a position in Mexico City, he selected Hispanic female Irma Macias. Walser failed to explain how Kathleen had arrived before Irma, or that he gave Irma lower ratings, or that he counseled her and recommended that FBIHQ counsel her and administer additional psychological evaluation and improvement. He placed a copy in Irma's personnel file. Walser also recommended counseling for Sam. In his efforts to prove how "fair" he was, Walser unfairly abused Mormon support employee Kathleen Horne.

The court recalled Sam to testify that the FBI discriminates against Hispanics in subtle ways. Walser discriminated against Frank Quijada, a Hispanic, on his application for Legat Panama without Frank even realizing it. Both Roger Toronto and Frank applied for the position when they both were in Mexico City. Both men had similar recommendations, yet in the last paragraph on Frank's application, Walser wrote that, since Frank had already served time in Mexico, he could not complete the full term in Panama. That statement was unfair, as the same condition existed for Toronto as it did for Frank, and Walser did not include the statement in Toronto's recommendation; this led the career board to rank Walser's Mormon co-religionist over Frank, yet neither received the position.

The OPR investigators Tom Kirk and Joe Smith told Sam that the gun matter should not have risen to the level it had. Dave Flanders, the head of OPR, referred to it as a "chip shot," meaning no issue. Deputy Assistant Director Gary Penrith reviewed it, saying that there was nothing to it other than Sam having not advised Walser. However, in actuality, Sam informed Walser on the day of the gun transaction in 1985, and Walser even saw the AR-15 in the trunk of the bureau car. OLIA, OPR, and the administrative services division thought the incident might rise to the level of a letter of censure, but Buck Revell escalated it into a demotion, removal from office and probation.

An exhibit dated December 8, 1986, was a letter directed to William H. Webster from Bernard E. Hobson, Assistant United States Attorney (AUSA) assigned to El Paso. Sam sought assistance from AUSAs in San Diego to pursue the extraterritorial prosecution of a fugitive who shot San Diego, US Border Patrol Agent William Beaumet. The San Diego AUSAs turned down the extraterritorial prosecution because of the extensive paperwork involved and because it would provide no statistical accomplishment for the office.

Sam instead found AUSA Bernard Hobson of El Paso interested in pursuing justice in prosecuting the case, and their efforts met with success. Walser block-stamped AUSA Hobson's letter and sent it to Sam to be initialed. Sam made a copy of the letter showing Walser's initials and nothing else. When Sam reviewed the documents in discovery, Sam saw that Walser later wrote in "Atta boy, good show." This, after the EEO complaint, was another example of Walser's "CYA" habit of covering his ass.

Although EAD Buck Revell ordered the demotion, censure, and probation of Sam, John D. Glover testified that he was the final decision maker in demoting Sam because of his alleged criminal activity in the sale of two weapons in Mexico City. Unmindful of his own gun incident, Glover refused to give Sam the opportunity to present an oral appeal because he found Sam's action "atrocious." The Merit System Protection Board instead reversed the "atrocious" actions of the FBI based on Glover's and the FBI's manufacturing of facts. Even when the DOJ stated that Sam's actions were legal in the US and did not appear to be illegal in Mexico, Glover moved forward with the three charges against Sam without sustaining a charge of illegal activity. Glover failed to evaluate the supporting documentation and the mitigating polygraph taken by Sam that disproved the allegations of insubordination and lack of candor. Glover neglected his duty to evaluate all evidence as both an EAD and a law enforcement officer. He also violated Title V procedures in refusing to allow Sam an oral presentation. Glover stood his position; he would not buck Oliver Revell's decision.

23

Leopoldo J. Montoya

Leopoldo J. Montoya, born and raised in Mexico, lived there until he finished high school. He received a degree in electrical engineering from UTEP. Leo worked for Stone & Webster, a company that built nuclear power plants. He also worked as an industrial engineer for Rockwell International and worked on constructing the B-1 Bomber. He joined the FBI in 1976 under the Spanish language program. Leo received orders to the San Francisco division but spent four months in the El Paso Division because of a medical hardship.

Leo found it odd that, when he first arrived in El Paso, SAC Warren C. Debrueys used him as his chauffeur several times. He asked one of the senior agents if such a duty was customary. Their advice to him was to leave the office early and stay out of the SAC's sight, so Leo left the office early to complete investigative work. This strategy seemed to work; the SAC never had the chance to ask Leo to drive him again.

In October of 1982, Leo applied for and became a Technically Trained Agent (TTA). The TTAs support the wiretaps in their divisions and handle other technical aspects of investigations. A TTA initially studies under a qualified technical training agent who explains the operations and uses of equipment, and provides on-the-job training with constant hands-on experience. After initial training, TTAs complete additional training at Quantico. About a month into the TTA program, Leo received orders to monitor a Title III. He monitored conversations, reviewed tapes, and translated for eight months. This affected his TTA training program as it took him away from hands-on experience with the equipment, and he fell behind.

According to legal counsel, TTAs are not supposed to monitor Title IIIs because of the sensitivity and the classification of the certification. The FBI held the deposition Leo gave for the civil suit in a secure location, since it required a security clearance. Even after the FBI certified Leo as a TTA in 1986, FBIHQ—again in violation of policy—ordered him to work a Title III in Atlanta.

Leo saw non-Hispanic Spanish speakers who never sat on wires sent to their office of preference; this did not happen with native Spanish speakers. Native Spanish speakers supported other agents by conducting and translating interviews. Supervisors never liked that the Hispanic agents assigned to them did not acquire the stats of those not forced to travel on TDY assignments.

Leo received a letter of transfer on June 22, 1984, which sent him to San Juan, and he noted that his ability to speak Spanish, not his TTA qualifications, resulted in his transfer. His San Francisco supervisor sent a message to headquarters to void the transfer, as the supervisor believed that San Francisco required Leo's skills more than San Juan did. In Leo's opinion, Puerto Rico was a hardship office.

There were two separate declarations in Leo's file noting he had an accent, something that Leo found to be petty and discriminatory, as it came from a professional agency. He also anticipated retaliation from his participation in the class action. An accent could handicap a person, block advancement, create a biased stereotype, or in Leo's case, result in an assignment as his boss's personal chauffer.

Ms. Black, on cross-examination, stated that Leo had just helped a Hispanic case agent when he worked his most recent Title III. Leo countered that the circumstances of the Title III caused him delays with his own work and that his supervisors had ordered him to take the assignment. Leo also stated that investigative situations forced Hispanic agents to help Anglo Spanish speakers on wires because their Spanish was deficient. Although Legal Division mandated that TTAs cannot serve on T-IIIs, management ordered Leo to do so. Meanwhile, the other TTA in the San Francisco office—a pilot—took on pilot assignments, which, as Leo pointed out, are always voluntary and are never in violation of any policy. Leo's assignments to T-IIIs were neither voluntary nor legal. Leo did not file an EEO complaint because, he testified, "They did not work."

24

Luis Antonio Monserrate, Jr.

Luis Monserrate, Jr. served in the US Army, attended Russian language school, and worked with the Army Security Agency for four years in a variety of capacities. He left the Army and completed college on the GI Bill. He received a commission in the Air Force through the ROTC Program and served in the Air Force for seven years as a pilot with two tours in Southeast Asia. Luis worked as a pharmaceutical representative before becoming an FBI agent under the modified program. In training, he took the Russian and Spanish language tests, passing both. In new agents' class, management entrusted him with a deep undercover assignment in Los Angeles, an assignment that involved his entire family and lasted nine months. He served in San Juan for six years before transferring to the Atlanta division. Luis was a Technically Trained Agent (TTA) and a pilot, and he spoke fluent English, Spanish, German and Russian. Luis also worked on Major Cases such as the naval personnel murders, the bombing of the Air National Guard base, the terrorist ambush of ROTC personnel, police corruption, and a major armored car heist.

An undercover assignment in LA required his Russian language proficiency besides his knowledge of electronics. Luis went in feet first, with no training prior to the total immersion of himself and his family in the assignment. He received a general briefing as to the targets but received no kind of psychological evaluation. The FBI promised to set him up with an appropriate lifestyle and equipment commensurate with the level of the undercover assignment. However, when financial problems arose, he had to pay medical bills out of his own pocket since his insurance was under his real name.

The undercover assignment terminated earlier than anticipated because the FBI faced a lawsuit in a similar case in which they had placed an agent on the board of directors of a corporation. Luis wanted to go right back to work as an agent, but his boss, Roger Castonguay, told him that the bureau had gone to great expense to set him up in his undercover role, so he was to remain undercover and in time receive another case assignment. Instead, the office assigned him to fixed surveillance, and he watched closed-circuit television feeds.

The FBI never got around to giving Luis a pilot's license under his assumed name and he became involved in a minor aircraft accident. When he completed the Federal Aviation Administration (FAA) accident report, he gave his real name and listed his employer as the Federal Bureau of Investigation. Castonguay admonished him for lack of judgment in revealing his identity. Chastised, he returned to being an agent. Meanwhile, under the stress of his undercover assignments and the related financial worries, his marriage dissolved.

25

Sandra I. Chinchilla

Sandy Chinchilla graduated from the University of Puerto Rico in 1972 with a BBA concentrated in accounting, management and marketing. Hired by the FBI in April of 1976, she served in the San Juan division for two and a half years, then with the Boston division for the nine years preceding the civil suit. She entered the bureau under the accounting program. Later she took the Spanish language exam and received a level 5 rating. She worked the "Taco Circuit" on twenty Spanish language specials, which ranged from thirty to ninety days.

Sandy testified that there were numerous downsides to working T-IIIs, as they are sometimes in difficult locations in which an agent sits for a period of eight to twelve hours, five or more days a week. Often there were no bathroom facilities nearby, and when agents are by themselves, they cannot leave the post. A disproportionate amount of T-III assignments are discriminatory because they do not allow the agents to complete the other work assigned to them, and because management did not force Anglo Spanish speakers to cover Spanish-speaking assignments the way Hispanics were forced.

Sandy worked undercover and assisted other agents with Spanish-speaking assignments, but received no training and evaluation on her undercover work, which went unacknowledged and uncredited. Sandy requested a transfer out of Boston, but the office told her that they needed a Spanish speaker and refused her request. Meanwhile, she saw non-Hispanic Spanish speakers transferred out of the Boston Division and one non-Hispanic agent in the process of learning Spanish transferred from Boston to San Juan, where they needed Spanish speakers.

Sandy became a relief supervisor in 1978, but her supervisor told her that, since she did not have experience working the desk, she could not become the primary relief. Non-Hispanics with less time often received appointments as primary relief supervisors. Sandy lacked experience on the desk because of her workload and because she was busy assisting other agents in undercover work. She asked many times to attend MAP, but management refused to grant her requests. She received excellent and superior performance appraisals that did not help get her to San Juan, her office of preference (OP). Sandy applied for a supervisory position in San Juan and then for an ALAT position but did not get either one. She requested undercover training and informant development training, but FBI management turned her down. She never filed a complaint because she feared retaliation, acknowledging that the FBI is a large and powerful organization.

On cross-examination, the DOJ brought out that the Boston division had Sicilian and Chinese speakers required to work Title IIIs in their language. No other Hispanic female in her area performed undercover work on drug cases, dealt with Colombians, Cubans, and others. Meanwhile, non-Hispanic female agents worked the applicant and white-collar crime squads, which were much less dangerous assignments. The DOJ brought out that it cost the bureau over $40,000 back then to move a special agent from office to office, then to replace that agent the FBI would incur an additional $40,000 expense. Sandy reported that her light undercover work, even though it was not deep cover, still meant that the job required her to be available twenty-four hours a day, as "it is full undercover with these people; they don't know who I am."

On redirect, Tony Silva asked if the $40,000 the bureau claimed to expend on a transfer was any different for a Hispanic as compared to a non-Hispanic. He made the point that transferring a non-Hispanic agent to San Juan cost exactly the same amount it would have cost if

Sandy had received the transfer. San Juan and the bureau both acknowledged that there was a critical need for experienced Spanish speakers in Puerto Rico. Frequently, on undercover assignments in Boston, investigative situations forced the FBI to use Massachusetts State Police troopers to monitor conversations, since Sandy's fellow FBI agents could not understand Spanish and could not tell what was going on with Sandy's undercover operations. If Sandy needed help, under those conditions, she would have been forced to speak English and blow her cover.

Larry Potts served as ASAC Boston when Sandy Chinchilla sought reassignment to the San Juan office in 1987. Sandy reported that her father was ill, and she requested a hardship transfer to San Juan. Potts requested that Sandy commit to a five-year transfer to get her OP, which she was willing to do, but FBIHQ once again denied the transfer. Potts acknowledged that both Kevin Klemm and Sandra were accountants but that Klemm transferred out of Boston to San Juan, despite his limited Spanish. James Esposito, the SAC San Juan, testified that he chose Kevin Klemm as an accountant over Sandy.

Larry J. McCormick, who served in the Transfer Unit at FBIHQ, testified that Sandy could not transfer to San Juan because Boston needed a Spanish speaker and she was their only resource. Despite there being over eight hundred Spanish speakers in the FBI, for some unknown reason the FBI could not incentivize or compel a single one to transfer to Boston.

26

David Martinez

David Martinez, born in Marfa, Texas, attended college at Sul Ross State University where he obtained a Bachelor of Science in biology with a minor in physical education. He worked in El Paso for three years before joining the FBI in 1975. He worked in New York City for twelve and a half years, and he was a firearms instructor at the FBI Academy in Quantico, Virginia, for the seven months before the trial. Judge Bunton acknowledged that he knew David's parents and that, as a lawyer, he once represented the family.

David came into the FBI under three programs: the language program, the science program and the modified program. His science background did not appear in his file, but he showed a level 4 rating under the Spanish language program. He did not consider himself a good Spanish speaker because his family did not speak Spanish at home, and he only learned Spanish by taking classes in high school and college.

David received transfer orders from New York to San Antonio, Texas. He asked for the Austin RA, but the SAC denied him the opportunity to go to Austin or San Antonio. "I later heard from the Assistant Special Agent in Charge who told me I had a choice of three resident agencies. I could go to McAllen, Brownsville or Laredo. None of which I find attractive at all. Those offices are considered by many to be hardship resident agencies, not sought by many agents." He received orders to Laredo, Texas, and declined. The deputy assistant director in charge of transfers told David that, because of his refusal to accept the transfer, the bureau would punish him and defer his OP for two years and he would remain in New York. David thought this was unfair because, soon afterwards, the San Antonio division sent new agent John Wright, an Anglo Spanish speaker, straight from Quantico to the Austin RA. After thirteen years in the FBI, David had seen Hispanics stereotyped and restricted to certain kinds of work, such as wiretaps and surveillances.

A native Spanish speaker is brought up in a Spanish-speaking household in which Spanish is the primary language, and English is a second language. A native speaker is raised in the native culture. David was not. Hispanics work many wiretaps where shifts are twelve hours on, twelve hours off, often seven days a week. Managers expect Hispanics to help other agents with their caseloads, and supervisors still expect them to complete their own work. David discussed with his supervisor the fact that the Spanish language was more a hindrance to him than a help; "and in many instances I was just laughed at, was my answer." Discouraged, he felt that taking the issue any further would have just been futile. David knew of Spanish-speaking Anglo agents who removed themselves from the language program at their own request. Dorothy Shafler was an FBI qualified Spanish speaker who knew the language so well she had even taught Spanish before she came into the bureau. The FBI allowed her removal from the Spanish-speaking list.

David understood that, if an agent attended language school, they would then have a three-year commitment to use and receive work-related assignments in that language. If a person has a language ability and the office needs that language, the agent could move up the OP list, but as David said "the bureau very often hides behind the five words: the needs of the bureau." David worked twelve Spanish-speaking T-IIIs and, although Spanish language specialists and contract employees also worked as translators, David saw no translators at all on the Title IIIs he worked.

Ed Guevara was an agent in the New York office whom David first met on a TDY "Taco Circuit" assignment in Miami in 1979. Ed approached David to counsel him on an EEO complaint that Ed contemplated filing. David said,

> We discussed the ramifications of him going formal with a complaint, what the procedure would be. I got in contact with Helen Burgosa, who was more or less in charge of the EEO program in New York. He wrote a memo, which I gave to Helen. Ed did not file a formal complaint fearing retaliation and reprisal. I have seen the bureau subtly be very vindictive, cruel and mean. In many ways, the FBI can make life hard for an individual and their career. And it is not beyond reason that in the FBI, because of that you can be given the worst duties around, be given the worst hours around, be made to work TDYs and sent out of the district to disrupt home life, family life, personal life, where they literally push you to the point of quitting or to consider quitting, and I have been there.

On cross-examination, David testified that his Spanish language abilities never helped him to obtain any position. Spanish had nothing to do with his becoming a relief supervisor. Spanish had nothing to do with him being a firearms instructor. The DOJ attorney asked David to read in court a memo he had written: "Although there are hostage negotiators in the New Rochelle office, none of them to my knowledge speak Spanish. Since we have a responsibility for the Bronx, where Spanish is a primary language for many, it may prove beneficial to the bureau and to the New Rochelle office to have a Spanish speaker." Even so, David did not receive the position for which he applied.

Charlie Parsons, testifying on the eighth day, said he had identified a staffing problem in the border resident agencies of San Antonio and, with the director's approval, added ten agents. At about the same time, the director awarded first office agents in New York City with transfers to their OPs after having served for an extended period. Parsons denied David Martinez the Austin RA or the San Antonio Division, but instead offered him Laredo or McAllen. Meanwhile, Michael T. Hanley, who worked in New York City with David Martinez, transferred directly to the Austin RA. Jerry Adams also went to the Austin RA.

Parsons stated that narcotics squad experience, which David had, was important for transfers to the border RAs. Agent Leo Martinez and John Wright attended the same new agents' class. Hugo Rodriguez questioned Charlie Parsons,

> RODRIGUEZ: So we have Mr. Wright with five years law enforcement experience, Mr. Leo Martinez with no experience. They both speak the Spanish language according to the FBI. Mr. Martinez is Hispanic. Mr. Wright is Anglo. Mr. Wright is Mormon and Mr. Martinez is non-Mormon. Please tell the court where Mr. Martinez is assigned?
>
> PARSONS: He is slated to go to McAllen.
>
> RODRIGUEZ: McAllen? Where is Mr. Wright assigned?
>
> PARSONS: He is slated, if he has not already reported, to go to Austin.

27

Lionel Anthony Chavez

Lionel Chavez, born in Manhattan, New York, and raised in Miami, Florida, received his bachelor's degree in education from Bethany College, West Virginia, and his master's degree in criminal justice from Rollins College in Winter Park, Florida. He taught for three years and then began a career in law enforcement by becoming a sheriff's deputy. He joined the bureau on November 7, 1979, under the modified program with his first office of assignment in Los Angeles. Lionel attempted the Spanish language test and failed.

Lionel received a Spanish-speaking assignment and told his supervisor he did not speak Spanish, unaware this information would displease the boss. Assigned to the fugitive squad, he resented his training agent, Wayne Cassidy, who called him the "token Cuban." He also recalled agents Ralph Difonzo and Wayne Cassidy calling Luis Monserrate "a fat, stupid spic." He considered returning to the sheriff's department but after finding success locating several "old dog" fugitives (cases that had been around for years) he stayed on with the bureau.

Lionel once had a fugitive lead, and with his supervisor, Cassidy, unavailable, he covered the lead, informing the office about where the fugitive had gone. He concluded the interview and, to his surprise, discovered Cassidy and other agents waiting outside. Cassidy scolded Lionel and told him that if he did not straighten up, he would get rid of him. After that, everything seemed to go downhill for Lionel. His caseload declined from tracking fugitives to following leads and requesting telephone subscriber information. On one case, in which he developed all of the lead information to locate a fugitive, when the time came for the arrest, the other agents did not even include him. When he was working a case involving the interstate transportation of stolen property, supervisor Tyrone Miller told him that, since he had a Cuban background, he should instead be speaking Spanish and investigating false immigration "green cards."

Lionel became a firearms and police instructor. He tried out for the FBI's LA SWAT team under Myron Hitch but learned Tyrone Miller had informed Hitch that Lionel, who had excellent evaluations, was incompetent and not a good worker. Lionel tried out and scored in the top five, but Hitch rejected him. He applied for a defensive tactics school but when accepted, Hitch blocked him from going to Quantico for training. He reapplied with strong recommendations for the SWAT team.

Hitch told him that he could either be on the SWAT team or he could be a defensive tactics instructor, but he could not do both. This surprised Lionel because two non-Hispanic SWAT team members did both. Lionel later joined the SWAT team and, in preparation for the 1984 Olympics, Hitch asked him to cover some venues, which meant that he would take pictures and gather information about where the athletes would stay. He declined and told Hitch that he had forty some odd agents assigned to the SWAT team, and he did not want to take anything away from them.

Lionel, who had a scheduled training at Quantico, did not respond to a SWAT incident on a Sunday as he was due to fly out of town on Monday. Other members also did not report. Hitch told other agents that he had planned to remove Lionel to make him an example for refusing to cover venues. Ron Frigulti, a non-Hispanic, refused to do venues as well. Hitch removed Lionel, but not Frigulti, from the SWAT team without ASAC Jim Nelson conducting any kind of review.

George Vinson then became the training coordinator in LA. When Lionel was training local police officers, his squad secretary told him to watch his back, as the secretary had overheard Hitch and Vinson speaking about getting Lionel transferred. Soon afterwards, Vinson told Lionel that he needed to see the ASAC because of reports alleging that Lionel was not getting along with the police officers and that he was not a team player, that he had a bad attitude, and that contrary to what he might believe, Myron Hitch had nothing to do with removing him from his SWAT position.

Don Kinder, a defensive tactics instructor, tried to intervene, but Vinson told him to shut up or he too would be on the way out. Lionel transferred to an FCI squad working Middle Eastern matters, and his fellow squad members learned that Lionel had a "bad jacket," which meant that he was trouble and untrustworthy. Because Kinder came to Lionel's aid, agents also shunned him, and Kinder suffered in assignments and soon became depressed.

Lionel found several letters of commendation that Vinson failed to include in his personnel file. The letter from Hitch that criticized him as not being a team player and caused his removal from SWAT also did not appear in his file. However, Lionel kept copies, and he introduced them as evidence to the court.

On cross-examination, Lionel testified that, when he worked for Don Leighton, he was restricted from working major sources. Leighton told squad member Greg Hoeschen that Lionel had a "bad jacket." According to Lionel, other SWAT members missed assignments and, during some assignments he missed, he was busy providing instruction at various police agencies. Lionel did not file an EEO complaint because he believed that witnesses like Don Kinder and those who spoke up for Mat would suffer.

Myron Hitch testified that, in January 1985, he had prepared a memo listing the reasons for removing Lionel from the SWAT team. The 1984 Olympics required the office to do site surveys of twenty-five Olympic venue sites. Lionel did not participate in those surveys or assist, indicating he had other priorities. Lionel also had not responded to any call-ups to incidents. Hitch testified that he had never referred to Lionel as a "token Cuban," but admitted he had used the word "beaner" when speaking to a fellow agent. He verified that Frigulti, a non-Hispanic SWAT team member, never did venues or call-outs but remained on the team.

George Vinson testified that he had learned from Captain James Faranato of the San Bernardino Sheriff's Office (SBSO) that Lionel taught a defensive tactics class and that Lionel was unhappy with a student in the class, and that incident resulted in Lionel not teaching any more classes for the SBSO.

Vinson recommended that Lionel transfer to an investigative squad because he showed up late for police instruction classes. Vinson maintained that he forwarded all commendation letters to the appropriate supervisor, but read in court a letter of commendation that had somehow not made it into Lionel's file.

28

Elizabeth Rodriguez

Elizabeth "Liz" Rodriguez received B.A. and M.A. degrees in teaching English as a second language. She came into the bureau under the Spanish language program, serving in the New York and Tampa divisions. A week after arrival at her first office, management sent her to San Juan, Puerto Rico, on a special assignment. Travel regulations allow agents from thirty up to ninety days to get their personal affairs in order when they arrive at a new office.

When Liz returned from that first TDY assignment, the FBI shipped her out to Tampa, where they needed a Spanish speaker. She requested a thirty-day extension, but the ASAC in Tampa denied her request since he wanted her to work a Title III in Orlando. She worked in Ocala for seventy-five days before the T-III wire shut down.

Since she never had an opportunity to house-hunt, she assumed that, once she stopped working the wire, her relocation time would take effect. Her supervisor informed her that her allotted time had now expired, and she would have to look for a home on her own time. During the year and a half she spent in Tampa, she worked every Spanish-speaking special, both in-house and outside of the division. She knew of no other agent in her class who had been refused time to find a place to live.

Liz's supervisor assigned her to a fugitive case but then sent her away to a special in San Juan. When she returned, the office reassigned her to the white-collar crime squad. About a month and a half after that assignment, her office sent her on another special and, given leads to cover, she recalled only one white-collar crime case assigned to her. While on TDY to San Juan, she did not utilize Spanish as she was on surveillance most of the time. She believed that she had been sent to San Juan because of her appearance and because she was from Puerto Rico.

When Liz received her first performance appraisal in Tampa, her supervisor gave her a rating of "minimally acceptable" in informant development because she had no assets and no informants. Liz responded that it was difficult to develop informants while working TDYs and without assigned cases. She asked her supervisor to rate her on her special TDY assignments, but he said he had no choice and the rating would have to stand.

The applicant recruiter told her that ratings apply to the same elements for all agents, but if she went on specials, she deserved ratings in that category. She drafted a memo and sent it to the SAC instead of to her supervisor. The SAC instructed Liz's supervisor to remove that element from her evaluation for that period. Her supervisor then warned her she was not to discuss the matter with any other Hispanic agent in the office.

Left with no cases, Liz assisted other agents and RAs with interviews and surveillances. Her supervisor seemed upset when her name appeared on official interview reports such as FD-302s, but he did not assign her any cases. She testified that she most often worked with female agents, as male agents appeared uninterested in working with female agents.

In the New York division, there were Anglo Spanish-speaking agents who have never been on special TDY assignments or language Title IIIs. Liz ran into the same group of agents who worked Spanish-speaking wires. Tampa considered Liz a first office agent, even though she served in the New York office for six months.

On the ninth day of the trial, Richard Ross, a former ASAC in Tampa, testified that he considered Liz a first office agent, even with six months in the New York office, and assigning an experienced agent to Liz upon her arrival in Tampa for twenty days would have been standard policy. Ross said that, since he assigned Liz to a wiretap, her training period had started after completing the wiretap assignment, but he could not recall assigning her to an agent upon completion of the wiretap.

Ross concurred that all agents are entitled to administrative leave for house-hunting purposes, and he did not know why his office denied Liz administrative leave and required her instead to take annual leave to find housing in Tampa.

There was a time in the bureau when supervisors made calls to FBIHQ and did all they could to advocate for the rights of their personnel. If FBIHQ refused the request, then the supervisor would "fix" it or provide a "handle" on the QT (quiet). The saying was, "no harm, no foul." Your troops came first. There appeared to be pettiness and insensitivity in the lack of willingness to grant Liz the administrative leave she needed to go house-hunting.

29

Federico Villalobos

Federico "Fred" Villalobos, born and raised in Kenosha, Wisconsin, worked as a US Customs Officer on February 1, 1987. He served as a police officer while earning a degree in criminal justice. He first entered the FBI on May 19, 1975, first going to Miami, then the New York office, where he remained until his resignation in 1987. Fred spent thirteen years as an FBI agent and received outstanding evaluations. He failed the language test upon entry, but in 1978, the FBI ordered him to take another Spanish language test. He received orders to report to a TDY assignment in Peoria, Illinois, for a T-III. Fred took a three-minute, so-called "test"—after which, the bureau informed him that he was now fluent and certified and could get to work. The needs of the "Taco Circuit" were calling.

The "Taco Circuit" was the contemptuous FBI nickname for the system of permanent transfers, temporary assignments, and undercover assignments, in which Hispanic Spanish speakers became acquainted. Fred worked over two dozen "specials," with each lasting thirty to ninety days, for two straight years of his FBI career. Fred's frustration with the FBI grew, as he could not rise above the street agent level to a management position; he had problems even getting out of New York City.

When non-native, Spanish-speaking agents decided that they wanted their name removed from the list of Spanish speakers, they only had to ask and they no longer had a commitment to Spanish-speaking assignments. That policy did not apply to Fred or to the other Hispanic-surnamed agents. When Fred arrived in Miami, all Spanish-speaking agents or agents with Spanish surnames ended up on a squad known around the office as the "Tamale Squad." Fred could not get off the Tamale Squad for the entire three years he spent in Miami. Fred testified that only one female agent of Mexican descent, Alice, whose married name was Days, did not receive assignments to Spanish-speaking specials.

The FBI never did a good job of identifying and utilizing all Spanish speakers with non-Hispanic surnames, and this forced agents burdened with Hispanic surnames to bear the load. Fred recounted a story about agent Don Valdez, who transferred to Newark because FBI management assumed from his name that he spoke Spanish. However, when he informed FBIHQ that he spoke no Spanish, they did not rescind the transfer orders. When Don arrived, the Newark supervisor learned that he had no Spanish-speaking agent, but instead a Filipino.

Although Fred served as the principal relief supervisor for the "Tamale Squad," he never went to MAP for assessment. Fred applied for a position as an assistant legal attaché in Mexico City but again encountered rejection. An official from FBIHQ once interviewed him about a sensitive, deep undercover assignment in an unnamed foreign country and told him to prepare for immediate transfer. However, the transfer never came.

Fred testified that being a Spanish speaker was a detriment to his professional career. "It was difficult leaving the bureau as there is a certain amount of prestige in being a member of what is considered to be the number one law enforcement agency in this country. The FBI has high esteem throughout the world. Therefore, it was a very difficult decision to make. But, I don't regret my decision." Fred accepted a reduction in grade to work in a more agreeable and non-hostile environment—the US Customs Service, an organization that treated him with respect and dignity.

Ms. Gulyassy produced a Kenosha Police Department document to counter Fred's testimony about his lack of ability to speak Spanish. It stated that Fred "often" functioned as an interpreter. Since no other Spanish speaker worked for Kenosha PD, it would be difficult or impossible for an evaluator to assess the level and proficiency of any spoken Spanish. Fred explained that Spanish speakers may be considered fluent in some areas, but not in others, adding that when he flunked the entrance exam he was doing his level best to pass, since he very much wanted to become an FBI agent.

Fred accepted a reduction in grade to leave an organization that offered him no opportunity for promotion and gave him indigestion from his time on the "Taco Circuit" and the "Tamale Squad." Once he found sanctuary with US Customs, he became duty-free of T-IIIs.

30

Gilbert Mireles

Gilbert "Gil" Mireles, a graduate of New Mexico State University with a B.S. degree, entered the FBI on October 16, 1972. In his first office, San Diego, he worked fugitive and bribery cases. One special bribery case involved corruption of government officials along the entire length of the Mexican border. While in San Diego, he received transfer orders on two occasions, but his ASAC killed both orders. Upon termination of the corruption special, he transferred to San Juan, Puerto Rico, where he worked bombing cases and terrorism. He served in San Juan for two years before transferring to Miami in 1977, where he worked white-collar crime and then foreign counterintelligence. A new foreign counterintelligence squad formed, and he served as the squad's acting supervisor for three months and later as the principal relief.

Gil volunteered for an undercover assignment in San Antonio, Texas, which dragged out for two years, but it took more than a year to finalize the paperwork for his official assignment. Supervisor Joe Gannon informed Gil that the other non-Hispanic agent working undercover received his orders within a month. Gil did not receive the training or psychological evaluation mandated by bureau policy before his undercover assignment in San Antonio. No one monitored his undercover activities, nor did anyone provide reentry counseling.

He attended MAP I in 1981, receiving one contingency. He received no assistance in removing the contingency and found it inconsistent with his performance evaluations and commendations, which all stated that he possessed outstanding management abilities.

Gil received no training prior to Foreign Counter Intelligence (FCI) assignments. FCI training is important because agents face professionals from other countries whose jobs are to subvert our government. Jim Freeman provided Gil with about five minutes of training as a relief supervisor when he showed Gil where to initial teletypes and airtels. Gil's performance appraisals were all superior or above, except for his first one and last. The SAC told Gil that he was one of two agents considered for the next FCI desk, but Gil did not get the promotion. He applied for other jobs but never got those either. Gil noticed other agents admitted to the career development program (CDP) mere months prior to the advertisement of positions, and they would win those positions without having ever acted as supervisors, principal reliefs, or reliefs.

In 1987, ASAC Julian De la Rosa, who had been in the bureau for twenty-five years, asked Gil on three occasions if he would become an EEO counselor. Gil refused the position, as he feared the repercussions. De La Rosa convinced Gil that he was just the type of person the EEO needed: conscientious and serious, someone in whom people could confide his or her fears. Flattered, Gil accepted and attended a three-day EEO training. The following week, San Antonio SAC John W. "Bill" Dalseg summoned Gil into his office. Mel Jeter, head of the EEO program, wanted an experienced Mexican-American agent to travel to El Paso on an EEO matter. Jeter gave Gil authorization to travel to El Paso to conduct the interview but restricted him from interviewing any others and from traveling anywhere but El Paso. Gil later learned that he was to interview El Paso ASAC Mat Perez.

Gil had never met Mat until he arrived in El Paso and told Mat he was there to counsel his EEO complaint. Mat, knowing the bureau retaliated against counselors sympathetic to EEO victims, told him, "I am sorry about what this is going to do to your career." Mat then asked which of his issues Gil planned to investigate. Gil called Jeter and asked him what issues he should discuss with Mat, and Jeter told Gil to investigate all allegations.

Later, when Dalseg was preparing to transfer from San Antonio to Savannah, Dalseg told Gil that if he had known in advance that Mat Perez, a GS-16, was the complainant for the EEO case in El Paso, Dalseg would have prevented Gil from becoming involved. Mat and Gil spent all of the first day discussing a single issue. The following day, they continued with the second but could not finish because both had scheduling issues. They agreed to meet again on another day when both had open schedules to handle the third issue.

When Gil returned to San Antonio, ASAC Dodge Frederick assigned him to a T-III listening post in McAllen. Gil thought this strange because in both Miami and San Antonio, when he had requested TDY assignments, management had informed him that he was not expendable. He informed Frederick of the pending EEO investigation and that the investigation had mandated deadlines. Frederick, unconcerned with Gil meeting EEO investigative deadlines, sternly ordered Gil to report to the Title III.

Later, Frederick noticed Gil at his desk while Gil was on the phone with a Spanish-speaking informant. Frederick left him a note to see him after the phone conversation. When Gil reported to his office, Frederick told Gil that he would put up a sign like the one he had in his LA supervisory office, in which he had no one but Spanish speakers on his squad. The sign said, *Aqui no se Habla Español, Cabrón,* which translates as "You don't speak Spanish here, asshole." Frederick then repeated the phrase. Gil explained that he did not appreciate Frederick's comments as he translated the word *cabrón* to mean "son of a bitch." Gil then told Frederick he would be happy to abide by his wishes and not speak Spanish at work and there would therefore be no need to go to McAllen for the T-III.

From that point on, Frederick and his minions in the office labeled Gil a "Mexican malcontent" for counseling Mat and being so uppity. Frederick informed Gil that, as Gil's supervisor, he had a right to know which issues Mat planned to pursue in his EEO complaint. Gil refused to tell. He observed Frederick's animosity toward Mat. Frederick even had the audacity to call Mat and ask about the issues behind Mat's EEO complaint. Mat told Frederick that he was familiar with EEO policy and suggested that Frederick not interfere. Frederick told Gil, "I guess you have to go to El Paso, and I guess now I will be subject to an EEO complaint because Perez is going to say that I interfered."

Mike Appleby circulated a petition around the office for the court interveners, those agents who attempted to prevent the disclosure through discovery of FBI personnel records, and asked agents to sign. Gil refused to do so. Appleby opposed the class action, but he believed that the Hispanics would win the suit, although not because of any discrimination against Mexicans. On that point, he declined to elaborate further. Appleby said that Hispanic agents embarrassed the bureau because of their association with groups like the League of United Latin American Citizens (LULAC), which he equated with the Black Panther Party.

Gil had a heated discussion with Appleby following Gil's deposition, as Appleby demanded to know what Gil had said about him. Gil explained,

> So I told him I raised my right hand and I swore to tell the truth, and that is what I did. I attributed a disparaging remark to you concerning undercover work that monkeys could do what I was doing working undercover. Appleby said he knew because FBIHQ told him. He said, "I do not like that you mentioned my name in this EEO hearing. You have known me for a long time; you know I am not discriminatory." We were arguing, and he used many obscene adjectives I should not use here.

In Gil's sixteen years of service, disparaging references to Hispanics were common. He heard SAC Dalseg refer to Hispanic agents as "fucking Mexicans." He also heard ASAC Dodge Frederick make jokes about Mexicans to the point that one clerk told him it "was getting old." Dalseg would often tell his Hispanic ASAC, "Get your Mexican ass in here."

Gene O'Leary was Gil's immediate supervisor. He asked Gil to come over to his squad because of his work record; he saw Gil as an asset. When Gil and other Hispanic agents returned from their depositions and submitted their travel reimbursement vouchers, he testified, "He tore apart and separated our vouchers and held them out and stated that they were going to be sent to a special person back at headquarters because they were to be handled differently." Gil saw this as retaliation as FBIHQ planned to process the vouchers outside of normal channels and create delays.

On cross-examination, Ms. Simon brought out Gil's last performance evaluation that slid because Gil did not have informants. Gil and his supervisor discussed his performance two months before the appraisal, and O'Leary told him he would get a superior rating if he developed an informant before the scheduled rating. Gil reopened a productive informant, whom O'Leary had signed off on and sent the paperwork to FBIHQ for approval. However, on the evaluation, Gil did not get a superior rating in that element.

Gil noted that, in his sixteen years of experience, he had seen that some agents did not have to apply for a specific position because they had a "hook." Before the trial, Mickey Drake received a promotion to GS-14 from the San Antonio Division. Drake told Gil that he never put in for the position but instead received an unexpected call from FBIHQ.

Gil never filed an EEO complaint himself because he saw the unfairness and ineptitude inherent in how the FBI investigated such complaints, particularly in the case of EEO counselor Arnie Gerardo. O'Leary told Gil, "The only mistake Arnie made in the bureau was to get involved with Mat Perez," adding that Arnie's problem was insignificant and certainly did not warrant removal from a supervisory position. Gil told O'Leary that agents and support staff were afraid to get involved in the EEO process. Ms. Simon's last question was, "But they haven't suffered any because they haven't filed them, have they?"

31

J. Antonio Falcon, Jr.

J. Antonio "Tony" Falcon, born and raised in Puerto Rico, received an education in the Spanish language at the University of Puerto Rico, where he majored in accounting and finance. He joined the FBI on January 12, 1976, and served in San Juan through 1982, working a variety of cases. He transferred to San Diego, where he was a SWAT team member, a principal firearms instructor, and the principal liaison agent with Mexico. Tony worked civil rights and fugitive cases and all of the most important cases involving Spanish-speaking subjects. He was the SWAT team leader but remained on scene after an operation to conduct interviews in Spanish.

Tony received the videotape created by class members. The videotape contained a preamble at the beginning from one of the attorneys asserting attorney/client privilege. He shared the videotape with other Hispanic agents. Tony found out that after he had provided a copy to agent Ronald Orrantia, Orrantia had given the videotape to either SAC Tom Kuker or to ASAC Tom Hughes. Either Kuker or Hughes made a copy of the tape and sent it on to Ed Sharp, Section Chief of the Administrative Services Division.

At this point in Tony's testimony, Ms. Simon objected to questions leading to the intervention hearing, from when a group of agents and the FBI Agent's Association (FBIAA) had tried to block personnel files from discovery. She stated that the intervention had nothing to do with the merits of the Title VII claim. Hugo then addressed the court,

> RODRIQUEZ: Your Honor, the intervention effort was instigated in Washington, DC, out of the Administrative Services Division after Director Sessions told every FBI agent they would not be appealing your decision on release of records. It was instigated in Washington, DC, through Mr. Hughes and Mr. Kuker. They asked the Administrative Services Division to conduct investigations on the class members and us. It was done in reprisal and retaliation, to stigmatize these people and to involve us in a collateral issue only because of their ethnicity. We will indicate that to the court.
>
> SIMON: Your Honor, Mr. Rodriquez has been making these same claims for several months. He has not come up with any proof. We will request an offer of proffer before he goes on with this line of questioning and takes more time up along these lines.
>
> RODRIQUEZ: Your Honor, there is nothing in the rules that indicate I must proffer it. It is reprisal and it is retaliation, because of their ethnicity.
>
> THE COURT: I will overrule. However, let us get to it. I passed on that intervention once. I do not want to mess with it again.
>
> RODRIQUEZ: We are not concerned with the subject of the intervention, Your Honor. We are concerned how the intervention was originated and how it has affected their lives.

Tony testified that, in April of 1987, Kuker and Hughes met with all of the agents in the office to advise them of the class action lawsuit by Hispanic agents and to assert that private data, such as home addresses and history in agent's personnel files, would doubtless become public information. They maintained that the Soviet Union and any hostile country or criminal group facing investigation by agents would then have access to this information. No agent wished to see such information provided to the public or to terrorist groups such as Los

Macheteros, a violent Puerto Rican terrorist group involved in bombings and murders.

Both Kuker and Hughes asked Tony if he was interested in speaking in favor of the defendant's court intervention to block the plaintiff's discovery requests. Tony, and many others, did not know that the magistrate had issued a protective order on the personnel files of FBI agents and the details on protecting the files provided to the plaintiff attorneys. Agents signed and circulated the intervention around the office during working hours. In their panic, zealous agents failed to understand that the Hispanic agents, their attorneys, and the court all had Top Secret security clearances.

The FBI, at government expense, authorized Tony and the other agents to travel to El Paso to testify for the interveners. Later the FBI informed Tony that he would have to repay the US government for that travel, although he had received advance authorization from both his SAC and ASAC. Hughes told Tony that FBIHQ had reviewed the intervention and disallowed travel at government expense. Tony and all of the others who had traveled to El Paso instead received reimbursement from the FBI Agents Association, which had set up a trust fund for the intervention against the class action suit. Tony, despite being a member of the class action, went to the intervention because management asked him to go, and Tony did not wish to go against management's instructions.

Founded in April of 1981, in response to the growing recognition that FBI management had railroaded and left field agents hung out to dry, the FBIAA united field agents to protect and advance their interests and professions through logic and compelling arguments. In irony, the purpose, mission, logic and argument disappeared when the disoriented FBIAA did not support Hispanic agents and took its first recorded failure by siding with management.

EAD John Glover testified that he reviewed the videotape sent to FBIHQ despite its preamble addressing it, and the label marking it, as attorney-client privilege. He said that he reviewed it anyway to determine the substance of the tape and decide on a course of action.

Agents who were non-class members believed an intervention would be necessary to prevent the possible injustice of the dissemination of their personal data, which would allow the information to fall into the wrong hands. They wanted to restrict the release of privileged information to the plaintiffs, and they intended to make a claim for related expenses. Hispanic agents spent their own money on lawsuit expenses with no expectation of reimbursement, but they spent their money on principles in which they believed—a stronger FBI.

The FBI oath implies that the oath-takers are dutiful and intellectual citizens with characters conscientious of the concepts of that in which they are about to embark. The FBI oath also implies you are a part of a team—a pack—and what better team to join than a federal agency responsible for the dogma of federal laws and the credence of the US Constitution.

However, the oath is not implicit, but explicit, when the oath taker "without mental reservation or purpose of evasion" affirms no diversion from the US Constitution or US laws, even to the extent of being independent from the rest of the pack if it strays from the tenets of the US Constitution. Material marked and identified as attorney-client privilege is, under US law, deserving of respect and of its own due process—no sworn officer should dishonor and violate the sanctity of their oath to uphold the law. There was no noble cause involved in the disrespect of the confidentiality of attorney-client privilege, given that attorney Jose Silva stated in the videotape that the FBI would, in due time, review it through legal discovery. The American public deserves unwavering ethics from its sworn officers.

32

Louis Edward Barragan

Louis Barragan received a B.B.A. from the University of Texas at El Paso and served as an officer with the El Paso Police Department for four years before working for the Border Patrol as an agent for seven years. He joined the FBI in 1985 and transferred to Tampa after graduating from the academy.

Louis opted out as a class member because he thought that the discrimination he encountered did not rise to the level of the experiences of discrimination he had heard from other Hispanics. Between the certification and before the trial, he changed his mind and joined the class action, as he bore the brunt of ethnic and racial slurs, in which other agents called him and others a "spic," a "lazy spic," a "dirty Mexican," a "lazy Mexican and a "wetback," among others.

Louis had sixty to eighty hours in Equal Employment Opportunity training when he was with the Border Patrol and knew how to identify discrimination. He testified, "And I recognize this to be what occurred to me, exactly that, racism." He had a difficult time in deciding to join the lawsuit and testify. Louis still had his whole career ahead of him, and a lot of hope for the FBI.

Louis chose to work for the FBI because he thought it was an elite professional group. He did not know where his career would go following his testimony. He had never expected such racist attitudes from a group of supposed professionals such as the FBI. Louis expected to find trained professionals with a high standard of decorum in the workplace. He did not expect what he encountered.

Louis did not report the slurs he heard from other FBI agents and never filed a complaint. The Border Patrol mandates sixty to eighty hours of Equal Employment Opportunity training for all of its agents to assist them in understanding workplace interactions and in dealing with undocumented workers. This amount of EEO training should not have seemed excessive to the FBI after so many documented incidents of agents unlawfully crossing the border into slander. Closing one's ears to such speech was no solution.

33

Gregorio Rodríguez

Greg Rodríguez graduated from Pan American University in 1968 and received his master's degree in education from Western Illinois University. He taught at Highland Community College in Freeport, Illinois. Greg entered the FBI in 1974, serving in the Chicago division, a top twelve office. Greg transferred to San Juan, serving there from January 1978 to December 1980. He transferred back to Chicago for seven years before his transfer to San Antonio in March of 1987 for an undercover assignment.

On assignment to San Juan, Greg worked from the Ponce RA, about fifty miles south of San Juan. Greg requested a hardship transfer to a regional area in Texas to be close to his mother-in-law, but FBIHQ denied the request. About eighteen months into his Puerto Rico assignment, Greg informed SAC John J. Hinchcliffe that he wanted to stay longer than his two-year contract as he enjoyed the work, he liked his quality of life and playing golf, and he had made friends with Chi Chi Rodriguez. Hinchcliffe informed Greg that he planned to close the Ponce RA and transfer Greg back to the San Juan division. Greg then decided that if he had to sell his house in Ponce and make a move, he would opt out of extending. Hinchcliffe told Greg, "Well, just don't come crying to me when you don't get what you like." Greg wanted New York or Miami if he could not get his office of preference, San Antonio.

When Greg received his transfer letter, the SAC told him, "You're not going to like what you got." Greg thought that his transfer back to Chicago, his previous office of assignment before Puerto Rico, was unfair because other agents did not transfer back to their original top twelve offices. Homes like the one he had sold in Chicago for $52,000 were now selling for around $90,000. He wrote a letter to Director Webster requesting reconsideration. Assistant Director Richard Long told Greg that his transfer back to Chicago was due to his experience and their need with the Fuerzas Armadas de Liberacion Nacional (FALN) terrorism organization. However, FBIHQ and the Chicago Division did not coordinate their responses, since Greg received a letter from Chicago SAC James O. Ingram welcoming him to his new assignment working car thefts. Greg suspected that Hinchcliffe engaged in something devious and retaliatory in his transfer.

Once back in Chicago, Greg soon developed a Colombian drug case following a thirty-eight-day wiretap, and his investigation resulted in the conviction of sixteen perpetrators, the seizure of ninety pounds of cocaine, and the recovery of over a million dollars in assets. It looked as if Greg's future would include a letter of commendation with an incentive award—as he learned that the AUSA received $1,800 following the indictments—but instead Greg received nothing. Greg also saw other agents receive large incentive awards related to cases with minor statistical results, while his case received much acclaim and proved to be big news in Chicago.

Greg transferred to San Antonio to work an undercover assignment and became involved in an accident in an undercover car. He called his case agent and received instructions to use his undercover driver's license. At the time of the accident, Greg had just picked up his wife at the doctor's office. She had contacted him on his pager advising him that she had received treatments with instruction not to drive and had no way to get home. Greg considered this an emergency. Greg, in strict confidence, advised the police officer about his undercover assignment and informed him that his wife had no undercover identification, only her authentic identification.

Five months later, the FBI sanctioned Greg with a thirty-day suspension without pay. Meanwhile, first office agent Jim Fogel of the San Antonio division crashed on a Saturday night at 7:30 p.m. while driving an FBI rental car, a Nissan 300ZX sports car. He also had his wife in the car. Fogel claimed that they went to the gas station on Saturday night, although the car was due back to the rental agency on Monday. Fogel, off duty and not working undercover, did not need to turn in the leased car that evening or have his wife with him. Fogel caused $18,500 in damages to the car. Greg's accident occurred late on a Friday afternoon. Greg filed his report when he received the police report. In spite of the similarities between the two accidents, agent Fogel received merely a letter of censure.

When Greg returned from his deposition concerning the trial in El Paso, the payment policy of the San Antonio division for vouchers under $500 abruptly changed. His $300 voucher, and those of other Hispanic agents, went instead to FBIHQ and now would take three to four months to process before they got their money back.

Jerry Donahoe, Chief of the Administrative Summary Unit (ASU), testified three days after Greg and stated that the Title 31 statute confirms the restriction of a government car or government rental strictly for official use only. He said that agent Fogel was not in violation of Title 31 policy but that Greg Rodriguez violated Title 31.

> RODRIGUEZ: Mr. Greg Rodriguez was undercover, wasn't he?
>
> DONAHOE: Yes.
>
> RODRIGUEZ: Mr. Fogel was off duty out on a Saturday night at 7:30 p.m. with his wife, correct?
>
> DONAHOE: He was out with his wife. I do not recall the time.
>
> THE COURT: Let the record reflect it is better to be out at 7:30 p.m. on Saturday night with your wife than somebody else's wife.

Q: Because the SAC said he was out getting gas he decided not to discipline him, correct?

DONAHOE: No. Because that is what his statement was and we believed his statement.

Q: And there were no gas receipts indicating he had gotten gas, correct?

DONAHOE: I believe there were.

Q: After, post-accident, isn't that correct?

Greg had no entitlement to an outside appeal, as he was not a military veteran entitled to an MSPB hearing. Appeals for adverse actions against an agent by the Administrative Summary Unit are internal. Records reflect that the MSPB regularly reversed the decisions of the FBI.

34

James M. Garay

James "Jim" Garay, born in Los Angeles and raised in the Hatch Valley of New Mexico, obtained his accounting degree at Western New Mexico University in Silver City. After completing military service, he joined the FBI and served in San Diego, San Juan, and Albuquerque. Jim served as an EEO counselor but terminated that position because he thought the EEO process to be a sham and a farce and that the bureau proved incapable of investigating itself. He served as a media representative and interacted with television, radio, and newspapers reporters. He also served as the copilot for the FBI Albuquerque office and provided aerial support.

While in San Diego, assigned to the accounting squad, Jim's supervisor told him to complete an accounting correspondence course. He passed, but Jim paraphrased what FBIHQ told him, "Essentially you are no longer an accountant; you are a Spanish speaker." Jim, with a university degree and two years of accounting experience, knew of no Hispanic allowed into the FBI with a two-year degree, yet the FBI often recruited Anglo accountants who held two-year associate degrees and two years of work experience.

Jim was one of the class action members who participated in the videotape presentation that advised agents as to the organization of the lawsuit in the fall of 1987. In 1988, he appeared in Magistrate

Ruesch's courtroom to testify for the certification of the class. His performance ratings slipped, falling from exceptional, to superior, to fully successful and continued to drop.

Jim became a pilot at his own expense and never sought reimbursement from the bureau. He believed that upper management instructed ASAC Leroy M. Teitsworth and Supervisor Patrick McCormick to pressure him. Teitsworth removed Jim from his media representative position, copilot position and applicant coordinator position, but management never removed him from his Spanish-speaking duties, wiretaps and special TDY assignments.

At a firearms qualification, McCormick rushed to score Jim's target when the line finished firing to ensure that he qualified. No one other than a firearms instructor had ever scored Jim's targets. Jim felt this to be a personal affront to his integrity, initiated because he had become part of the lawsuit.

After joining the lawsuit, Jim stated, "All of a sudden I am dirt. The inspectors are after me, my supervisor is after me, and suddenly they provide me with an unfavorable performance rating. I am put on DRs [daily reports] where I must account for every fifteen minutes of my workday." His latest performance appraisal showed an unacceptable performance rating.

Jim received a significant deficiency report following the 1986 inspection of the Albuquerque office. Management censured him and placed him on probation. Teitsworth removed him from probation after Jim's reevaluation, but scolded him for delayed reporting and a lack of caseload management. Teitsworth rated Jim as minimally acceptable but later downgraded Jim to unacceptable and placed him on daily reports. Jim felt this was retaliation, as Teitsworth well knew that Jim participated in the class action.

Teitsworth testified that he was not a member of the class action but the FBI's PINS database listed him as a Hispanic agent. He never took a Spanish test and, although he spoke Spanish, he admitted that he had never worked Spanish-speaking assignments. He did not know if his surname had anything to do with it. Teitsworth testified that he did not remember telling Joe Hisquierdo that he did not want the FBI to know he was a Hispanic who spoke Spanish.

Hugo had Teitsworth read from an exhibit:

> In March 1987, Supervisory Special Agent Stuart Senneff retired and supervisory responsibilities for Squad 4 were given to Relief Supervisor Armand A. Lara, while awaiting the new supervisor. SAC William Brannon indicated that both former Supervisor Senneff and SA Lara had advised him that SA Garay was performing well, noted delinquencies and that SA Garay was working nights and weekends to meet deadlines assigned him. SA Lara confirmed that SA Garay had been adequately addressing his assignments. On May 12, 1987, SSA Teitsworth arrived in the Albuquerque Division and assumed supervisory responsibility for Squad 4. On June 15, 1987, responsibility for white-collar crime investigations went from Squad 3 to Squad 4. Because SA Garay was performing acceptably on applicant matters, and that the white-collar crime program was in need of an experienced special agent accountant, SAC Brannon removed SA Garay from applicant investigations and assigned him to white-collar crime under the supervision of SSA Teitsworth. SSA Teitsworth, promoted to ASAC on December 7, 1987, assumed supervisory responsibilities for Squad 2. ASAC Teitsworth brought white-collar crime matters with him to Squad 2, and SA Garay was transferred from Squad 4 to Squad 2 on January 11, 1988.

The court noted that the record spoke for itself.

Teitsworth gave no reason as to why the inspectors did not record Jim's ancillary Spanish-speaking duties on the inspection report. While on the inspection staff, Teitsworth assisted Gary Hart, the agent who illegally obtained a grand jury subpoena for Mat's administrative inquiry. The FBI promoted Teitsworth to an ASAC position in Albuquerque in December of 1987 following an October 1987 letter that he had sent to FBIHQ voicing his disapproval, as a Hispanic, of the lawsuit.

35

Michael A. Rodriguez

Mike Rodriguez entered the FBI on November 13, 1983. Before entering the FBI, he was the International Marketing Director for Westinghouse Electric Corporation and oversaw Latin America. He supervised a workforce of a hundred employees. Mike joined the bureau through Pittsburgh, receiving assignments to San Antonio and a deep undercover operation in Washington, DC, and then he headed to Quantico as a new agent class counselor before going to San Juan. He took the Spanish language test and received a 4+ rating.

Mike felt his undercover assignment (UCA) to be discriminatory because of the method used in his selection. FBIHQ gave Mike two options: he could elect to work undercover in the Washington, DC area or transfer to New York City. Instead of accepting the transfer orders to New York City, he accepted the undercover assignment. Upon completion of the UCA, which lasted nineteen months, FBIHQ told him he could no longer remain in Washington and work criminal cases. He did not want to work intelligence matters or UCA, so he transferred to San Juan.

In San Juan SAC Harry B. "Skip" Brandon III assigned him to Foreign Counter Intelligence (FCI) although Mike informed him of his ongoing interest in working criminal cases. A communication and a telephone call had gone to San Juan recommending Mike for criminal work, but Mike understood that SACs do as they please. Mike told Brandon that he could have stayed in the Washington Field Office (WFO) if he wanted to work FCI. Mike and his wife had a baby on the way, they owned a home, and they were happy there. His wife, who made $35,000 a year, had been willing to give up her job because she knew that Mike wanted to work criminal cases. Brandon told him that he would have to prove himself and told Mike, "Make your bones and we will see."

When Mike was a field counselor at Quantico, just prior to class graduation, his wife, five months pregnant, began to bleed profusely. Mike received orders to San Juan, but his wife's physician recommended she refrain from traveling. Mike called ASAC John Phillips to request an extension because of his wife's difficult pregnancy. Quantico had already agreed to assign him to another class to counsel in the interim, yet Phillips told Mike that the SAC in SJ refused to grant an extension. Mike followed orders and flew to San Juan while his wife bled and puked during the whole flight.

Mike refused to complain and kept a stiff upper lip. Lynn Bedford, a Mormon agent assigned to San Juan, vacationed in Phoenix when his wife was four months pregnant and experienced symptoms similar to those of Mike's wife. Brandon, however, provided Bedford with a temporary TDY assignment in Phoenix for four months and reassigned all his cases. Mike told Supervisor John Williamson that he considered this unfair and disparate treatment, and Williamson informed Brandon.

Brandon asked Mike if he was unhappy that he granted Bedford time in Phoenix. Mike responded,

> No, to the contrary, I know what he is feeling. My problem is not with him, I just think that he is probably getting favoritism because he is Mormon and I did not. The SAC asked what I was trying to say. I just thought it was unfair. He asked me four times what I was trying to say. The conversation ended when he said, "Young man, next time you come in here with a complaint you get your facts straight. I will check your story with ASAC Phillips!" And I was told to leave.

Mike never heard another word.

When Mike applied for the Career Development Program, management told him that he lacked experience as a manager, although he successfully managed a hundred employees at Westinghouse. The second time he applied, management told him that he did not have enough work experience, although he trained a class of new agents at Quantico. When he applied for a position in San Juan, the San Juan career board met, all of the supervisors approved Mike as their top selection but Phillips informed them that he refused to take Mike's name into the SAC for signature.

Mike testified, "I have not been given the opportunities I think I am qualified to be given. There are many qualified individuals in the FBI, they may not all be Hispanic, they may not all be Mormon, they may not all be whatever, but I am just as good or equal as they are. And I have the experience." In reference to his fear of retribution, Mike responded, "Well, there is a little joke going around the squad area on why I am receiving the National Business Employment Weekly every week and sending out resumes. Yes, I do."

Mike thought his work as a field counselor would prove to be a stepping-stone to improved positions within the FBI. He was one of the youngest class counselors ever selected, due to his past management experience and qualifications. Mike earned two incentive awards for leading his squad in statistical accomplishments for two straight years, and he received an additional incentive award for his undercover work. However, when Mike applied to be a relief supervisor, he competed against a Mormon agent, Jerry McDonald, and Mike lost out despite having more experience.

Larry J. McCormick testified that he was not aware that Mike Rodriguez had requested a delay in his transfer to San Juan. He reported that FBIHQ invariably approves temporary hardships based on pregnancies.

In his testimony, Julian De La Rosa denied telling Mike that he had a good case for discrimination and that he should pursue the EEO process. He claimed not to remember telling Mike, "I don't disagree with all the aspects of this lawsuit." De La Rosa also did not recall telling Bill Carlson that the FBI would never promote him because he was Hispanic or that he would never file an EEO complaint because it would not do him any good.

De La Rosa, with twenty-five years of service, received his promotion to SAC after the Hispanic agents filed the lawsuit. He was not a member of the class action, as he testified that the FBI did not discriminate. In his deposition, he admitted he had observed in different FBI locations derogatory cartoons or posted quotes demeaning to Hispanics. De La Rosa claimed he had learned to speak Spanish after attending FBI language school. However, the FBI personal information database showed: Julian De La Rosa—Hispanic, 6/24/63, zero Spanish proficiency.

There was laughter in the courtroom when the judge addressed De La Rosa, who, following his testimony, opened the closet door behind the courtroom, entered through the door, and then timidly reemerged. Judge Bunton told him not to worry about coming out of the closet.

36

Antonio Franco

Tony Franco received a Bachelor of Science degree from UTEP and at the time of his testimony, he had twenty-four years of law enforcement and firearm instructor experience with the US Army Military Police, the El Paso Police Department, and the FBI. He joined the FBI on October 17, 1977.

Within a few months of joining the FBI, Tony worked a sensitive deep undercover (UC) criminal investigation. He did not volunteer for the significant case that took two years of his life to resolve. He received no UC training, nor did he ever receive any type of psychological evaluation prior to entry into this sensitive undercover operation. Because of the UC assignment, Tony had a contract placed on his life, and his family lived in danger. The operation succeeded, and several other agents traveled around the country, taking credit for it and lecturing about it, although Tony was the agent responsible for its success. After the UC assignment was over, the FBI relocated both Tony and his family.

Agents who serve in undercover assignments receive special consideration in office of preference transfers. However, FBIHQ informed Tony that he had no entitlement to such special consideration, as he was a first office agent. Upon transfer to the San Antonio Division, he requested the Austin RA, where there was an opening. FBIHQ again told him no, that the Austin RA was for college boys. The petty tyranny of the FBI made no sense to Tony. SAC Charlie Parsons testified that Jerry Adams had twenty years in the FBI before his transfer to Austin, making him at least forty-three years old at the time. Tony was younger and closer to a college age, but he was Hispanic.

Tony served for five years in the McAllen RA, with its Hispanic population, and while there, he served on several other undercover operations. To get back to El Paso, management forced him to work yet another undercover assignment. When he received orders to El Paso, there was a caveat that the transfer would take effect after the UC operation ended. When Tony arrived in El Paso, he watched as at least one non-Hispanic, with less time on the seniority list, was able to OP transfer into El Paso.

Tony requested to join the SWAT team, because of his former military and law enforcement experience and his marksmanship abilities, after accomplishing a perfect score known as a "possible." The SWAT team leader did not want Tony because he was a first office agent, yet several non-Hispanic first office agents served on the SWAT team. He did not file an EEO complaint because he did not want the label of a troublemaker or a malcontent.

A perfect firearms "possible" is difficult to attain, and the names of agents who shoot a possible receive recognition on a permanent acknowledgement board at Quantico. When Tony shot a possible, hitting 100% of his shots, the firearms instructor strode over to view the target, then stared at Tony and told him "nobody shoots a possible on my range." He then downgraded Tony to a 98%.

On the sixth day of trial, Executive Assistant Director John Glover testified that all undercover assignments were voluntary and by special agent request. Joaquin Garcia, Tony Franco, and Mike Rodriguez had all testified that they did not volunteer for their undercover assignments.

Larry J. McCormick testified that the FBI manual states that assignment to an undercover operation does not warrant an office of preference transfer. The FBI only considers OPs when an individual stands number one on the seniority list of that office. He was unaware that

SACs promised agents their OP if they went undercover. McCormick stated that Tony did not have to do two undercover assignments to get his OP, but that Tony had two undercover transfers. Tony transferred from the McAllen RA to El Paso following his second undercover assignment. McCormick thought Tony's transfer was counterproductive, as San Antonio had staffing needs in the border RAs.

On the eighth day of trial, Oliver "Buck" Revell testified that all long-term undercover agents receive training and testing cycles at Quantico and reaffirmed undercover activities are voluntary. Class action members testified that they never received such training and that many did not volunteer for undercover assignments. Revell, the executive director in charge of investigations over the criminal and intelligence divisions, testified that he was not aware that the FBI, through the United States Marshal's Office, deputized non-FBI agent personnel to sit on FBI wires.

37

David C. Gomez

David Gomez, born in Los Angeles, attended the University of Southern California and received an undergraduate degree in political science and a graduate degree in public administration. He became a detective with the LAPD before joining the FBI in January 1984, under the modified program due to his police experience. David first served in the El Centro Resident Agency, a two-man office that had earlier suffered the shooting deaths of both of its agents. El Centro is located 120 miles outside of the San Diego Division on the Mexican border. David then served in San Juan.

To David, the FBI had always represented the ultimate experience in law enforcement. When he first joined the FBI, other agents warned him not to emphasize his Spanish language ability because of the likelihood of transfers and discriminatory assignments. He took the Spanish test when he applied and paid no mind to the advice he had received because he very much wanted to get into the bureau, but he failed the Spanish test. At the academy, his instructors ordered him to retake the Spanish test orally and he discovered, much to his surprise, that he suddenly qualified as a level 3.

David spent two years in the El Centro office, which he considered a hardship office especially for a first office agent. After about a year, his senior partner transferred into San Diego, and David spent his last year in El Centro working alone. During his first week on the job, David worked a TDY assignment on a T-III that lasted 120 days. When he completed that wire, his SAC told him he had to go San Juan for a sixty-day special. He informed the SAC that he had just completed a four-month T-III and knew plenty of non-Hispanic Spanish speakers in the division whom the office did not assign to any Title IIIs or San Juan specials.

David's partner in El Centro, Robert Watkins, a level 3 Spanish speaker, told David that he had never worked a T-III in all of his eight years with the FBI. Watkins later went to a specialized language school in Burlington, Vermont, for an intensive Spanish course, yet the bureau never tasked him to work Title IIIs. The SAC told David "that I should learn to accept the fact that as a Hispanic, as a native Spanish speaker, that I would be eventually assigned to the San Juan Division. The sooner I accepted that fact, the better off I would be, and the sooner I transferred to San Juan and got it over with, the better it would be for my career. Then I could get to my regular FBI career."

A T-III narcotics matter, on which he worked 160 days, resulted in 90 indictments against a Peruvian narcotics cartel. David made several of the arrests himself, including the arrest of the armed and dangerous mastermind of the cartel. He learned that many individuals in the San Diego Division received monetary incentive awards for their work on the case. Those who did not receive financial awards received letters of commendation. David received neither. The case agent told him that everyone contributed but apologized to David, stating he could do nothing. It was hardly a surprise to David when he discovered that none of the Hispanics who worked the case received an incentive award.

From San Diego, David requested an assignment to a top twelve office but instead ended up in Puerto Rico. When he arrived in San Juan, the ASAC told him that the domestic terrorism squad was his new assignment and that he should avoid a group of individuals on that squad whom he considered rabble-rousers. He thought David was an impressionable young agent and later referred to the agents he disapproved of as "the Mexican Mafia." David later learned that those agents tried to work within the system to make changes and alleviate the hardships, but the ASAC did not appreciate their efforts. San Juan had many more personnel issues than the mainland US offices. The irony was that the FBI transferred David to San Juan because of his Spanish language skills, but he worked on an FCI squad investigating groups where he required a foreign language translator himself.

As an LAPD detective, speaking "Spanglish" and being Hispanic proved helpful, and David never once felt discriminated against as a police officer in Los Angeles. "It wasn't until I became an FBI agent that I actually started to realize that there is intrinsic institutional discrimination and disparate treatment that is applied by the bureau against Hispanics and Spanish speakers."

Dave testified,

> There are many subtle ways the bureau can act against you in the future for testifying here. My supervisor, an individual I respect much as an honest person with much integrity, illustrated one way to end a career. He told me that, instead of being highly recommended for a promotion to a position or being an extremely well-qualified candidate, you become a good candidate or a qualified candidate, which would drop you from any further consideration at the career board level.

Fluency in any language is relative. What some considered fluent in Los Angeles may not be fluent in Miami. Word meanings and dialects differ. David asked about work in a legal attaché position, and the FBI placed a notification of "Spanish" on his request. However, David was interested in any Legat, not just those in Spanish-speaking countries.

38

Albert Nava

Al Nava, born and raised in El Paso, Texas, obtained his bachelor's degree in psychology at the University of Texas at El Paso and a master's degree in administration and supervision from the Education Department at Inter-American University in San Juan, Puerto Rico. He had been in the FBI for sixteen years with assignments in Jacksonville, Florida; San Juan, Puerto Rico; and El Paso, Texas.

Al said non-Hispanic agents transferred out of San Juan to their office of preference or office of choice with less time spent in San Juan, while Hispanic agents never did. He knew that Lynn Bedford, a Mormon, served two years in San Juan before transferring to his OP in Phoenix, Arizona. Al noted that many agents transferred to San Juan from New York City. They were non-native Spanish speakers who had attended a six-week or six-month language school and were desperate to get out of New York City. He remembered Bob Booth, Bill Murphy, and Bill Myer as agents who all spoke some Spanish. Al became an "Anglo helper," assisting these agents with their cases, while still shouldering the responsibility for his own caseload. Those agents all left San Juan in two years or in less than five, and transferred to their office of choice.

Al spent six and a half years in San Juan, all the while trying to get back to El Paso, his office of preference. While Al was in San Juan, the FBI developed the five-year plan in which an agent who served five continuous years in San Juan received an office of preference transfer or, at the least, a transfer choice of three offices. However, when Al's five years were up, the FBI told him there were just too many GS-13s in El Paso and he would have to wait another year and a half in San Juan to get his transfer.

When Al applied to become an agent, the FBI gave him the Army proficiency language exam in Spanish. This comprised multiple-choice questions, some essay writing, and an oral section that involved speaking into a tape recorder on a given topic. Ten years later the FBI ordered him to take another Spanish exam. When Al questioned the reasoning behind it, SAC Ronald A. Hoverson told him that the FBI needed to update all records and that they planned to test attorneys in the theory of law and accountants in accounting practices. Al protested because he had serious doubts the FBI was testing everyone with a specialty. In response, Hoverson threatened him with insubordination charges and disciplinary action. Al took the test under protest. Two months later, he learned that he had received a score of level 1. The high proficiency score is a level 5. After reviewing his personnel file during trial discovery, he discovered that, somehow, someone had changed his proficiency score to a level 3.

Under cross-examination, Al confirmed that the Puerto Rican five-year plan did not exist upon his arrival in San Juan. He could not remember the name of the person who informed him that there was no room for more GS-13s in El Paso.

39

Alvaro Cruz

Alvaro Cruz, born and raised in El Paso, Texas, graduated from Bel Air High School, and then from the University of Texas at El Paso and joined the bureau on October 20, 1975. He served in San Francisco, San Juan, and El Paso.

Al learned from the bureau transfer policy that first office agents in small offices would remain there for three to five years. He was in San Francisco, a top twelve office, where agents expected to stay throughout their entire careers until they qualified for their offices of preference (OP). He had been in San Francisco for nine years when, in 1984, he received orders to San Juan with four other Hispanic agents from San Francisco—none of whom had requested transfers. The FBI did not transfer non-Hispanic Spanish speakers from San Francisco to San Juan.

Al said of his time in San Juan,

> Three or four other special agents undertook a project, in which we tried to improve the situation in San Juan. The contract was a four-year contract in San Juan and we felt this was a hardship office. We thought that maybe we could try to improve the situation by bringing it back to a three-year contract and bringing out some benefits for those individuals that wanted to stay longer. My SAC referred to me as a member

> of the Mexican Mafia and a rabble-rouser and treated me as such. I should mention the bureau accepted this proposal and is now implemented in the San Juan Division.

As a GS-13, Al considered himself an "Anglo helper." He testified,

> I have been in the bureau thirteen years, and basically given assignments which reserve me for certain tasks such as T-III wires, surveillances and such. A good example of that was recently here in the El Paso Division, [when] the front office told me I would be handling some civil rights investigations. The acting ASAC told me he hated to burn two agents for this type of violation. However, the present agent doing the investigations could not speak Spanish. Therefore, a Spanish-speaking agent needed to assist the other in Spanish-speaking interviews. I mentioned I spoke both English and Spanish, and therefore he would only have to assign and use one agent: me. But two agents are still being used.

Al had proven that he had the ability to handle cases on his own as an agent, yet investigative situations forced him to cover leads for Anglo agents. By not assigning cases that required Spanish abilities to non-Spanish speakers and assigning them instead to Spanish speakers, Spanish-speaking agents would develop more statistical accomplishments, and those statistics seemed to concern FBI supervisors at the time.

On cross-examination, Al testified that he did not receive preferential treatment on his OP to El Paso, as he was number three and there were four openings. Assigned T-IIIs, other miscellaneous tasks, and assisting on cases assigned to others never allowed him to rise to his full potential. Ms. Gulyassy told him that the record reflected he had spent 65% of his time in El Paso working investigative cases other than T-IIIs. Ms. Gulyassy did not add in Al's "Anglo helper" time. The DOJ seemed to argue that being away 35% of the time on T-IIIs or that a 65% effort toward accomplishing his agent caseload was an acceptable practice of work.

Al testified that discrimination came from the top down and its source was the FBI decision-makers. When asked if discrimination came from his supervisor Gary Webb, whom the government attorneys noted married a Mexican-American woman, Al responded that men could marry a person of a different ethnicity and still manifest hostile feelings toward that race or ethnicity. Spouses of the same nationality may also harbor abuse and hostility.

40

John Hoos

John Hoos served as a special agent in the Los Angeles Division. Born and raised in Baltimore, Maryland, he graduated from the University of Baltimore with a bachelor's in management and a master's in criminal justice from California Lutheran University. Prior to entering the bureau in May of 1969, he worked as a steel sales representative in York, Pennsylvania. He enlisted in the United States Army, serving in the Military Intelligence Branch with a tour of duty in South Vietnam. He served in Columbia, South Carolina; New York City; and Washington, DC for six months of Spanish-language school. He then transferred to San Juan before transferring to Los Angeles. John is not Hispanic, but due to what he had seen and heard, he believed that the FBI discriminated against Hispanics. He never went on any Spanish language TDY assignments.

By 1982, John served as the media coordinator for the LA Division. He answered to the SAC and to the Senior Administrative ASAC, a position held by the lead plaintiff, Bernardo M. Perez. In his role as media coordinator, John answered all media inquiries from Los Angeles and around the world. He was the point man for all media coverage of the 1984 Olympics. Mat's office and ASAC Christensen's offices were right across from John's office, so John could see and hear almost everything that went on, in addition to his unrestricted access to top management.

John felt, at the time of the trial, that he was one of the most regarded media representatives of the FBI. The job was very stressful and not a sought-after position, as it takes a special type of personality to handle such a visible position. However, with John's sterling qualifications, he carried it off with aplomb. John, his SAC and ASAC interacted daily. A media representative must keep a close relationship with his SAC. A media rep must also have the ability to make snap decisions about what to say to the media. There is one opportunity to get it right, which makes it stressful. John worked closely with SAC Bretzing, who granted John absolute access. In Bretzing's absence, John went to the administrative ASAC to outline his daily interactions with the media.

John served in Los Angeles for fourteen years before Mat arrived. There was always an introduction of each new ASAC or SAC to core employees. John testified that Mat was the sole individual whom Bretzing never introduced to the FBI LA office as an ASAC. SAC Richard T. Bretzing instead gave Mat the cold shoulder.

In Bretzing's absence, John met Mat to discuss ongoing investigations to prepare responses to media inquiries. John testified,

> Numerous times, I can't began to tell you how many times it was, that I would go to see Mat and he had no idea what was going on in the division with cases and FBI issues. He was unaware of information I was giving him. In my experience, the Administrative ASAC of any large office, of any office, should know what is going on as the number one ASAC. Mat was kept in the dark about numerous investigations.

John learned that Bretzing had kept Mat oblivious while ASAC Christensen and ASAC Nelson, the two ASACs junior to Mat, had the facts on all of the cases and their statuses. John would often inform Mat of a media inquiry, and Mat would answer that he had no knowledge of that investigation. "It is just a clear example that Bretzing was not informing Mat, his number-two man, of what was going on within the division. He should have been," added John. After Bretzing arrived in LA, he promoted a fellow Mormon from supervisor to the ASAC level.

John testified,

> There was a time where Mat and I discussed doing a recruiting segment on Spanish speaking TV, KMEX Channel 13, in Los Angeles. I set up the interview. Mat and another Hispanic agent, Aurelio Flores, appeared live on KMEX TV. This program crossed the country to over two hundred stations by satellite dish. Our office switchboard lit up requesting applications. We got calls from our New York Division, San Francisco Division. It came right down to "what the hell" is going on in Los Angeles; we are getting all of these phone calls from all over the country. What it was, was Mat was on national TV talking about job recruiting for special agents and clerical, support-type individuals with the FBI. It was a tremendous success. Mat later advised me Bretzing had chastised him. I asked for what. He said Bretzing advised him his job is not recruiting, his job is sitting behind a desk, being administrative ASAC of this office. He did not want him to do it anymore. Coincidental to Bretzing's feelings on Hispanic recruiting, within the last six months there was a Hispanic job fair for law enforcement positions. Over five thousand Hispanics attended this job fair. The FBI was invited and all other local and federal agencies. The FBI did not send a representative, even though they were invited. Bretzing would have decided on sending a representative to that job fair. The Los Angeles Division not only lost an opportunity, but the entire bureau lost out in not attending the Hispanic job fair. We definitely need more Hispanic recruits.

In 1983, a kidnapping developed in Alhambra, an area of responsibility of the West Covina resident agency. Mat responded. He served as the senior FBI official on the scene; second in command was Chuck Sawyer, supervisory special agent of the West Covina resident agency. The investigation proved successful, and Mat received enthusiastic commendations from all local law enforcement officials.

John testified,

> However, shortly thereafter [Mat] advised me in conversation and showed me a memo that was written by Bretzing

> wherein Bretzing again chastised him for numerous items. One I vividly recall is that the attire that Mat wore during the investigation, the attire being casual—jeans, cowboy-type shirt. The way the investigation was going, it would not have been very appropriate for Mat to wear his traditional three-piece suit with a watch chain hanging out. Mat was not photographed or videotaped. Immediately, Mat moved to the fifteenth floor of the Los Angeles office.
>
> Previously, Bretzing and Mat had their offices on the seventeenth floor, which are the administrative offices of the LA Division. The sixteenth floor is for steno pools and many closed files. The fifteenth floor is the first working area for the street agents. This is where Bretzing moved Mat. There was a supervisors meeting one morning, and Bretzing announced that Mat was being sent down to the fifteenth floor as ASAC Christensen was elevated up to the seventeenth floor as the Administrative ASAC and also held the same duties of ASAC in charge of foreign counterintelligence. The entire supervisory staff just rather looked at one another, thinking this is extremely unusual. I knew it was definitely reprisal against Mat.

John further added,

> Mat is a very outgoing individual. Bretzing is on the other side, an introvert, and a cold type individual I would describe [as] out for one person and one person only: himself. Mat had a tough time of getting in to see Bretzing. When he did, it was brief, to the point. It seemed that the other ASACs spent considerably more time in conversation with Bretzing than Mat did. There were meetings between Bretzing and the two other ASACs where Mat was never invited. One time I remember I walked in to see Mat and I said, "Are you aware that Darryl Gates, the Chief of Police of Los Angeles, is coming to the office this morning?" and he said "no." That is a rare occasion when Darryl Gates comes to the FBI office in

Los Angeles. Gates appeared and Mat was not invited to that conference.

John testified,

> Right after Mat filed his EEO complaint, I was summoned one day by two agents from our headquarters, names of which I do not recall other than I do know they were from the Legal Unit. We went into an interview room, they identified themselves and said, "We are here for the bureau, are you aware that Mat has filed an EEO complaint?" I said, "Yes, I know." They informed me that Bretzing would like [me] to testify on his behalf. I said time out. Are you aware that Mat asked me to testify and I have agreed? The two of them looked somewhat dumbfounded, walked out of the room, and came back and they said, "Well, I guess we cannot use you."
>
> My comment to them was, I will never forget this, is that, you know, this is a catch-22 situation, I am damned if I do and I will be damned if I don't.

John decided that he would testify to what he had seen in the office, what he had heard, and what the FBI had considered normal procedures and how those procedures changed when Mat arrived. In his testimony regarding the EEO hearing, agents asked John numerous questions about his knowledge of Mormon activities or Mormon business that Bretzing conducted on government time. John responded, "When my testimony was over, the attorneys for the government were upstairs [in a] real quick meeting with Bretzing, I'm sure to inform him of my testimony."

John's close relationship with Bretzing deteriorated. As the media coordinator, the first thing John checked each morning was Bretzing's calendar to verify his availability for interviews or to discuss issues with the media. The day following John's testimony, he discovered he no longer had access to Bretzing's calendar. He had to ask Bretzing's secretary for his schedule and other resources. Bretzing's secretary turned cold, refusing to provide routine information. John noticed that Bretzing never visited his office again. Bretzing's attitude had changed. Fred Reagan, the assistant media coordinator, also had similar experiences in getting information.

John said, "Numerous times I would go in when I had access to the calendar and see the secretary's handwritten notation 'LDS speech.' I knew Bretzing was out doing Mormon speeches before a Mormon group on government time." There were many such notations on the calendar. His secretary also told John that besides Bretzing's numerous Mormon meetings, she also had to type letters dealing with Mormon matters, and that she also had a list of about ten Mormon Church officials she had instructions to put through when they called, even when Bretzing held meetings or conferences with police officials.

When Bretzing's secretary was absent, Mat's secretary had standing instructions to do the same. John said, "There was a conversation I had with Mat where he said ASAC Christensen told him he questioned how Bretzing held down two jobs in reference to the Mormon Church and the FBI." As John understood it, Bretzing served as the Church of Jesus Christ of Latter Day Saints Bishop in the Ward of Ventura County and directed the church's food storage warehouse, which assisted needy Mormons.

John testified that, after the EEO hearings,

> It was extremely difficult to do my job, and I had to rely on other avenues for information. Many times the media representative must make snap decisions and sometimes the voice of authority for the SAC as needed. Much like Mat, I could not get information through normal channels. Bretzing called me into his office on November 14, 1985—one year to the exact date after I testified at an EEO hearing against Bretzing.
>
> Bretzing advised me he was removing me from the media office after five years and three months of service. I was very surprised. I asked him why. He said, "I have no confidence in you; you have made yourself scarce since the 1984 Olympics. And I just attended a manpower conference somewhere back in Washington, and I am reducing the number of media reps from two to one."

John asked Bretzing if he could have his notice of removal in writing, and Bretzing informed John that he deserved no such entitlement. Bretzing said that he had conferred with John Mintz, the legal assistant director at FBIHQ, prior to his decision. John then said to Bretzing, "I am seriously considering that you are removing me from this position because of my testimony on behalf of Mat in the EEO complaint." Bretzing smiled at John and said nothing.

Bretzing asked John which squad he wanted. John told him either the applicant squad or foreign counterintelligence (FCI), but not a drug squad. He went to the applicant squad but six months later stumbled onto a drug squad through orders from Bretzing. John spoke with one of the supervisors on another FCI squad, who told John that he had excellent rapport with the FCI ASAC and that he would try to transfer John over to his squad. The FCI ASAC told the supervisor that the SAC wanted John on the drug squad. Bill Baker, former Assistant Director of the Office of Congressional and Public Affairs who answered directly to FBI Director Webster, told John, "Bretzing got you for your testimony, and you will never be able to prove it." Baker offered John a position at FBIHQ.

John had four and a half years to go until retirement and believed that the FBI would try to "get" him for his testimony. He also thought that they would go after the Hispanic agents who testified about their personal interactions with Bretzing.

Fred C. Reagan testified that, on November 14, 1985, he met with Dick Fox, Mr. Haas, and John Hoos. Yet, he claimed that he could not recall telling John Hoos, "You were screwed by Bretzing for testifying in Mat's EEO." Reagan did not acknowledge if his selection as the media representative over John Hoos resulted from any retaliatory motives.

James Nelson testified that unauthorized articles in the press appeared but had no information, much less proof that John leaked the information. Nelson could not recall the content of the unauthorized articles or address the possibility that they could have originated with someone other than John.

Richard T. Bretzing testified that he removed John Hoos from his position as Media Coordinator because of efforts to secure more people for investigative assignments. Bretzing claimed to have lost confidence in John. In the months preceding the decision, his ASACs, supervisors and other sources informed him that John made disparaging remarks and held Bretzing up to ridicule in a disloyal fashion. The media coordinator kept close daily contact with him, and he felt he did not need to have somebody disloyal to him in such close contact. Bretzing claimed the decision was discretionary, merely coincidental that John's removal occurred one year to the day after he provided a statement to support Mat's complaint.

John chose not to file an EEO complaint because he saw what Mat went through and considered the EEO process to be a total whitewash. One of Mat's EEO complaints regarded the harassment of witnesses, but the FBI and EEO did nothing. When informed by one of the government's attorneys that Ms. Tyrell, Bretzing's secretary, had denied under oath that she had made comments about Bretzing working on Mormon matters on government time, John responded, "I am under oath too, counselor."

John Hoos had the *fidelity* to his oath of office, the *bravery* to face up to domination, and the *integrity* to be explicit about the facts. John Hoos, an unselfish man of honor, was determined to do the right thing and paid the price for it.

41

Aileen Ikegami

Aileen Ikegami served as Mat's secretary while he was ASAC in Los Angeles. She testified that, when Mat arrived in Los Angeles as the administrative ASAC, the SAC did not introduce him to the office through an all-employee SAC conference, as was the custom. Instead, Mat arrived, went to his desk and got to work. Aileen followed Mat downstairs from the seventeenth floor to the fifteenth floor when Bretzing moved Christensen into Mat's office.

After Mat left the Los Angeles office, Bretzing retaliated against Aileen by removing her from executive secretarial duties and instead made her supervisor of the telecommunications center. The duties of a telecommunications supervisor and an executive secretary for an ASAC are worlds apart in terms of status, as the communication supervisor handles oversight of the young adults that work for the bureau in support positions.

Aileen believed Bretzing removed her from her position as ASAC secretary because of Bretzing's perception that she was a loyal employee of Mat and because of her deposition in which she stated that the FBI discriminates against Hispanics. The Los Angeles office had a single Hispanic supervisor. All of the other supervisors, except for one black and one Asian, were Anglo. The LA office had many Hispanic employees.

As secretary to the ASAC, Aileen often saw Bretzing's calendar when Bretzing's secretary was on leave or away from her desk. She noted that Bretzing scheduled several Mormon Church activities during work hours. Aileen also received many phone calls for Bretzing from people who identified themselves as representatives of the LDS Church, many from one particular person who identified himself as the church secretary.

Francine Tyrell, Bretzing's secretary, gave Aileen a long list of names of specific high-level Mormon Church officials with immediate access to Bretzing with no regard as to his activity at the time. Tyrell informed Aileen that, besides her regular FBI duties, her responsibilities included writing letters addressed to various Mormon groups and updating Bretzing's biography, which detailed his Mormon background and activities for advance distribution to the various Mormon groups to which Bretzing regularly spoke.

Mat, who came to Los Angeles as the senior ASAC in charge of administrative matters, suddenly found himself demoted to ASAC of criminal matters, a lower-grade position. FBIHQ allowed Mat to keep his pay grade, but Bretzing forced him downstairs to the fifteenth floor, a shocking action that no one in the Los Angeles office had ever seen. Aileen followed Mat down because of his grade level. If she had taken the secretary position with ASAC Christensen, who was at a lower pay grade than Mat, it would have lowered her pay grade as well. Aileen instead maintained her grade level and salary by sticking with Mat.

Aileen testified,

> When told that I was not going to be going back to the old job as ASAC secretary upon Mat's departure, I asked why, with the OSM, Office Services Manager, telling me that she thought it had to do with loyalty in some way. I asked her who issued my field instructions. She said it had to come from Mr. Bretzing; he was the only one who could make such a determination, such a transfer. I believed that, because I had gone with Mat and preserved my grade, I was no longer trustworthy as far as

Mr. Bretzing was concerned and not allowed to work in his office.

It was clear that Bretzing gave preferential treatment to Mormons, as he gave a break to Bart Brooks, a Mormon pilot out of Point McGoo, who was caught stealing Valium from a drugstore. Mat summoned Brooks into the office with his supervisor, and Brooks admitted to taking the drugs but claimed he had no addiction. He saw danger in having Brooks, potentially under the influence, fly FBI aircraft. Mat offered Brooks the opportunity to participate in a drug rehabilitation program, which Brooks refused.

Further investigation determined that, on several previous occasions, Brooks called the pharmacy, posing as a physician and requesting that the pharmacy process or renew narcotics prescriptions in Brooks' name. Mat drafted a communication to the bureau and recommended firing Brooks, as the FBI fired agents who were caught stealing. Bretzing then interceded and advised that he considered such a sanction to be too harsh. Christensen and Bretzing instead took charge; they brought Brooks back from the field office for several months and then returned him to Point McGoo. The supervisor at Point McGoo informed Aileen that he planned to draft a memo for record to avoid any potential liability. Afterwards, Bretzing transferred the Point McGoo supervisor back to the LA office, but Brooks remained in Point McGoo.

Because of her testimony, Aileen anticipated further reprisal. She informed the court that she did not complain about her reassignment to telecommunications because she expected that no one would care to listen. She moved forward to do the best job possible wherever she landed and in whatever she did.

Under testimony, Bretzing admitted that he removed Aileen Ikegami from the administrative ASAC secretarial slot to a supervisory slot in communications after she provided a statement of support for Mat.

42

Joseph E. Yablonsky

Joe Yablonsky, born in Newark, New Jersey, joined the FBI in February 1952, when he was twenty-three years old. He retired from the FBI in December of 1983, having served for almost thirty-two years. Joe testified that the FBI discriminates against Hispanics and that discrimination was present in the FBI, just as it is everywhere in the bureaucracies and institutions of America.

Joe worked for the bureau back in the days when there was little investigative policy and the bureau expected case agents to take the initiative. He worked undercover (UC) and developed many scenarios from information that arose from informants. Joe played the role of crook, or fence, or whatever role it took to catch a criminal. He transferred to Miami in 1966 and worked many UC cases. In 1973, he transferred to FBIHQ, assigned to the interstate transportation of stolen property unit because of the great success of his UC investigations.

Joe petitioned the bureau to adopt a UC agent-training program in the criminal area. He developed the curriculum and seminars himself. The classes were composed of experienced and inexperienced agents, all with specific, required prerequisites. Joe considered certain predisposed personality characteristics to be absolute.

One can be a highly qualified investigator but have difficulty acting a role. He recommended that a designated unit control and run

UC investigations throughout the country. Joe recommended that agents possessing the needed characteristics submit a form with personal information to input the data into a computer database to help divisions select the right agent for an assignment, like a casting call for a role in a Hollywood movie. Joe transferred to Boston as the ASAC and later became SAC in Cincinnati. He retired out of the Las Vegas office.

Law enforcement circles knew Joe as "the father of UC." Joe testified,

> When a person of ethnicity such as a Jewish agent, Italian or a Hispanic performs a role of UC, he is in effect, in most occasions reinforcing a stereotype of a group. I notice that some peers and superiors of UC agents view that agent as the person of the role he plays, rather than being one. UC agents are nontraditional in terms of capabilities of doing investigations through UC as opposed to the traditional method—so they are looked upon differently.
>
> If they develop an important case, wonderful, but just let something go wrong, which is likely to happen because it is very difficult to predict the behavior of our criminal adversaries in certain situations, you can bet they are going down on them harder than they would otherwise. There is a tendency, and I have seen this, if a minority type, such a Jew or Italian or Hispanic does something spectacular, it is usually not looked upon as spectacular as it might be in somebody from the general population. However, if he does something wrong, it is usually magnified. What did you expect?

As SAC in Cincinnati, Joe assumed a UC identity and within three days recovered three million dollars in bearer bonds. Instead of FBIHQ agents considering the success of the case, they were critical. The ABSCAM bribery investigation, in which FBI agents posed as wealthy Arabs, garnered a tremendous amount of criticism and caused the FBI to refine all of the nuances that go into UC work: the legalities, procedures, record keeping and so forth. Some subjects prefer dealing with people in their own language. However, anyone who can play a role can buy narcotics.

When Joe refined the elements of UC work, he sought agents with a minimum of five years investigative experience and could develop a specific mindset as an investigator. They must also maintain loyalty to the institution, not suffer an identity crisis but still play a successful role, stay mentally alert and adapt quickly. There is also a long list of issues UC agents are forced to cope with, including security, family issues, backup, technical issues, and the fact that they never have a script to follow.

The agents who raise their hand to go to FBIHQ watch their p's and q's, gain favorable relationships, and advance in the bureaucracy. The fact that they are not star performers becomes inconsequential. When Joe was in the bureau, there were agents placed on supervisory desks because they had trouble working the streets, so the field offices transferred them to FBIHQ to shuffle papers.

On cross-examination, Joe said that he did not know what the statistical averages were for using non-Hispanics and Hispanics when he was in the bureau. He observed that, more often than not, management was more likely to approach a member of a minority group before they sought anyone else to work UC. Joe first met Mat on UC assignments out of Miami. Mat and Dick Castillo posed as wealthy Mexicans interested in buying a valuable Rembrandt painting stolen from a museum in Montréal. Over the course of the investigation, Joe developed respect for Mat both as a person and as an agent. Joe testified that Mat was the type of person one would want as a friend, as he was a man of principle. However, over the years, they spoke more infrequently, and Joe never developed a close relationship with Mat.

The bureau placed Joe on probation just prior to his retirement. The entire political and economic establishment in Las Vegas attacked him because he initiated an investigation of a federal judge with political connections. Joe said he was not testifying because he was embittered but because he loved the FBI, and if there were inequities in the bureau, he wanted to see them corrected.

The DOJ was foolish to bring up in court that Joe had been on probation before retirement in an effort to discredit his testimony. Joe spoke of a program he had developed many years before that was still in use by the FBI. Hugo and Tony knew the real value of Joe's testimony on undercover policy, management's reactions to UC agents, and the effects of UC assignments on FBI agents.

43

Joaquin Manuel Garcia

Joaquin "Jack" Garcia attended college at West Texas State and played college football for the famous Coach Joe Kerbel. He graduated from the University of Richmond with a bachelor's degree in Spanish. Jack was born in Havana, Cuba, and when he graduated from the university, he tipped the scales at 305 pounds. Jack was an FBI double agent—not because of any spy activities or his size—but because he became an agent twice, on February 4, 1980, and again on May 4, 1980. On the first occasion, after he left his job as an investigator at the Union County New Jersey prosecutor's office, he weighed in at 280 pounds when the SAC Newark swore him in as an FBI agent.

At his first new agent's class at Quantico, instructors called out Jack, yanked him out of class, weighed him and discovered that he tipped the scales at 280 pounds. The instructors informed him that he did not meet bureau weight standards and did not represent the correct image of an FBI agent. Quantico gave him two options: resign, with possible reinstatement after losing weight, or have the FBI fire him and have no possibility of reinstatement. He accepted option number one.

This was the first time an agent had been accepted and sworn in and then been informed he exceeded bureau weight standards. It was also the first time Jack felt embarrassed and humiliated in front of his peers. As a former college and semi-pro football player, his physical ability at his weight allowed him to sail through all of the FBI's physical fitness programs. The difficulty arose because his 280 pounds caused a perception problem for the FBI—not because Jack lacked any ability.

After the experience with Jack, the FBI instituted a new policy of weighing candidates prior to swearing them in as agents. Although Jack knew of instances in which agents in training recycled to positions in FBI field offices—becoming translators, technicians or clerical personnel—the FBI failed to offer Jack any type of employment, instead forcing him to resign. Jack became so anxious after his resignation that at first his weight ballooned.

Special Agent Jim Pledger sent Jack a letter affixed with signatures of all of his Quantico classmates, informing Jack that the class believed the bureau was wrong in not allowing him to be recycled and was wrong in its actions. They wanted to see him come back. Quantico also failed to offer Jack any guidance or counseling.

Management did not resolve the problem, since Quantico identified it as physical fitness related. Had a medical reason prevented Jack from completing the training, he might have understood, but they refused to give him an opportunity to complete the class with his fellow agents because of his weight. On the day he resigned, officials told him he was to leave the FBI facility by sundown. Judge Bunton commented, "That was a brave fellow that told you." (When Jack first took the stand, Judge Bunton noticed Jack's prominence and quipped that, if he had to choose people to be on his side, he wanted Jack.)

After leaving a good job with nice people who threw him a going-away party, Jack was embarrassed to no end to work for the number-one law enforcement agency, perform well on all of the required physical tests, and then discover that the FBI wanted to can him because of his weight. It was not because he lacked integrity, not because of an absence of aptitude or ability, and not because he lacked ambition. It was because his weight presented a perceived unsuitable image of FBI agents. Jack risked his health with an unhealthy starvation diet—a diet that caused him to urinate blood.

Jack later returned to Quantico. He shed a lot of weight during the intervening three months. After graduation from Quantico, he worked in Newark in applicant, bank robbery, fugitive and terrorist matters. He worked a ninety-day special in San Juan and then served three and a half years as a deep UC operative for the New York Division. When Jack resurfaced, FBIHQ transferred him to the Philadelphia Division.

Working as a deep undercover operative has its drawbacks. Jack explained,

> As a UC operative, I worked a very sensitive operation that, if the court allows me I would rather not go into, due to its nature. However, it did not have me involved with any forms of administrative dealings in the FBI—by that I mean no exposure to agents. There was no exposure to normal, everyday things, like taking any physicals or firearms training. I received no prior training in working undercover or a psychological evaluation, nor was the assignment monitored. The case agent or handler would visit with me to rehash the operation and what exactly was I accomplishing.

A "handler" is a case agent who handles the administrative portion of the undercover case. Jack's handler met with him, and they broke bread together.

The SAC, ASAC, and several supervisors would also conference with Jack, and none ever mentioned his weight. However, just when he made reentry, his weight again became a problem for FBI supervisors, even though Jack had no problem with physical ability.

When his undercover assignment ended, Jack returned to Quantico for tests and evaluation and met with an individual from the behavioral science unit. He gained weight in his undercover capacity, since for the previous three and a half years, he had maintained a very lavish lifestyle, with access to a generous expense account and open tabs at New York's finest restaurants, and Jack neglected none. The FBI also provided Jack a with a penthouse apartment, access to limousines, swanky jewelry, and $21,000 watches. As Jack recounted, "You name it, I had it. If I gave you my undercover name, you are guaranteed a table in New York City." The UC assignment never required Jack to look like an FBI agent. He ate at the finest restaurants in the city, while most Hispanic agents worked deep-fried "Taco Circuit" duties.

Jack testified,

> When you are in FBI space, everyone is kind of a clone; everyone looks alike. The FBI never counseled me for any type of weight gain during the operation. There were never any physicals or any restrictions to this weight. The weight program since day one has been the play with all forms of problems regarding my weight issue. I do not choose to be like this and certainly do not want to offend some managers, especially in Philadelphia. I developed some eating habits during my undercover role and have been on every imaginable diet. Learning the FBI could remove [fire] me from the rolls of the FBI because of my weight is hindering me in losing weight. Being undercover in a dangerous situation, I was constantly nervous.

Jack felt that, if his weight were to be a problem for the FBI on future assignments, his managers might at least have counseled, monitored or informed him. Jack considered his physical capabilities to be on par with the physical requirements of the FBI, although there were managers who assumed he was lethargic because of his weight. He received high performance appraisals and passed all of the physical and firearm requirements. However, he did not have a "Rabbi" to protect him, as do some overweight agents who sail through with no stress or duress. On regular duty, the humiliation he underwent and the constant hostile environment made it difficult to accomplish his work. Jack knew of an assistant director and an ASAC who were both overweight, and neither faced harassment.

Jack also did not receive his office of preference upon reentry, despite the fact that SACs, ASACs, and supervisors assured him that he would. He received no incentive award or commendation for the three and a half years he spent undercover while sacrificing time with his family and associating with people he despised. On his transfer orders, a discriminatory caveat stated that Jack was not to work Cuban matters of any substantive nature. When an Anglo works deep cover on a substantive matter involving Anglos, the FBI never excludes that Anglo agent from all future work involving Anglo cases.

When he met with the behavioral science unit, Jack found its behavior contradictory to that of the Philadelphia Division. After his arrival in Philadelphia, Jack worked in a highly visible position on the applicant squad in which he met with high-profile business people, judges, accountants and lawyers, but the SAC removed him from that position.

Jack then filed an EEO complaint and asked for protection against SAC Wayne Davis until they processed the complaint. The requested protection instead resulted in attacks from his ASACs and supervisors. He felt uncomfortable knowing that Davis had transferred SSA Arnie Gerardo from Allentown to New York. Jack reported that, within the division, anti-Hispanic posters and comments trailed after Arnie, an agent whom Jack knew to be an excellent worker and a good administrator.

Wayne Davis testified that he prevented Jack from becoming a relief supervisor because of his lack of experience and concurred with FBIHQ instructions advising Jack not to work Cuban matters. In response to questioning, Davis admitted he did not know of any black agents whom the bureau instructed to never again work cases involving blacks.

44

Arnold R. Gerardo

Arnie Gerardo had twelve years of local law enforcement experience by the time he joined the bureau on March 8, 1976, under the Spanish language program. Arnie served in the bureau for eleven years. He first worked in LA then transferred to the FBI Academy, serving as a management instructor with responsibilities in the Management Aptitude Program, the DEA, and secretarial training. He provided executive development instruction to all levels, including SACs and police chiefs throughout the country.

Arnie received many letters of commendation. He transferred to the Personal Crimes Unit, where he coordinated FAA matters, including the airline anti-hijacking program and bank robbery matters in the southwest, which included Los Angeles. One particular year Arnie's unit investigated 1,900 bank robberies, besides kidnappings and extortions across the southwest. After a year, he transferred to the organized crime section, where he managed organized crime/drug enforcement matters in addition to serving as the primary acting unit chief.

Arnie's performance appraisals were exceptional—the highest ratings possible in the FBI. Never did he perform at a level that reflected any deficiencies that required a need for attention. Still, Arnie received no promotion until management suggested that he apply for the Allentown, Pennsylvania Resident Agency (APRA) of the Philadelphia Division, a small agency comprising fifteen agents, four support employees and an accounting technician.

In 1982, when Arnie transferred to the FBI Academy's Personal Crimes Unit, he worked for Unit Chief Drew Clark, who appeared to be a very thorough supervisor. However, Arnie heard puzzling statements that he found hard to understand. One day, when Arnie spoke with Clark and discussed work, Clark stated that he thought Arnie had a "minority chip" on his shoulder. Arnie, who—at age forty—had experienced no comments of this nature during half a lifetime in law enforcement, and he asked Clark to repeat what he just said. So Clark did. After thinking about it, Arnie then visited Section Chief John Schreiber several times and requested a transfer, although he never mentioned his conversation with Clark. No transfer materialized.

Arnie applied for a dozen different supervisory positions that he never received, although he had high qualifications—more qualifications than some selectees did, but sometimes he felt the selection was justified. In the interim, Arnie found a change in his workload, assignments and so forth. He realized that management had taken it upon itself to make it difficult for him to do his work. Arnie saw an opening for an organized crime section slot that did not need career board approval, but again he did not get it. Arnie filed an EEO complaint against Clark within the training division and moved to the organized crime section, where he worked for Shawn McWeeney. He was finally able to accomplish his work, and he received many letters of commendation and two more exceptional ratings.

It was during this period that Arnie received a telephone call from Mat Perez in Los Angeles seeking EEO counseling. Despite some difficulty, Arnie assisted Mat with his complaint. Mat submitted his complaint, and afterwards Buck Revell summoned Arnie into his office. Arnie was unaware that he had infuriated Revell because he had helped file a complaint against one of Revell's managers. Arnie testified,

> I thought he was referring to some memo that I had written relative to the complaint I had filed. He says, "I am referring

to the complaint you filed regarding Mat Perez." I said, "Mr. Revell, with all due respect, sir, we really shouldn't be discussing that. That is a private matter really between Mr. Perez and the EEO administrative process, and those involved in that process." He told me anything that affects his division is his concern, and I do not want you involved in that. The time I spent on preparing the EEO complaint and the phone call was off duty time, weekends and at night. I am doing my job, as Mr. McWeeney will attest, earning high ratings.

He threatened me and told me that, in his division and in the personal properties crimes section, there had been no discrimination. I told him I differed with him, there had been discrimination against me and I reiterated the statement about Mr. Clark. He asked why I did not tell him. I said, "Everyone up the line, including Wayne Gilbert, your deputy assistant director, knew of that. I assumed you also knew of that." He said, "I can tell you one thing: discrimination does not exist in my division." He implied it made him look bad. He said he was part Indian and that he had one or two Oriental stepdaughters. That was his answer to my having indicated we had discrimination in the personal properties crime section.

He brought up Mat Perez again and I said, "That is between Mr. Bretzing and Mr. Perez and the administrative EEO process, Mr. Revell, and I really don't think we should be discussing it." He pushed it on three or four occasions. He said, "You better have been right about your allegations or you will suffer the long-term consequences of your actions." I advised him at that point in time I fully knew of the consequences and that I was willing to accept those consequences. At that point, I thought there would be an objective investigation conducted into Mat's complaint.

Arnie then left while McWeeney stayed in the office. Arnie wrote a summary of his conversation with Revell. McWeeney later told Arnie that Revell indicated to McWeeney that perhaps Revell overstepped his bounds, that Arnie was doing a good job and was a good agent, and that maybe they should forget the whole thing and put it behind them. Arnie agreed, but after giving the matter more thought, and knowing Mat's conviction in his complaints against Bretzing and the bureau, Arnie drafted a reprisal complaint, even though he sought career advancement and knew that Revell wielded inordinate power.

Arnie received encouragement to apply for the Allentown Resident agency position, so he figured the Buck Revell incident must have been over and that he was better off going to Allentown. Philadelphia SAC Phil Hogan mentioned that they had several problems in Allentown; two agents had drunk driving incidents, another was fired after he was discovered wearing women's clothing, and yet another transferred out of the office because of administrative problems.

Allen Tolan, the ASAC assigned to supervise Arnie, was not happy with Arnie's assignment to Allentown. The local police chief and officers at the National Academy informed Arnie that Allentown had a reputation as a party resident agency and that agents spent the workday playing golf. Although the statistics for the office were good, in terms of the community, the FBI's high standards for professionalism appeared to be lacking. SAC Hogan gave Arnie instructions to monitor and do his best to reduce the number of negative activities.

Arnie discovered how much the Allentown RA lacked in both resources and equipment. This was now his office. SAC Hogan transferred to ADIC New York, and SAC Wayne Davis replaced him. ASAC Tolan often played golf with the agents from Allentown, and Arnie had to work around that connection. One day, Tolan told Arnie to meet him at the same hotel where Arnie met informants. At the hotel, Tolan told Arnie that agents had complained that Arnie was too strict. Arnie referred to his FBIHQ experience and advised Tolan that the RA needed more discipline but that he would be sensitive to the issue. Afterwards, Arnie traveled to Virginia for three days with his family.

Upon his return, Arnie learned that Tolan had traveled to Allentown to discuss the situation with the Allentown personnel, although Tolan failed to render Arnie the courtesy of discussing the visit with him in advance. Upon reviewing his personnel file for the trial, Arnie found a memo from Tolan that contained negative comments. The memo said that Tolan counseled Arnie on various areas of complaint; however, no such incidents existed. The statements in the memo were not regarding Arnie's work but were instead personal attacks. This happened after Arnie had been in Allentown for several months and, after a SAC gave him specific instructions about discipline problems, now an ASAC was enabling the lack of discipline.

The relief supervisor for Allentown was Bill Jones, an agent who applied for the SSRA position at the same time as Arnie. Tolan, most of the agents in Allentown, and Deborah Wycoski, Arnie's secretary who received her position through the patronage of Jones, all supported Jones for the position.

Wycoski was a good secretary, but Arnie believed her to be undermining him, and she was uncooperative regarding work-related issues. He spoke to her about her work performance. When she still did not make adjustments, he spoke to her again. She refused to respond and cried. The following Monday, an agent complained that he heard that Arnie made Wycoski cry. Arnie asked if he planned to act as her legal representative, since he was the legal rep for the office. Arnie then told him he had issues with Wycoski's performance and that he alerted her to those issues. The following week Wycoski filed allegations of misconduct against Arnie.

Arnie realized the Philadelphia office received misstated facts and inconsistencies on various incidents wherein the Philadelphia office initiated an administrative inquiry on him. ASACs Tolan and Robin Montgomery advised Arnie that there was a complaint pending. Arnie suspected they had come because of his secretary's performance counseling, but they advised Arnie that there was an allegation having to do with a voucher. Arnie told them that he traveled to Philadelphia for file reviews and, on his way home, he stopped for dinner and charged it on a voucher. The second complaint alleged that Arnie took his daughter to the doctor's office in a Bucar, a bureau vehicle, during working hours.

Wayne Davis requested Arnie's removal from the SSRA desk, and it developed into a major administrative inquiry. Normally field offices conduct investigations into voucher allegations. FBIHQ received the statements from Philadelphia's voucher investigation and made a judgment call that the five-dollar charge for dinner was a violation, as Arnie returned to Allentown before 5:00 p.m. The voucher investigation uncovered errors in the time frame of the voucher but no financial errors, as official travel continuing after 4:00 p.m. rated three meals.

FBIHQ went through all of Arnie's past vouchers, including his transfer voucher. Arnie testified, "That was common practice there with the prior SSRA, since we were about sixty miles or so from the Philadelphia office. Then those vouchers would go to Philadelphia for review by someone assigned to voucher processing before any submission to FBIHQ for payment." Therefore, it was a check-off system, but one for which Arnie was not privy. The FBI could not prove the allegations. So Davis added an allegation that Arnie allowed relief supervisory agents to sign off on mail and on vouchers. Tolan advised Arnie that this was standard for efficiency.

The upshot was that Arnie was demoted from GM-14 to GS-13, suspended for thirty days without pay, and transferred to the streets of New York, all based on findings that Arnie lacked candor, took his daughter to the doctor without taking sick leave, and that he allowed uncertified relief supervisors to sign off on bureau mail. The punishment for these alleged offenses seemed excessive compared to sanctions in similar situations that Arnie had seen, heard, or knew happened to others.

Arnie suffered retaliation for his participation and representation of Mat's EEO complaint. Everything moved downhill when Revell warned Arnie that consequences were coming. The evaluations, awards, and progress halted because Buck Revell, a man of influence and power, ordered Arnie to back away from Mat's EEO assignment. Three times, Revell warned Arnie of dire consequences.

Arnie at one time applied for a supervisory desk in Los Angeles under SAC Bretzing. Arnie qualified with high marks, and McWeeney supportively asked Bretzing for his consideration. McWeeney told Arnie that Bretzing indicated he was unhappy that Arnie became involved with Mat. Arnie did not get the job, as Bretzing laterally transferred an LA division agent to that desk.

Arnie's disciplinary transfer to New York created a severe financial hardship for Arnie's family. He appealed the action up the chain of command to Webster, Ed Sharp and others. The appeal never worked out—there were long-term consequences for Arnie. After seven months in New York City, Arnie received several job offers. On May 10, 1987, Arnie accepted a position as a Special Agent with the US Customs Service. US Customs promoted him to a higher grade, placed him in charge of fifteen investigators and he received several incentive awards.

On cross-examination, Arnie testified that his rating of minimally successful in the element of supervision of subordinates was because of the resistance to his choice for the position and because he encountered several individuals who required supervision on performance. The FBI did not follow performance appraisal guidelines in allowing Arnie time to remedy the alleged deficiencies. Arnie allowed the relief supervisor to sign his vouchers as instructed by his ASAC and SAC.

Oliver "Buck" Revell testified that he brought Arnie Gerardo into the office to tell Arnie that he did not want him to engage in any rumormongering regarding SAC Bretzing and to inform Arnie that he had no authority to act as counselor to Mat Perez. Revell testified that he was unaware that Arnie was an EEO counselor. After that incident, Revell denied Arnie's request for a field supervisory position, stating Arnie had not served the minimum time in the division at FBIHQ.

After Revell testified, Wayne G. Davis, SAC Philadelphia, testified that he was unaware that Arnie Gerardo taught management skills for two years at the FBI Academy and throughout the country. Davis was also unaware that the previous SAC in Philadelphia had instructed Arnie to deal with the issues involving the drunks and the golfers in the Allentown RA.

Davis claimed that he could not recall if Arnie's dinner voucher was less than five dollars, but added that he believed Arnie to be untruthful. He testified that Arnie had agents act as relief supervisors—in violation of FBI rules and procedures—even though, in doing so, Arnie may have followed the instructions of his ASAC.

Davis's administrative inquiry recommended Arnie's removal from his supervisory position and his transfer to another division, and it stated that Arnie had lost effectiveness and could no longer work as a supervisor. He added that he would make the same recommendation in any similar case. Davis then reviewed exhibits in which one black agent and one Anglo agent committed, what he also claimed to be, serious and egregious acts. Davis read exhibits 836, 837, and 838, which concerned similar allegations brought against his own ASAC and another agent. But in those instances, Davis chose not to fire, demote, or transfer either agent.

While he served as an FBI agent, Arnie accepted and endured the verbal abuse and obstacles placed in his way because of the prestige of the agency, the money, the investigative work, and the many added perks that being an agent of the FBI offered. However, the system within the FBI required change, as the exploitation and manipulation of misinformation, internal investigations, administrative inquiries, the Office of Professional Responsibility (OPR), and the abusive and unbalanced mien that resulted caused the FBI to remain insulated from any outside pressure.

In an organization with normal standards, multiple educational degrees, strong work ethics, exceptional performance, external commendations, experience, an instinct for justice, and a passion for advancement, one can expect the cream to rise to the top. But the lumps that Arnie received from an organization for which he would have given his life proved to be enough to impel him to take his services to US Customs, a place where he would be entitled to a full cup—instead of a half measure.

45

Paul P. Magallanes

Paul Magallanes earned both a bachelor's degree from St. Mary's College in Winona, Minnesota, and a master's degree in Administration of Justice from the American University in Washington, DC. He joined the FBI in 1968 and celebrated twenty years in the bureau at the time of the trial. He had extensive experience in FBI undercover work and wiretaps, and general investigative experience including foreign counterintelligence. He transferred four times before serving in Los Angeles.

Paul testified earlier in El Paso for the class certification hearing and the hearing concerning the temporary restraining order. Paul testified that he and other Hispanic agents did not receive the polygraph examiner's position in Los Angeles and described how the procedure violated standard regulations. After Paul appeared in court in December 1987, the LA office denied him an opportunity for assignment to the applicant squad to recruit Hispanics. Paul requested reassignment away from the drug squad, where he worked for six years. Paul developed a medical back problem, but it was not the real reason Bretzing placed him on limited duty.

In December, when he returned to LA from El Paso, ASAC Gary Lisotto informed him that there were no vacancies on the applicant squad. On January 4, 1988, Lisotto confirmed the selection of Roberta

Burrows for the applicant squad, and then claimed that the office needed a younger agent on the same squad. When Paul questioned Lisotto on the importance of Hispanic recruitment, Lisotto responded, "Well you know, it's a long trip from East Los Angeles to Westwood." Westwood is the upscale neighborhood where the FBI office is located, while people stereotype East Los Angeles as a lower-class, Mexican-American community. Paul countered that Hispanics live everywhere in Los Angeles, including Westwood and Santa Monica, and were not restricted to East Los Angeles. Lisotto shrugged it off.

In July, Paul learned that he faced an administrative inquiry and was the subject of a possible criminal investigation because, during his deposition, he asserted his rights under the Fifth Amendment on the advice of his counsel. On another matter, Lisotto initiated the administrative inquiry because he claimed that Paul took leave without submitting a leave slip or requesting authorization. In early February of 1988, Paul had taken a half an hour of leave.

A week before the trial, Lisotto told Paul that the administrative inquiry for the alleged unauthorized leave was no longer active. Paul asked for a copy of this communication but never received it. In reviewing his personnel file in the lead-up to the lawsuit, he discovered that he had been the subject of another administrative inquiry back in 1985 when an FCI supervisor accused Paul of espionage, charges similar but unrelated to those made against Los Angeles agent Richard W. Miller, the convicted Soviet spy. The LA division initiated the FCI inquiry because a billing record under investigation showed a call to Paul's telephone, then reviewed Paul's telephone calls. The LA office documented everything regarding Paul's work—they kept "book" on him, meaning they looked at where he went, people he met with, and whom he called.

Paul believes that the actions taken against him—the denial of the polygraph examiner position, his transfer from an RA to the main field office, the confiscation of his gun, the removal of his assigned bureau vehicle and all of the administrative relief problems he encountered—were due to his participation in the class action suit. Paul, who had twenty years of unblemished service investigating dangerous cases, did not deserve the treatment he received from management.

In court, Paul reviewed the submissions by the government of the list of medications taken by ASAC Lloyd Dean for Dean's back pain issues. Paul learned that Dean took drugs similar to the ones Paul took for his own back problem, that no one ever placed Dean on limited duty, that no one confiscated Dean's gun, that no one transferred Dean to another assignment, and, finally, that no one removed Dean's government vehicle. There was never any indication that anyone ever questioned Dean's leave status. Then again, ASAC Dean was not Hispanic.

On cross-examination, Ms. Black attempted to show that there were differences between Dean's and Paul's back problems. The Judge told her not to bother, as he had reviewed the relevant documents.

Gary A. Lisotto testified that Paul Magallanes traveled to New York for a TV program at the advice and direction of an attorney. Lisotto did not know if Paul had contacted his squad during the time he spent in New York or if he advised his squad on how to contact him while he was away. Lisotto had no background in medicine and claimed that, because of this lack of medical training, he could not verify whether the two government doctors or Paul's personal physician had ascertained if Paul was fit or unfit for duty.

Mark Codd, who served at FBIHQ, testified that the FBI needed Spanish-speaking agents and Hispanics but admitted he did not send agents to recruit Hispanics at a minority-recruiting fair held in Los Angeles. He did, however, testify that he sent representatives to an event organized by the Los Angeles Chapter of the Urban League, an African-American organization. Hugo questioned Codd as to why the FBI could locate fugitives and terrorists throughout the country, yet the FBI cannot find Hispanics to hire as agents. Codd did not respond.

Bretzing later testified that he had approved the removal of Paul Magallanes from the Ventura RA, the confiscation of his weapon and the suspension of his authority to drive a government vehicle because of medication he took for back pain, despite two government doctors and Paul's personal physician never having made such a recommendation. On the stand, Bretzing acknowledged he knew of Paul and Mat's relationship and EEO complaints.

46

Yvonne Shaffer-Perez

Yvonne Shaffer-Perez, plaintiff Mat Perez's wife, joined the FBI in San Juan in 1977 as an English/Spanish stenographer-typist, evidence vault clerk, high-security communications vault clerk and security patrol clerk of the San Juan Office.

Director Webster, through Assistant Director Colwell, instructed Mat to stop dating Yvonne after the bureau named Mat SAC San Juan, and a security allegation against Yvonne surfaced. Yvonne was unaware of the allegation yet knew that the FBI did not want Mat to see her. She requested a transfer off the island, as she did not want to cause him problems and because she now sensed an uncomfortable atmosphere around the office.

FBIHQ offered Yvonne a position in the Legal Attaché's Office, United States Embassy, Mexico City, but before she left for Mexico, FBIHQ ordered her to DC for additional training. Not realizing these orders were a ruse, Yvonne arrived in DC to discover that the Office of Professional Responsibility (OPR) had initiated an administrative inquiry, and— following several unethical and illegal interrogation sessions—she learned of the allegations against her. The interrogators warned Yvonne that she must not contact an attorney, or contact Mat Perez, and that she was not to speak of the investigation to anyone, not even her own parents.

The first question from OPR was, "How many times have you been to bed with Mat Perez?" She responded, "It is none of your business." Marty Ford accused her of passing secret information to the Socialist Party of San Juan. As the twenty-three-year old daughter of a US Air Force aircraft mechanic, Yvonne tried to imagine anything in her past that led the FBI to entertain such wild ideas but came up with nothing. Yvonne felt desperate, cornered and confused.

She thought it was her duty to assist her interrogators to prove her innocence and for her family, and for Mat. She was a virtual prisoner because of the restrictions placed on her while she was in Washington, where she faced interrogation daily. OPR coerced Yvonne into "voluntary" polygraph examinations. They informed her that she showed deception on one specific question. They grilled her on whether she visited Jamaica, which she denied. She knew she had never visited the island. Yvonne was unaware that Jamaica was a country often used by the intelligence service of Fidel Castro's communist Cuba as a place to meet with their informants. The FBI gave her the third degree on her sexual activity with Mat. Art Czintos, a former coworker of Mat's from the Los Angeles Office, asked Yvonne, "How's the cocktail party going?" as they shuffled her from one office to another for further questioning. Rodney McHargue, a former San Juan supervisor, chimed in—to curry favor with his bosses—and accused Yvonne of being "a whore."

The FBI pressured Tom Kelly, a high-ranking FBI official and friend of Mat, with whom Yvonne stayed while she was in town. Forced, Kelly reluctantly asked Yvonne to leave.

While puzzling over the alleged polygraph inconsistencies, EAD Buck Revell confided to Yvonne that he too had not passed polygraph examinations in the past, but corrected the problems. He played the part of "good cop," dripping with sympathy. Revell lied, as he was not a close friend of Mat's, stating, "You can confide in me..." Yvonne refused to take the bait.

Instead, Yvonne accused her interrogators of violating her rights and lying to her. They realized they might have exceeded authority. Yvonne spoke with a female attorney from Director Webster's office, telling her that she felt violated and emotionally raped.

The attorney promised to look into the matter and passed along the word that the FBI's behavior had been unprofessional and that heads should roll for such abusive behavior. No heads rolled. In a moment of weakness, Marty Ford told her she either "was completely innocent or she was the best spy Fidel Castro ever had." The bureau terminated the inquiry, but they did not permit Yvonne to go to a foreign assignment because of the unresolved question about Jamaica on the polygraph exam. They told her, however, to pick any domestic office for her new assignment.

After tossing and turning her way through yet another sleepless night, Yvonne realized that she no longer wanted to work for the FBI and called Mat to tell him what had been going on. The next morning, she submitted a letter of resignation. FBI management professed surprise and told Yvonne that she had no reason to quit or even be concerned for her job, as she was innocent of the allegations. OPR told her the intelligence and criminal divisions wanted to talk to her. Relieved that FBIHQ had dropped treating her as an inanimate object, she mistakenly accepted talks with Divisions Five and Six before she returned to Puerto Rico, thinking the talks regarded job prospects and relocation.

However, the entertainers pulled strings for an encore to quiz the puppet about her sexual relationship with Mat. Strung, manipulated and frazzled, the strings snapped and the show ended as she came to life with her last words as she left the stage; she told the manipulators to shove it.

She had enough theatrics and caught a 4:00 p.m. flight back to Puerto Rico. She married Mat one month later. Yvonne continued to suffer as the attacks on Mat continued. Yvonne never filed an EEO complaint, saying, "EEO complaints...everybody knows it is worthless."

Ivan M. Ford testified that he could not recall certain facts as his memory had lapsed in the eight years since he had interviewed Yvonne, yet he informed the court of the exact date of the allegation and the exact dates of which Yvonne was at FBIHQ. Ford remembered that they polygraphed Yvonne three times and that Yvonne volunteered for each of them. Ford did not recall Yvonne asking for an attorney, since the interview was only an administrative inquiry and an administrative inquiry does not require Miranda warnings. Court records proved Ford and David Flanders, the agent in charge of OPR, had read Yvonne her Miranda rights.

47

David Velazquez

David Velazquez, born and raised in Brooklyn, New York, received his education at Columbia University. Three months after his graduation from Columbia, in August of 1982, he entered the FBI as a clerk in New York and became a special agent in 1984. He worked in El Paso before transferring to San Juan, Puerto Rico. He came into the FBI under the language program. Dave worked as a language specialist even before he came into the FBI and performed the same exact job as an FBI agent as he had as a language specialist.

While in San Juan, Dave provided an affidavit to support the class action lawsuit. SAC Esposito called him and his wife, Priscilla Velazquez, who was not an agent, to his office on July 16, 1987, at 5:10 p.m. Dave testified,

> He closed the door and immediately showed me a copy of my affidavit. He said he had it in his possession for approximately one week. He said he did not know who placed it in his inbox. Esposito said he had read it several times during the week and that he had grown more and more excited with the contents of the affidavit during the week. He questioned me as to the specific contents of the affidavit, the venue of the case, the attorneys involved, number of Hispanics involved, the judge involved. He said he took specific exception with one

> paragraph in the affidavit, which obliquely referred to his engaging in retaliation against Hispanic agents.
>
> Esposito said that though he admired Mr. Perez for all the pain and heartache he had undergone in proceeding with this litigation. However, he thought that the lawsuit had no foundation. He said he took exception to my running a quote, "underground newsletter," and that if I wanted to say something about the lawsuit I could do so in an open forum in the office. The trouble with that was he was leaving one week later. He was very angry. His facial expressions led us to believe he was upset at me and my wife.

Esposito never informed Dave as to why he had requested Priscilla's attendance at their meeting, as this intimidated both Dave and his wife. Esposito then ordered the two leave his office without saying what he planned to do with the affidavit. Several months later, when David informed his new SAC and ASAC that he would travel to El Paso to testify, ASAC John Phillips admonished him to remember that the bureau has a long memory.

Under cross-examination, Dave admitted that he felt too humiliated at the time to contemplate going before an all agents' conference to address the lawsuit, let alone call such a conference on his own. He did not consider Esposito sincere when he told Dave he could announce the lawsuit at an office conference. Dave recalled a San Juan special and successful assignment in which an award would have been the normal standard procedure, but instead he received no acknowledgement.

On day seven of the trial, Esposito, an attorney familiar with attorney/client privileges, spoke of the class action lawsuit and his meeting with lawsuit participants David and Priscilla. Esposito claimed to have received an unsolicited letter, government exhibit G-1798, stating that David feared retaliation for his participation as a class member. Esposito acknowledged that he summoned David and his wife into his office and told them of his disappointment that David would think that Esposito or any other FBI agent would retaliate against him for his participation. Exhibit G-1799 was a document regarding David's activities, which Esposito unnecessarily reported to the Administrative Services Unit.

48

Primitivo Rios, Jr.

Primitivo "Jay" Rios, born in San Juan, Puerto Rico, graduated from Florida Atlantic University. He had ten years of experience in law enforcement prior to joining the FBI in 1979 through the Miami Division, where he began as an agent. Within two years, he transferred to San Juan, then back to Miami and again to San Juan. He worked criminal, FCI, and TDY specials. While in Miami as a first office agent, he worked on the Mariel Boatlift, interrogating Cuban refugees and covered three "Taco Circuit" TDY assignments in less than two years. After failing the language test, Jay came in under the modified program because of his law enforcement experience. In 1984, he took another language test and received a level 4 rating.

Jay was in San Juan during the inspection period involving SAC Mat Perez. "The mood before, prior to the inspection, was that it was general knowledge amongst the support personnel, the street agents, that the inspection squad was coming down and they were going to be looking to get Mat Perez. When there is a hit on someone, it means someone is going after that target. Sometimes nobody knows." He said it was general knowledge throughout the bureau that there was a hit on Mat. Jay did not believe Mat deserved the hit from the inspection staff because of all of the Major Cases that developed in San Juan. Confirming the sense of impending doom in San Juan was John

Guido, an inspector's aide, who declared within earshot of several agents, "We are going to nail these turkeys' hides to the wall."

Under cross-examination, Jay testified that, when he completed his two-year contract in San Juan, even though he had already served in a top twelve office, he received orders to New York City. The FBI wanted to make an example of him and demonstrate that, if an agent only stayed two years, they would ship him to New York City, no matter his OP. Most non-Hispanic agents, however, received their OP following a mere two years in San Juan. In Miami, where he wanted to work criminal cases in his second assignment, Jay instead went on the FCI squad derisively known as the "Tamale Squad" with eighteen other Spanish-speaking agents.

On the eighth day of the trial, Terrance "Terry" Dinan testified that he had headed the inspection staff when Mat was the SAC in San Juan. Dinan lived with EAD Lee Colwell. He claimed that he never spoke to Colwell or to the director about Mat serving in San Juan or spoke with either about the allegation of an FBI contract on Mat, although his inspection team found thirty-four findings of noncompliance in San Juan attributed to Mat's leadership.

The inspection staff reported thirty percent of the office's permanent investigative staff were under-assigned, but Dinan could not answer why the FBI, following this determination and with Mat leaving, continued with the mass infusion of temporary duty agents to work the four designated Major Cases. Dinan testified that Mat had abrogated his authority, and that this was a significant contributing factor to San Juan's poor performance. He testified that he was unaware of the FBI removing any other SAC for administrative shortcomings or deficiencies.

Despite having served as a lead inspector and as a SAC, Dinan postured difficulty in understanding the FBI term and the associated definition of a "Major Case," which did not amuse Judge Bunton:

> RODRIGUEZ: How many Major Cases have you originated in the Cincinnati Division since you have been SAC?
>
> DINAN: In five years, how many Major Cases?
>
> RODRIGUEZ: Yes, sir.

DINAN: Okay. Define that for me.

RODRIGUEZ: Major Case?

DINAN: Give me a better feel.

RODRIGUEZ: Major Case as captioned by the FBI.

DINAN: Where we concentrate people, put more than one person on it or something?

49

Raymond P. Yelchak

Raymond P. Yelchak retired from the FBI after serving as SAC in El Paso. He began his employment with the FBI in July 1956 and worked as a clerical employee for six years; for two and a half of those years, he clerked with great pleasure and much respect for Director J. Edgar Hoover. Ray attended George Washington University, Catholic University and graduated from Southeastern University in Washington, DC. As an agent, he worked in Louisville, Kentucky; the Covington RA; Dallas; Buffalo; and then FBIHQ before becoming ASAC in Philadelphia. After he was promoted to GS-16, he served as SAC in Sacramento for six years, until 1986, when he transferred as the SAC to El Paso. Ray retired on August 16, 1987.

Before coming to El Paso, Ray made the rounds with FBIHQ officials over a two-day period and received briefings on operations in El Paso. One high-level FBI official, Buck Revell, told Ray that El Paso was an international-type border city with much work in narcotics. Revell also spoke to him about Mat, a GS-16 ASAC in El Paso, characterizing him as a no-good troublemaker. Upon arrival in El Paso, Ray found Mat Perez to be an extremely well-qualified, well-educated, bilingual and highly competent assistant. As the SAC, he observed Mat through two performance appraisals; his first rating for Mat was excellent and his second rating for him was outstanding overall. Although Mat had concerns that FBIHQ was out to get him in retaliation for filing complaints about discrimination, Ray thought that Mat was well balanced, levelheaded, had no kind of a chip on his shoulder, and created no divisiveness between Hispanics and non-Hispanics.

Ray sent a letter to Director Webster that outlined several instances in which he believed that there were clear acts of reprisal taken against Mat. With an active civil action, Mat asked if he could attend a news conference held by his attorney at a local television station. He planned to take annual leave; he would be off duty and would say nothing. Mat did not want to risk accusations of insubordination or any other charges, so he wanted to make sure all was right and above-board. Ray spoke to the head of EEO FBIHQ, Assistant Director Ed Sharp, EAD Glover, and Deputy AD Milton Aldridge of Congressional Affairs. No one was willing to go on record and provide Ray with any guidance.

Time passed and the day of the press conference arrived. Ray again called Aldridge, who was in John Glover's office, and Aldridge informed Ray that the FBI would not sanction Mat's attendance at the news conference, but that they also would not interfere with Mat's First Amendment rights. Glover ordered Ray to have the media representative of the EI Paso Field Division observe the news conference. Ray saw no need for this and objected, as Mat would be off duty and would not speak. The scheduled news conference was at a local Spanish-language television station. Ray thought that sending an FBI observer was improper, as some might interpret such an action as interference, intimidation, or as an act of reprisal, and it would be unnecessary since all television clips and related newspaper articles would be available for FBI to review both locally and at FBIHQ. Aldridge reiterated that those were Glover's orders. Ray told Aldridge that he would follow orders to avoid insubordination charges, but felt obligated to voice his concerns.

FBIHQ also sent a communication with a strong tone, insisting that Mat had not followed FBIHQ instructions related to a sensitive program he managed and that Ray should ensure that Mat carry out FBI orders. Ray testified,

> There was a threat of insubordination, and I viewed that with great alarm. I called Mat in and asked to see the referenced communication. He could not find one. We had no record of this referenced communication whereby allegedly they instructed us to do certain things within this program. After an exhaustive search of our records, we could not find this communication.
>
> We informed FBIHQ. Sometime later, we received another communication and as I recall now Revell signed these communications. The reply came with an enclosure. The enclosure was a poor copy of what appeared to be a rough, almost made-up type communication. It just did not fit. Mat could not have complied with those instructions because we had not received that communication.
>
> I was extremely concerned about that because it appeared to be, as we described it, a spurious airtel. Later it was determined the original communication was found some great time later, it had been misplaced and was found in the front office of one of the assistant directors. The timing of this did not fit. It did not make sense. It is almost as if this airtel did not exist, and then created to make it appear that Mat was not doing his work. I raised this in a letter I wrote to Bill Webster, and I expressed my concerns.

Ray recommended Mat with several commendations—FBIHQ refused to accept them. In one instance, Ray recommended a commendation letter for Mat from the director for his performance in the arrest of a DEA fugitive involved in a police shootout. Ray observed Mat at the scene with the SWAT team, the DEA, and two young first office agents, who all conducted themselves with a high degree of professionalism. Ray recommended incentive awards for the two first office agents and an individual letter of commendation for Mat. FBIHQ denied the requests. Ray protested to AD Sharp. Sharp granted the two agents their incentive awards and advised Ray that he could include remarks in Mat's performance appraisal, but nothing more.

In another instance, there were three armed and dangerous bank robbers in the El Paso area. Ray observed their arrest, which involved Mat's hands-on management, his supervision of the SWAT team, and control of the crime scene. Ray recommended another letter for Mat, but again to no avail. Mexican authorities requested FBI assistance with the capture of a high profile subject in another instance. Ray testified,

> Mat, in my absence, put that together and organized a very successful raid. Again, I made recommendations for recognition for the agents involved including Mat Perez, and again they denied it.
>
> Mat had a complaint and wanted Leo Gonzales, the most experienced EEO counselor in El Paso, to counsel him. FBIHQ denied Mat's request, stating Leo served at one time in a representative capacity for Mat; therefore, he could not serve as counselor.

Again, Ray did not agree with the ruling.

Ray had never believed that there was discrimination against Hispanics in the FBI until he landed in El Paso. Ray hoped that an emphasis on hiring Spanish speakers would improve conditions for Hispanic FBI agents. Ray testified,

> I saw the situation with Mat Perez, I saw the situation with Leo Gonzales. I heard from them about a number of other cases outside the El Paso Division, which I was not aware of. That caused me concern that it appeared to be a pattern there. I can't say there is discrimination against Hispanics across the board in the FBI, but there was a pattern there that I saw in Mat's case and Leo's case and other cases they brought to my attention after I arrived in El Paso that greatly concerned me.

Upon his retirement, Ray highly endorsed, with strong recommendations, that Mat replace him as the Special Agent in Charge of the El Paso office. FBIHQ denied Mat the position.

His support of Mat adversely affected Ray's career. Ray sensed it in the tone of communications arriving from FBIHQ, in the lack of response to specific requests, as well in the performance evaluations that Ray received when compared to the many collected before his arrival in El Paso.

When agents speak of "The Bureau," they mean agents in the field—the visible agents—those making arrests, and those who bring public recognition to the organization. FBIHQ itself is often somewhat anonymous. Ray explained, "For example, in FBIHQ communications we receive—there are no initials on them—and we don't know who necessarily ordered these communications. The bureau, in my view, is a handful, perhaps three or four very strong, highly placed individuals who manage the bureau, the FBI: Oliver Revell, John Otto and John Glover."

On cross-examination, Ray testified that he once filed an EEO complaint against Director Webster based on religious discrimination. When he was SAC Sacramento, John Mintz told Ray that the FBI was considering transferring him to Memphis, Tennessee. Ray reminded Mintz of the letter a doctor submitted regarding the health risk of moving Ray's wife out of the Sacramento area and that Webster had assured Ray that the letter would remain as the top serial of his personnel file. Mintz told Ray that he better update the doctor's letter. Before he could get another letter from his wife's physician, Webster sent Ray a communication ordering his transfer from the Sacramento office. In this communication, Webster attempted to impose his Christian Science religious beliefs and, in an insensitive tone, he instructed Ray to surmount his personal problems. Ray remembered that this Christian Scientist attitude manifested itself previously in the passing of Webster's wife—showing the same religious prejudice that FBIHQ now attempted to impose on Ray's wife. Ray testified, "He completely disregarded the letter from the doctor. I got the letter from him before he received the letter from the doctor. And I would like to add, Your Honor, my case is still pending and I don't know how much I have to get into it here today." Ray received an oral reprimand concerning the matter from John Mintz.

Ray also complained to Lee Colwell about his performance appraisal element of fully successful. Prior to his transfer to El Paso, Ray Yelchak had nothing less than outstanding and excellent performance appraisals. Ray believed that his lower performance appraisal resulted from his support of Mat and that the FBI's actions against Mat were in reprisal for his EEO complaints.

On the sixth day of the trial, EAD John Glover, Administrative Services Division, testified that, although he authorized incentive awards for SACs, ASACs, and agents, he did not accept the recommendation to honor incentive awards for SAC Ray Yelchak and ASAC Mat Perez for their participation in high profile cases in El Paso. Glover testified that Ray's support for Mat's litigation against the FBI had nothing to do with his decision.

Glover admitted that he had enhanced the work force in Dallas when they had a problem with bank failings. In stark contrast, Glover provided no adjustment to the work force in Puerto Rico after Mat Perez had requested help in San Juan with four major terrorism cases involving the bombings of US bases, destruction of US government property and the murders of US military personnel.

Revell testified that he summoned Ray Yelchak to headquarters to counsel Ray on Ray's problems. Revell told Ray that part of his responsibility in supervising Mat was to improve Mat's performance and ensure there was a coherent management team in the El Paso office. He claimed that he had never referred to Mat as a "no-good troublemaker." Revell also stated that the needs of the bureau are requirements that take precedence over individual needs, even over other sub-organizational needs.

John Otto testified that Ray Yelchak had identifiable weaknesses when he was SAC in Sacramento and seconded Revell's testimony that he brought Ray to Headquarters to counsel him about his own problems, not Mat's problems. Meanwhile, Glover testified that Ray misdiagnosed the merits of Mat's accomplishments.

In their opinions, Mat was in El Paso as an ASAC because Judge Webster, Dr. Colson, Bishop Bretzing and the three EAD's—Otto, Revell, and Glover—all believed that Mat needed administrative direction and because they sincerely wanted him to improve. The six executives thought it was in the best interest of the bureau to send their "problem SAC" to head an office with a "problem ASAC" who needed administrative help, and that somehow this was all justified by the "the needs of the bureau."

Ray's problems began when he chose not to march in lock step, but instead to use the steps he learned from the old-school, J. Edgar Hoover FBI that took a stance on civil rights that was in clear opposition to the Ku Klux Klan. It was Hoover's FBI, as it was Ray's—not the Judge's, not the doctor's, not the bishop's, not the three EAD amigos. Ray recalled that, under Hoover, agents proved their values to the rule of law as an FBI family and shared healthy thoughts, sound reasoning and respected exchanges. He refused to participate in tearing down one of his own agents, a man who had a legal right to file a complaint. Ray's job was to help people improve and become better able to accomplish the work of the FBI. He did not see a disease in Mat's Jesuit and FBI instilled values, administrative skills, or work ethic. Ray acknowledged that hardship was often one thing, which came from having principles.

50

Bernardo Matias "Mat" Perez

On cross-examination, Mat testified that he believed Director Webster to be a bigot because he refused to address the FBI's systemic discrimination and the sanctions the FBI imposed on Mat. He believed a person who acts unjustly against another person because of race, sex, national origin, or age is, by definition, a bigot. Although Mat acknowledged that he did not know what was in the director's heart, he knew Webster had supported actions against Mat and those around him. Webster and his staff impugned the rights and essence of the woman he loved, Yvonne Shaffer-Perez. Under Webster's rule, the FBI subjected Yvonne to illegal, unethical, and unprofessional interrogation when the administrative inquiry turned criminal while FBIHQ agents denied her access to an attorney.

Mat had no doubt that Webster had him demoted and ousted from San Juan, with the San Juan inspection staff ratifying Webster's FBIHQ agenda. Director Webster transferred Mat from San Juan to Los Angeles. Mat believed the inspectors had orders to magnify trivial items instead of focusing on the chaotic ongoing terrorism in Puerto Rico. The inspection itself did not have an anti-Hispanic agenda; instead, the inspectors went after the head of the office, the Mexican-American Special Agent in Charge. The inspector's findings proved in court unfair and dishonest, and they presented an inaccurate picture of the situation in San Juan. The findings led to disparate treatment that made the inspection process a part of an anti-Hispanic agenda.

In November of 1979, Webster appointed Mat as SAC in San Juan after he served as San Juan's ASAC for seven months. Mat considered Director Webster, Dr. Lee Colwell, and Buck Revell to be his mentors, making the experience such a searing betrayal. The review of the 25,000 pages in his personnel file revealed to Mat the existence of many treacherous acts. Headquarters officials said one thing to his face and wrote the polar opposite in his personnel file. Mat lamented,

> The worst thing about this type of action is that it causes severe self-doubt because the FBI is very strong. Not everything I am saying here points at Anglo versus Hispanic. Because 99% of all FBI agents are not, do not act in this way. However, these few in powerful positions have made these things happen. Yet I was struggling. I knew I was getting results. I was talking to my agents daily; they were agreeing with me.

Mat recalled his SAC in Miami, a chronic alcoholic, often threatened to fire or demote him, but Mat disregarded these incoherent ramblings. Each SAC is different, and FBIHQ gives each degrees of latitude. One might run innovative and unconventional operations, while others cannot. Mat acknowledged those who run FBIHQ have a right to insist that field offices follow FBI procedures, but FBIHQ controls both funding and resources, and it makes mistakes.

Mat testified that John Glover, the black assistant director, and people of any color, could be considered anti-Hispanic bigots if they followed discriminatory orders. He stated, "And if he does not stand up for what he thinks [is] fair, I think he is guilty of those actions."

In June of 1982, Mat landed in Los Angeles as the Administrative ASAC. Mat realized that, under Bretzing, race and religion were the determining factors in management decisions. Mat believed Bretzing's Mormon religion and the Book of Mormon showed an inherent bias against those whose skin color is other than white and is possible for anyone to discriminate against. He added that the American frontiersman "Kit Carson married a Native American woman, and after she died he married a Mexican woman, but he sure fought and killed

Mexicans and Indians." The Department of Justice, FBIHQ, and Bretzing united against Mat. Mat's performance would never satisfy Bretzing, who never wanted Mat in LA.

Mat received a letter of censure from Webster for the unauthorized disclosure of Bretzing's travel vouchers. He took the vouchers to his EEO hearing. The FBI forbids the transmittal of FBI documents to private persons without official approval. Mat did not have official approval to show the vouchers to his attorneys. Mat did not consider the vouchers related to an official FBI investigation, instead believing them to be government documents generated while working for the FBI. He thought the EEO process allowed him to give such travel documents to his attorney during an official EEO hearing in which FBI attorneys were present, and that it was his right to discuss them at the hearing.

The allegation of discrimination against the director was serious. Mat felt upset and insulted when the EEO program under Jeter elected not to send a full inspector but a Grade-14 agent with two hours of EEO training to handle his complaint. Mat told SA Burdina Pasenelli that it was unfair to him and Pasenelli for her to act as an EEO investigator and counselor when the allegations concerned the director of the FBI. Mat filed several EEO complaints against Bretzing and Webster charging disparate treatment, anti-Hispanic discrimination, religious discrimination and retaliation. The DOJ even tried to make it appear as if the director did Mat a favor by sending him from California to El Paso, as Mat was from California. Mat countered, "That is like asking a person 'would you rather be shot or hanged?' "

Dozens of Hispanic agents did not enter the FBI under the language program yet spoke Spanish with varying degrees of fluency, many well enough to use their language skills in accomplishing bureau investigative needs. Mat recognized that agents used their skills to the best of their ability to carry out the FBI's mission.

Mat, as a supervisor in LA, heard complaints from Hispanic agents of excessive workloads. He had also been a part of this system of discrimination as a supervisor, ASAC, and SAC. The system impinged unfairly on specific groups. As an example, in the El Paso office, Mat supervised nine agents, two of whom spoke Spanish. Non-Spanish-speaking agents could not work many kidnappings, bank robberies, or extortions. When he assigned cases to non-Spanish speakers, some investigative cases forced Spanish-speaking agents to cover their leads. Mat had to rely on new agents Luis Fraticelli and, before him, David Velazquez to handle most work in Spanish. Mat's other bilingual agent, Jim Beck, an Anglo, also had too many Spanish-speaking assignments and responsibilities. Failure to address overloaded agents was an act of discrimination and led to repeated EEO problems in the FBI.

The bureau refused to recognize the pressing need for Spanish speakers; race was not at issue in the beginning. The burden of running the Spanish-speaking investigations fell upon the short-staffed Hispanic agents. Mat theorized that, while Webster had no intention of laying an unfair burden on Hispanics and overworking them, the bureau never did enough to recruit Spanish speakers or use the Anglo Spanish speakers it had.

Mat clarified his position and affirmed that not every single Hispanic had excessive assignments and not every Anglo had too few cases, nor should anyone define the litigation as Hispanics versus non-Hispanics. One bureau-wide management perception came up that people who had a Hispanic surname ipso facto spoke Spanish, and management heaped upon them the Spanish-speaking assignments.

The Hispanic American Police Command Officers Association (HAPCOA), an organization of high-ranking Hispanics in law enforcement, requested in writing that Mat address their convention. The FBI claimed to be interested in recruiting Hispanics, and this seemed the ideal forum—a presence of experienced law enforcement officers. The FBI, in two separate communications, turned them down, citing excessive cost. The trip to Albuquerque from El Paso would have set the FBI back about $32, less than a full tank of gas. In response, HAPCOA offered to pay all costs. Still the answer was a big "No." The director of the FBI then confirmed that he could not let Mat Perez give a speech at HAPCOA because of his involvement in the ongoing litigation. Mat recalled a recruiting conference at which Webster informed Mat that he wanted to recruit more Hispanics. Mat advised him to stop hiring attorneys and hire Spanish speakers instead. The director made no such changes.

Mat's trial testimony closed with the discussion of several discriminatory letters that he had received. One letter from William C. Asbury, a field agent who appeared disabled in asking questions, claimed that the order for discovery far outreached the necessity for the court action, that the personnel information provided through discovery was not relevant, that the litigation was a disservice to all agents, that Mat was a disgrace and embarrassment, that Mat should resign, and that Mat's relationship with his wife, whom the letter writer claimed was a woman involved in terrorist activities, compromised investigative matters. This one letter illustrated the typical hysteria manifested by agents too lazy to learn the facts and willing to set aside any investigative talents they might have claimed to possess. Agents no longer cared for objective fairness. FBI team spirit became the priority over integrity.

On the Monday following Mat's testimony, Executive Assistant Director (EAD) John Glover testified that he would perhaps consider Mat for an assignment at FBIHQ before consideration for any SAC position. Glover said that, as an ASAC in Newark, he had recruited and given speeches for the FBI, but he did not approve Mat's request to recruit at and speak at the Hispanic American Police Command Officers Conference in Albuquerque because of the funding issue. He claimed his decision to forbid Mat to attend the HAPCOA conference in Albuquerque or even consider him for SAC had nothing to do with Mat's EEO complaints.

EAD John E. Otto claimed the bureau considered everything when they demoted Mat for administrative deficiencies, even the fact that he only had a staff of fifty-five agents permanently assigned to San Juan working four active FBI Major Cases of terrorism that included over 150 bombings, murders of US military personnel, and police corruption. Upon Mat's transfer to LA, Otto did not oversee Bretzing's supervision of Mat and received no reports from Bretzing. He had no answer as to why SAC Dick Held and Jim Esposito were able to handpick the agents they wanted and doubled the size of the San

Juan office. Otto provided no enhancements of agent personnel to San Juan while Mat was SAC.

On the eighth day of the trial, Buck Revell testified that Mat rose from ASAC to SAC too rapidly. Mat had seventeen years of experience, yet Revell testified that he did not think his own rise to SAC within twelve years had been too rapid.

Revell claimed that he learned on the day of his court testimony that the DOJ terminated the administrative inquiry against Mat. He claimed not to know whether the FBI recommended firing Mat because of those charges. He testified, "There was a determination as to whether he should be fired or not, but I did not read the memorandum." In reference to the DOJ and FBI producing a sixty-six page un-serialized document that recommended firing Mat, Revell testified that all documents and files contained serialization, but sometimes documents stay in folders until a case is completed and then is serialized. The maintenance of un-serialized documents in active case files contradicts bureau policy and is a violation inspectors would pounce on.

Revell said that he never failed the two polygraph exams rendered by an FBI polygraph examiner, as the adjudication process had not upheld the opinion of the polygrapher that Revell was deceptive. Revell testified that, while he had no authority to fire that examiner, the examiner left the bureau.

James Esposito testified on the seventh day, two days after Mat, that in 1981, Mat Perez served as SAC San Juan and had a complement of fifty-five agents and four Major Cases. In contrast to not providing Mat additional personnel, in 1983 FBIHQ increased SAC Richard Held's complement to seventy-five agents when there were only two Major Cases. In 1986, Esposito increased his complement to ninety-three agents.

The court disapproved of Esposito's refusal to answer questions directly, as he tried too hard to justify the decisions of the FBI. Judge Bunton warned Esposito and the DOJ six times not to discuss a program the judge had already heard in court and instructed Esposito to answer questions "yes" or "no" or face charges of contempt.

The FBI prioritizes and ranks their investigative programs. Esposito claimed he did not know if the inspection staff checked whether Mat had organized his personnel according to FBI investigative priorities, although he earlier testified that he had reviewed Mat's inspection report when he worked for SAC Held. In 1981, the FBI rated terrorism as tenth on their list of priorities; however, from 1983 to 1986, terrorism ranked as number one. Esposito confirmed a SAC has the authority to identify and rank the crime problems in his respective geographic territory and address them with the support of FBIHQ. The inspection staff and FBIHQ refused to give Mat such authority.

Esposito had the two-year tours of agents in San Juan extended to four years. This was the same plan that Mat proposed and FBIHQ denied. The director approved an October 1, 1969, field-wide program that transferred first office agents to a top twelve office or gave them a chance to go to San Juan for four years and then return to their office of assignment or an office of preference. Esposito requested more personnel, including an entire new management team, and maintained he did not want to staff the entire San Juan office with Spanish-speaking Hispanic agents, as he believed diversity to be important in all offices.

About thirty agents applied, of which Esposito selected three: James Rumchak, Steven Warner, and Tommy Nessa. He did not select Henry "Hank" Tenorio or any other Spanish-speaking Hispanic agents, despite his earlier testimony that San Juan's priority was Spanish speakers with investigative experience. Antonio Silva drilled Esposito:

> SILVA: And Mr. Rumchak does not speak Spanish, does he?
>
> ESPOSITO: That is right. But he was also a supervisor, which is a position that does not operate on the street, largely an administrative position. Fluency in a supervisory position is preferred but unnecessary.
>
> SILVA: You brought him in to supervise Hispanics?
>
> ESPOSITO: Well, participation in the career development program to be a supervisor is voluntary. We asked him if he would be a supervisor, if he wanted to be, and he said yes. He was not ordered to be one, because we do not have that

capacity within the FBI. We asked him to be the supervisor of that squad, and he accepted and he was selected at our request by headquarters to do that.

SILVA: The answer to my question is yes? You brought him in to be the supervisor of the Hispanics?

ESPOSITO: No, sir.

THE COURT: Obviously he was.

Three days after Mat testified, Richard T. Bretzing, who served as SAC Los Angeles during the time Mat was the Administrative ASAC, testified that no one had informed him of FBIHQ's intent to transfer Mat as his ASAC. No one informed Bretzing of Mat's alleged administrative shortcomings. He determined on his own that Mat did not have the competence or the ability to perform his responsibilities. Neither Bretzing nor any other FBI official provided evidence of any remedial training program to help Mat. He did not recall introducing Mat to the LA office. Regular "working lunches" Bretzing acknowledged occurred with his other ASACs, but not with Mat, his principal relief.

The conduct of career boards was important in the selection of the most qualified persons for promotion, according to Bretzing. He testified that Mat had failed to keep documentation or consider the dimensions of the selection process, yet Bretzing did not address the missing documentation on his fellow Mormons Miller, Brooks, and Spilsbury. Under oath, Bretzing claimed he had Mormon Church and social connections with Spilsbury but that he was unsure if Spilsbury was a Mormon.

Mat alleged that Bretzing had traveled outside the division to Salt Lake City, that there was a failure to notify other SACs of his visits to other divisions, and that Bretzing had set up a protective detail of Mormon agents in LA for a high-ranking Mormon Church official. Mat also alleged that Bretzing favored Mormon agents in assignments and promotions, and that the FBI office replaced a car battery in a car belonging to Bretzing's daughter. The record reflected that the FBI found the allegations unpunishable within forty-eight hours. The bureau quickly resolved administrative inquiries regarding Bretzing; Mat's were not.

Bretzing testified that there was no favoritism shown toward Mormons in the LA office while he was SAC. Yet, he kept a Mormon Soviet spy on the payroll, restored a Mormon thief with a drug problem to the position of aircraft pilot, anointed a Mormon non-applicant to a polygrapher position, and set up a Mormon agent protective detail for a high-level Mormon Church official. FBI management honored Bretzing's word, affidavits, and sworn testimonies on the impossibility of him discriminating, instead trashing Hispanic agents' complaints against him. Circumstances may have been different had Bretzing shown the same passion in the discrimination complaints as he did for the Mormon Church. He retired from the FBI in 1988 and accepted a security position with the Mormon Church. Bretzing had boasted, the year before he quit the FBI, "Active Mormons don't step down from anything."[6]

The Book of Mormon describes a group of people known as the Lamanites as being "dark and loathsome" as they are cursed with dark skin because of their inequities. Bretzing denied that Mormons are "white and delightsome" or "pure and delightsome" but said he thought the phrases were somewhere in the Book of Mormon. When asked if the "dark and loathsome" Lamanites can go to the same Heaven as "white and delightsome" Mormons, he responded that all persons go to Heaven eventually.

In 1983, Bretzing reorganized the LA office, switching Mat from administrative ASAC to criminal ASAC. This was following Mat's withdrawal of an agreement for a voluntary reduction in which he was to step down to an assignment as a supervisor in Houston. Bretzing requested that FBIHQ remove Mat from the LA office because of Mat's lack of credibility and the ineffectiveness of the relationship between the two. Bretzing claimed his decision had nothing to do with retaliation. Mat had been through a traumatic experience in his removal as SAC San Juan, suffering indignity and embarrassment. He desired to spare Mat additional embarrassment, so he offered him the alternatives of stepping down or facing removal.

In an airtel to the director, dated October 8, 1985, Bretzing alleged that ASAC Perez had made false statements in the R. W. Miller spy trial. The DOJ sent a communication to FBIHQ dated February 2, 1987, advising that the DOJ would decline prosecution of Mat Perez on perjury allegations regarding the two Miller trials. Bretzing testified that he counseled Miller while on administrative inquiry on the allegations that he was a Soviet spy.

John T. Hall swore there was no favoritism shown toward Mormons, and no anti-Hispanic bias or retaliatory behavior by Bretzing directed toward Mat or anyone else. Hall testified that his primary assignment was to assist administrative ASAC Mat Perez, but Bretzing reassigned him away to other projects and did not think that relocating Mat two floors downstairs, away from Bretzing's office, made any difference.

James Nelson, the criminal ASAC in LA, confirmed that, although Bretzing introduced Nelson to the LA division as ASAC, Mat did not have an introduction. Although Bretzing briefed Nelson on his duties, Mat received no such briefing. Bretzing did not censure Nelson for appearing at an investigation without a suit, but Bretzing censured Mat. Although Mat was Nelson's superior while he was ASAC Los Angeles in charge of investigations, Nelson never briefed Mat on his cases, nor did he remember briefing Mat on a $6 million undercover operation in Palm Springs. Nelson testified that Bretzing was fair with Mat and that he saw no evidence of favoritism toward Mormons or any anti-Hispanic bias from Bretzing.

Ricardo Leon Estrada served as Executive Secretary under Bishop Bretzing at the Mormon Church Ward of Los Angeles and claimed he had never observed Bretzing discriminating against Hispanics. In response to the question, "When a Lamanite repents and becomes a member of the Mormon Church, do they become 'white and delightsome?' " Estrada responded, "That's an incorrect question; I cannot answer it." (The Book of Mormon described Lamanites as being "dark and loathsome" because of God's curse on the descendants of Laman for their wickedness and corruption:

> And he had caused the cursing to come upon [the Lamanites], yea, even a sore cursing, because of their iniquity. For behold, they had hardened their hearts against him, and they had become like unto a flint; wherefore, as they were white, and

> exceedingly fair and delightsome, that they might not be enticing unto my people the Lord God caused a skin of blackness to come upon them.

In contrast, for the Lamanites who embrace the book of Mormon: "… their scales of darkness shall fall from their eyes; and many generations shall not pass away among them, save they shall be a white and a delightsome people.")

51

Benito Perez, Jr.

Benito Perez, Jr., no relation to Mat Perez, was an El Paso police officer with eighteen years of law enforcement experience. He testified that on April 11, 1988, at about 12:30 p.m., he and his partner, Ed Uribe, left their office on the way to their field assignments. He noticed a vehicle parked across the street from the City-County Building. Inside the vehicle there was an individual holding a dark object. As they approached, they noticed that the individual had a camera with a telephoto lens and was photographing a group of individuals on their way down the steps of the Federal Courthouse. The vehicle had California license plates and was light brown in color. Benito turned to his left and observed the group of individuals leaving the courthouse, one of whom was Mat Perez. That night Benito saw a TV news report about the hearing regarding the Perez civil suit.

The following day, Benito saw Mat and told him about the photographer, whom Benito believed to be a federal agent because of the out-of-town plates on the car. Benito provided Mat with the license plate number of the vehicle.

On cross-examination, Benito stated that he did not approach the vehicle, identify the driver or follow up on the license plate number, as he believed it to be part of a government operation. He disagreed with the DOJ counsel, as he believed that any representative of the media would have stood on the street in front of the courthouse to take pictures and that he would have recognized a reporter in town because of his vast experience as a police officer.

52

JOSEPH R. HISQUIERDO

Joe Hisquierdo became an El Paso Police Department officer in 1964 and joined the FBI in 1968. He first served in the San Antonio, Texas, Brownsville RA, then in New York City, San Juan, and San Francisco, where he served as a supervisor.

Joe testified that he had seen discrimination in action in the FBI. He informed SAC Bill Beane that the large contingent of non-Spanish speakers in San Juan was unfair, as Spanish-speaking agents performed the bulk of the work, meaning they conducted interviews, solicited confessions, and assisted non-Spanish speakers with their work. However, they received no credit, monetary compensation or recognition, while the non-Spanish speaking agents received credit as the actual case agents. Joe saw the daily friction in the bullpen where the agents worked.

Beane told Joe flat out that this meant Joe must be a racist who did not like white people. Joe responded that, if that was the case, he would not be in the office discussing the matter with him and that he did not deserve a racist, troublemaker, nonconformist label, or told that he displayed negative attributes just because he had stated an uncomfortable truth.

During a subsequent inspection, the inspection staff, on a pretext, censured and placed Joe on probation in retaliation for his statements in the meeting with his SAC. Joe also saw Anglo, non-Spanish-speaking agents transferred to their office of preference and Anglo Spanish speakers who "forgot" their Spanish to be excused from wires and TDY assignments.

Joe made this heartfelt plea to the court:

> I have been in the FBI for 20 years. This badge and these credentials do not say pilot, they do not say Anglo, they do not say Spanish speaker, they do not say Puerto Rican, and they say nothing but that I am an FBI agent. For twenty years, I took to heart what you see on our logo, you know, fidelity, bravery and integrity. Promotions, assignments, transfers, the way we are handled in disciplinary matters in the bureau, there is no integrity.
>
> I only have maybe two to six years left in the bureau. I, with the 311 agents, want to see the bureau become better. I love the FBI; I am proud to be a Spanish-speaking agent for the FBI. I have a lot to offer the FBI, but I want to leave a legacy where the promotion system will be better for us, where the transfer system will be better for us, where the assignment of cases will be better for us, and when we have a grievance with the FBI we have a way to bring this to the attention of the FBI. They tell us here about the EEO we have available to us; it is a sham and a farce. There is just no way to bring these grievances to the forefront of our problems. I want to correct that. I want to make the FBI better so that when my son, like he asks me now about becoming an FBI agent and I tell him no. However, if we change it, then I will tell my son yes, I want you to be an FBI agent.

53

Edmundo Mireles, Jr.

Ed Mireles received a bachelor's degree in business administration from the University of Maryland. He had nine years of bureau experience at the time of the trial. He served five years at the Washington Field Office, and two years each in Miami and Quantico.

Ed was not a member of the Hispanic class action lawsuit and felt that if he wanted to sue somebody, he would sue as an individual. He explained that it was difficult for him to testify because, one year before the trial, he received the Attorney General's Award because of his actions on the day that two thugs shot and killed two Miami FBI agents in the line of duty. Ed had performed heroic acts while wounded.

Although the FBI recognized him for his heroism, he affirmed that, approximately four years prior to the lawsuit, he had suffered discrimination at the hands of the FBI. The DOJ attorneys and the FBI declined the opportunity to cross-examine his testimony.

At its beginning, Ed was unsure of the elements of the case; rumors, accusations, anger, and distrust ran rampant through field offices—it seemed the main goal was to vilify Mat—to label Mat as a traitor. Ed asked questions and learned the issues; he had issues of his own—perhaps they did not rise to the level of other agents—but issues still important to Ed and his family, so much so that he decided to support the case. Although it was not without conflict, not without heartburn, and not without question. He showed no fear on the stand, yet he testified with his head hung and his shoulders slumped. His voice cracked, and he rubbed his hands nervously as he told the court his personal experiences of discrimination—facing the similar problem of many Hispanic agents who had difficulty testifying to the truth of their FBI dysfunctional family.

Ed foresaw the outcome of the trial and thought that the bureau would be upset—upset that Mat would dare challenge management, upset that Hispanics would dare to sue, upset that the court was beyond their control, and upset about the negative publicity that would follow any revelations of discrimination and the violation of civil rights.

In his heart of hearts, Ed knew that the bureau acted with bias—bias against Hispanic agents—but unsure if the biases of the bureau stemmed from racism or if they were attributable to poor management and poor people skills. His testimony placed him in a difficult quandary; Ed disliked the word discrimination and attaching it to his beloved FBI and its agents made him sick to his stomach, yet he knew agents who were bigots—he had met them—and they were idiots. It was an era of egos, a time of arrogance, a time of power and a time when "Don't embarrass the bureau" applied to everyone but management, fixable problems went unrecognized, with management unable to admit to either the existence of a problem or the need for intervention.

A friend of Ed once told him that Ed appeared to be a supervisor's nightmare because he was not loyal to people but instead loyal to causes and principles. Ed regretted that the greatest law enforcement agency now had to own up to a problem—the mistreatment and mismanagement of its own agents—and the perpetuation of a culture of bias that led to the transgression of employee rights. The bureau could only become a better place and the organization as a whole would prosper when this era—in which the bureau treated support employees as peons, neglected to promote women, patronized blacks, and ignored Hispanic concerns—would end. The FBI needed transparency to learn from its own records; it needed to treat employees in a more fair and professional way. Ed would captain through his testimony, no matter the outcome, but he had a huge concern.

Ed wondered if the ideology of the FBI Family, the shared association of agents and support staff, would last. The concern for each other's work successes and failures—the shared joy at the birth of each other's children, at graduations, or weddings, group vacations, or just having someone listen and sympathize with problems, indiscretions, or divorces—was a worthwhile concern. Ed did not want his FBI Family to reject him again.

54

José Antonio Lopez

José Antonio Lopez, a US Marshal, Liaison in Organized Crime, Miami, joined the Marshal's service twenty-two years before the trial and headed the US Marshal's office in Puerto Rico from 1976 to 1981.

The FBI had several major ongoing investigations into the Puerto Rican Police and various terrorist groups while Mat was SAC in San Juan. When the Socialist and Communist parties picketed the courtroom, José worked closely with the Puerto Rican police. Mat's name came up when one of the officers stated that the Puerto Rican Police "had a camera on him [Mat], he had been under surveillance and that they really did him in." The officer told José that the police had even planted a microphone in Mat's bedroom.

In his opinion, although not in the opinion of the US Marshals Service, the Puerto Rican police had set Mat up because of the FBI investigation into police activities. Jose said, "The typical Latin manner is that we will neutralize him by going after his prestige, the job, or life." José saw these kinds of activities as a common practice in Latin America.

José, in defense of Yvonne Shaffer-Perez who worked for an attorney the FBI considered a socialist, testified that the University of Puerto Rico had a policy of assigning students, such as teachers, court reporters, or secretaries, to complete required public assignments as part of their practicum. Yvonne obtained employment with the attorney suspected of socialist ties through this same university practice. José's own mother, a teacher, and several other relatives experienced the same kinds of temporary assignments over the course of their educations. The university arranges these assignments, called practicums, and they last about a semester.

José worked well with SAC Clark Anderson of the FBI. The island considered Anderson an institution in Puerto Rico; he was a down-to-earth agent who was familiar with Puerto Rican culture. The transition from Clark Anderson to Mat Perez was easy since, when Mat arrived in Puerto Rico, he spoke Spanish, was interested in Spanish literature, Puerto Rican culture, show horses and scuba diving. He was a total professional and he responded immediately to calls from the US Marshals. One clear contrast was that José never observed SAC Anderson going out on arrests in the Puerto Rican community; however, he knew that Mat was more "hands-on" and that Mat supervised Major Cases from the street while he was SAC in San Juan.

55

Phillip E. Jordan

Phil Jordan, born in El Paso, Texas, was the SAC in the Dallas Division of the Drug Enforcement Administration (DEA). He had been with DEA for twenty-three years at the time of the trial.

Phil testified that an 1811 series agent under DEA regulations is a criminal investigator, synonymous with an FBI agent. The DEA is principally responsible for narcotics enforcement and works many cases in concert with the FBI; there is concurrent jurisdiction in the US on drug investigations. In 1981, FBI Agent Francis "Bud" M. Mullen, Jr. became the Administrator of the DEA. Phil identified Administrators John "Jack" C. Lawn and Deputy Administrator Tom Kelly as former FBI agents who transferred over to the DEA. There are over 2,500 DEA agents; approximately 278 are Hispanic. Hispanic DEA agents comprise more than 10% of the agency's workforce, compared to the FBI's 4%. The DEA employs approximately fifteen Hispanic GS-15s, about fifty Hispanic GS-14s and five Hispanic SACs. Phil credited Mullen, Lawn, and Kelly, all former FBI administrators, with promoting Hispanics in the DEA.

On cross-examination, Phil testified that he learned the purpose of his testimony ten minutes before he took the witness stand, and he was on annual leave when the court notified him to report to El Paso. The FBI and the DEA have ongoing joint investigations and task forces on drug cases. The DEA has nineteen divisions in the US and maintains a permanent presence in major cities such as Los Angeles, Miami, New York, Atlanta, Dallas, and Houston. Phil had never conducted a statistical survey of Hispanic representation in the DEA. He did not know the specific allegations and could not comment on any case. Phil confirmed that he had never been executive assistant director of the FBI, nor had he ever been a congressman charged with establishing the "needs of the bureau."

56

The FBI Resists the Verdict and Change

Hispanics of Mexican-American descent have an added reason to celebrate Cinco de Mayo because, on that date in 1989, Judge Bunton found the FBI guilty of employment discrimination against Hispanic agents. That evening, after the long-awaited announcement of the verdict as the trial ended in August 1988, Leo Gonzales and other Hispanic agents in El Paso went to Mat's house with their families to celebrate. While Leo himself celebrated with laughter and hallelujahs, the only white woman in the group cautioned, "You guys won, but none of you know what is coming your way." Barbara Cooper Gonzales, Leo's wife and a native of Port Arthur, Texas, suspected reprisals were still to come from a suspected angry "good ol' boy" network managing the FBI. There was reason for concern.

During the trial and in the interim before the judge rendered his decision, Hispanic agents heard through the grapevine that some Anglo citizens of El Paso had advised Judge Bunton not to rule in favor of the plaintiffs. Following his decision, they suggested he not award any damages. Judge William S. Sessions, a long-time friend of Bunton's and a fellow Texas judge who served as the Senior Judge for the Western District of Texas, had in the interim been appointed director of the FBI. He would now implement the changes ordered by the court with the implication that there would be a "hands off" remedy that allowed the FBI to make the requisite changes without strict court supervision.

In its findings, the court detected numerous flaws in the statistical database provided by the FBI and their hired expert, Dr. Rebecca Klemm. The bureau had neglected to keep systematic, accurate, or comprehensive records that may have been helpful in the FBI's attempt to disprove the findings of disparate conditions of employment experienced by members of the plaintiff class. Dr. Klemm based her statistical summary, titled "Temporary Duty Assignments and Spanish Language Usage," on the bureau's personnel information numbering system, combined with a competitive promotions database she prepared from career board minutes, her interviews with bureau personnel, and a summary of temporary duty assignments in 1987 and 1988 provided to her by the bureau.[7]

The court discounted the probative worth of several FBI exhibits. The evidence presented by the FBI omitted temporary assignments within a field office; there were often "informal," out-of-the-office, temporary duty assignments not reported to the bureau; summaries did not reflect joint wiretap assignments with the Drug Enforcement Administration or state police authorities; and there had been no systematic manner of classifying Spanish-language assignments. One incredible, erroneous exhibit produced by the FBI that compared Spanish-related assignments showed that there were no undercover assignments during fiscal year 1987 when there were many. The FBI could not rebut the testimony of class members assigned to Spanish-speaking temporary duty assignments in which the FBI did not use them for that purpose or in which management cautioned agents not to speak Spanish.[6]

Dr. Klemm asserted that Hispanics, on average, apply for the same number of positions as non-Hispanics with about the same success rate. The court reported,

> Dr. Klemm concluded that Hispanics have unrealistic expectations for advancement within the bureau. This is a monumental leap in reasoning. Dr. Klemm's conclusion did not account for the findings that: (1) Hispanics have been discouraged from

> applying for positions, (2) the promotional system has not fully documented the actual applicant pool, (3) the contribution of Hispanics to the bureau has not been reflected in the agent's administrative profile, and (4) Hispanic special agents have been prevented from training and from experiencing opportunities which better prepare them for advancement.
>
> The FBI did not incorporate performance ratings and MAP records, nor attempt to incorporate the disparate conditions of employment found by this court into the study. There was no consideration of differences in opportunities to acquire broad professional experience and training. The omissions from Dr. Klemm's model require this court to discount Dr. Klemm's database and her conclusion that Hispanics have unrealistic expectations for advancement. The court was unpersuaded by such testimony.[6]

In response to the Performance Appraisal System, the court found that "(1) Hispanic agents suffer disparate treatment in the conditions of their employment, and (2) those conditions affect their promotional opportunities in an adverse manner."[6] The court's findings related to Title III wiretap duty, undercover assignments, other temporary duty assignments, and ad hoc investigatory assistance to fellow agents utilizing their linguistic skills, concluding that the FBI failed to credit the contribution of Hispanic agents.[6]

On promotions, the FBI argued that first, Hispanics are not victims of discrimination; second, that the "needs of the bureau" require the appointment of the most qualified person to fill supervisory positions; and third, that class-wide incidents of promotional discrimination did not exist. However, the court determined that the FBI did not have in place the means to determine the most qualified person for promotion, and this prevented class members from gaining the professional experience and training afforded to non-Hispanics.[6]

The Management Assessment Program (MAP) was an effort to measure critical abilities that would ensure the success of field supervisors and enable using those measurements to select FBI supervisors. MAP was the best tool available, making subjective evaluations as fair, organized, and systematic as possible while providing an objective tool to evaluate candidates. However, while FBIHQ gave field offices the sole discretion to select those who would attend MAP, the FBI did not monitor the selection of candidates for MAP.[6]

With Legat assignments, the court received no evidence to refute the charges that a Hispanic never served in a non-Spanish speaking nation, even when Hispanics spoke additional languages. Hispanics routinely staffed only a single South American post in which conditions were hazardous. Hispanic agents received far fewer placements to Legat assignments in Spanish-speaking countries than their Anglo counterparts did, even though they are uniquely qualified for these. The bureau never articulated a legitimate business reason to justify the past practices requiring injunctive relief.[6]

The court found convincing evidence that, prior to 1985, the FBI ordered Hispanic special agents to submit to testing for Spanish language capability while non-Hispanic language speakers "opted out" of their language skill.[6] Spanish speakers with Anglo surnames were overlooked for Spanish-speaking assignments.

The judge of the court determined that the FBI EEO program had not accomplished the goals that Congress envisioned in devising the EEO program and warranted serious restructuring. The court targeted insufficient training for EEO counselors, the systemic failure to study FBI promotional processes, and practices that created a significant danger of retaliation by superiors in response to a grievance. The court identified the FBI EEO program as "bankrupt."[6]

In addressing Mat, the court found the articulated reasons given to justify adverse employment decisions to be a pretext for retaliation against him for protected EEO activity. Management infused Mat's performance evaluations with retaliatory animosity and played a role in the adverse employment decisions, as did the fact that the bureau illegally secured a grand jury subpoena and then used the subpoenaed materials in an administrative investigation of Mat without leave of the court.[6]

Perez served at the level of SAC in San Juan but received a demotion to the position of ASAC in Los Angeles. In Los Angeles, the SAC prevented Mat from accomplishing the job of administrative ASAC for what were discriminatory reasons and later, in retaliation for protected activity. His transfer to El Paso related to ongoing retaliation against him by supervisors within the bureau. The judge ordered Mat's promotion to the rank of GS-17 with the related compensation and privileges that attend that rank. The court also ordered the FBI to pay all attorney fees.[6]

The court implemented mandatory injunction of "Rightful Place Seniority" (RPS) as a remedy for Hispanic class members to present their requests justifying promotion. "Special masters" appointed were former US District Judge Susan Getzendanner; University of Texas professor Barbara Jordan, who was also a former member of the Congress from Texas; and W. Edwin Youngblood, an arbitrator and former federal administrative law judge in Fort Worth.

The judge authorized the Rightful Place Seniority Panel to recommend agents for promotion to a higher grade and position. They first had to consider the extent of an agent's superior rating for performance; second, the receipt of any special award or commendation that did not translate into an expected promotion; third, high MAP scores; fourth, evidence that fellow non-Hispanic agents with similar experience had been promoted; and finally, evidence of undercover work or temporary duty assignments to a degree that other investigative experiences or training had been foregone. The panel weighed the issues of each individual's degree of disparate conditions of employment, any causal connection of disparate condition to failure to advance, any undervalued contribution, and if the recommended position was commensurate with their experience and abilities.[6]

The court rejected the FBI's contention that certain disparate conditions of employment or promotional opportunities were justified because the entrance criteria for minority agents were credited points, a similar advantage provided to military veterans. However, the court gave the bureau the opportunity to respond to each charge of discrimination, and the bureau could produce evidence that some Hispanic agents were not yet ready for promotion. Prior to the hearings, the bureau promoted a few agents to demonstrate their approach of good faith.[6]

All Hispanic agents before the panel received promotions with the singular exception of Paul Nolan, who never served on a Spanish-speaking wiretap or any similar assignment.[8] Although the FBI promoted Ray Campos, Ed Guevara, and Armand Lara prior to the Rightful Place Seniority hearings, the legal division set out to rally divisions to dispel and counter the court's findings and resist the promotion of Hispanic class members through the RPS panel.

One such division was the Office of Liaison and International Affairs (OLIA), a group overseen by Buck Revell. Martin V. Hale and Stanley A. Pimentel of OLIA continued their ongoing efforts to thwart Hispanic class members' opportunities for Legat assignments. This was in direct contradiction of Director Sessions' memorandum, which stated, "There is no higher priority than to ensure that the FBI provide an environment which guarantees every employee the dignity which he or she deserves."[9]

In preparation for the RPS hearings, the legal division tasked OLIA to provide evidence to support the reason for the lack of Hispanic agents to foreign assignments as legal attachés.

On December 20, 1989, Pimentel, a unit chief in OLIA under penalty of perjury, drafted an official declaration to the court, which stated that Hispanic class members lacked sufficient FBIHQ time, which he declared to be a prerequisite for foreign assignments. He stated that, in the long history of the FBI, there had been three exceptions made, and he then named the three agents. Pimentel neglected to mention his assignment to a Legat position, an assignment he also received without ever having to go through FBIHQ. One can understand that errors might creep into a report in a time of extreme pressure and stress, but it did not appear to be a simple mistake. SSA Sam Martinez then produced a list of forty-five agents assigned to Legat positions, each of whom served in Legats without serving at FBIHQ, which showed a difference of forty-two names.[10]

Pimentel denied a plaintiff Title VII access to documents when he sought redress, denied access to supporting documentation in response to a charge when such documents existed in the file, provided false information to a career board to have two Anglos placed first and second in the selection process, and documented in writing that he opposed Judge Bunton's decision in the class action suit. He made false charges that a plaintiff compromised a Confidential Source Abroad (CSA), provided false information to demote a class member, initiated Office of Professional Responsibilities (OPR) complaints against a plaintiff, and continued to take these kinds of irresponsible actions against a class member no longer even assigned to the same division. In addition, he requested the removal of a plaintiff from a Legat office in retaliation for the plaintiff's attempts to secure his civil rights.[11,12,13,14,15] The bureau chose not to reprimand Pimentel for his pervasive behavior in denying opportunities to class members. Instead, he received a promotion, validating that attacks against Hispanic class members were signs of loyalty to their noble cause.[16]

Martin V. Hale, as the Deputy Inspector in Charge of OLIA, assisted John Walser in reducing the charges of misconduct and allegations of discrimination against him so that Walser could receive a bureau transfer to his office of choice. Hale refused to provide Sam Martinez a copy of the affidavit when he added a paragraph containing the text, "My perception of Title 18, Section 1001, of the US Criminal Code pertaining to the falsification of an official document is not limited to the altering of an existing document as described to me by Mr. Hale." Hale, by way of Buck Revell and the transfer unit, retaliated in orchestrating the transfer of Sam to Los Angeles, which was known as a hostile environment headed by a SAC under several EEO investigations.[17]

In another obvious attempt to prevent class member promotions, the OLIA neglected to report to the panel that, in September of 1988, Buck Revell and the OLIA acknowledged that the bureau had difficulty staffing Legat offices in countries because of the limited number of FBI linguists. In citing the need to optimize professionalism, they set in place a policy in which a level 3 rating would become the minimum level for a Legat representative in a foreign country, while level 4 became the actual "representational level."[18]

Revell's "Buck Board" paid no attention to the judge's ruling concerning career board hearings. Hale neglected his obligation to forward to the career board applications for Legat positions. On a matrix he and Pimentel prepared, they omitted the awards and commendations of class members, ensuring ratings and specialties were unlike those of non-Hispanic applicants in the matrix. The "fix was in" for the position of Legat Montevideo.[19]

Agent Stephen P. Walker was the innocent beneficiary when the "Buck Board" made him appear as if he walked on water and confirmed him to the Legat Montevideo position before the career board evaluated any applicant. The FBI tested Walker at a level 1+ rating in Spanish. One non-Hispanic agent had a higher language rating than Walker, while four of the Hispanic applicants, having met all other qualifications and experience, had a level 4 or above language rating in Spanish. Hale, who spoke no Spanish, represented to the career board that Walker, having undergone no additional testing, was now a "strong level 3 Spanish speaker." MAP records showed that several Hispanic applicants to Montevideo had no management contingencies while Walker did.

During an inspection in Mexico City, where Walker served as an assistant legal attaché, Special Agent Carlis Sabinson cited, "A review of files assigned to Mr. Walker reflected deficiencies." The inspectors noted that Walker violated policy by commingling his personal funds with the US government's petty cash fund for the Legat office. Further, the inspection found Legat Rick Lang's supervision of Walker was "less than effective and efficient." The report found Walker "effective but inefficient" in his investigative cases, although Hale reported to the career board and the Rightful Place Seniority Panel that Walker was effective and efficient in Mexico. Hale had embellished other achievements of Walker.

Even with Federal Court instructing the FBI career boards be tape-recorded, the "needs of the bureau" continued to work behind the scenes, displaying selected agents as if they walked on water and leaving others in mud. The FBI should have recognized that management had shaped applicants to beat the system, and this type of system was harmful to all agents and the agency.[20,21]

Through discovery, SSA Sam Martinez reviewed the career board meeting for a position in Mexico for which he had applied.

He noticed his name missing, which prevented any consideration for promotion. Sam reported the incident to the Rightful Place Seniority Panel (RPSP), telling the panel that he told Hale that Connie Adkins typed the application and that Hale failed to forward his application to the career board in retaliation for his ongoing EEO complaint. In response to the RPSP for clarification, Hale had his secretary Lynn Vissers-Leach produce a statement to the RPSP stating that she did not type the missing application and did not know of it. Neither Hale nor the FBI asked Connie Adkins any investigative questions.

Even after the judge ordered the recording of career board meetings, the FBI saw its way around the ruling. During one session chaired by John Guido on the selection of a Legat, Richard C. Staver waved his arm up and down toward Stan Pimentel, indicating he wanted the recorder off when a black candidate came up for discussion. After Pimentel stopped the recorder, Staver mentioned the candidate's sexual adventures while serving as an ASAC. The discussion continued among panel members until Sam informed the panel that a person's character should be part of the selection process as are administrative or OPR inquiries, and the judge's order made no exceptions to recording career board meetings. Guido ordered Pimentel to restart the recorder, and that was Sam's last participation in a career board meeting.

OLIA was not the only division or section at FBIHQ pressured to resist court-ordered remediation. From the trial, there were allegations of perjury on both sides. Mat learned of two separate investigations that addressed the alleged misconduct of agents during the trial. There were no actions taken on the allegations of misconduct filed by Hispanics against non-class members, although Hispanics testified in court with supporting documentation.

The EEOC did nothing when EEO officers themselves suffered retribution. The FBI coerced Gil Mireles, a presumable poster child for the FBI, into becoming an EEO counselor. Gil was the security officer for the Miami Division, the Hispanic program coordinator, a SWAT team member and instructor, the sniper team leader, and an FBI instructor for firearms and defensive tactics who had nothing less than great performance appraisals. He initiated a Major Case entitled CUBIR, served as the case agent and acting supervisor of the squad, all the while coordinating the law enforcement efforts of several agencies and military intelligence departments. However, when he followed up on a complaint of discrimination, the EEOC, the DOJ and the FBI turned against him, and his career went downhill just as it did with other EEO investigators and officers. Rather than welcoming counselors back into the group and acknowledging serious problems, management instead kept counselors at arm's length, threw them to the wolves, or forced them out of service. The leadership refused to change.

Director William S. Sessions, who inherited the shameful burden of the lawsuit from Webster, was the man tasked with making the changes ordered by the federal court. The lingering misinformation, animosity, and divisiveness from the court decision caused Sessions to send an airtel to all agents in January 1992 that provided a summary of Bunton's decision.[22] With DOJ consultation and concurrence, Director Sessions chose not to appeal the lawsuit, which many of the executive directors and SACs in the field offices begged him to do.

Director Sessions then discovered that the bureau was as dark as the deepest ocean, an unfamiliar and alien place, a place in which he, a good Christian who also believed in the perfectibility of man and who never doubted the good works of the FBI that he observed in his courtroom during his time as a federal judge, would be frustrated and stymied. It was inconceivable to Director Sessions that he should find himself drowning in a sea of sharks that snapped and bit and nipped and nibbled and nitpicked him out of office, a group he referred to as a "cabal."

Complaints and anonymous allegations funneled to the DOJ charged Director Sessions with ethical improprieties that resulted in a finding of "serious deficiencies in judgment." One criticism was that the director had used the FBI plane to travel to visit his daughter. No one in the FBI ever complained to the DOJ about Webster's travels to various field offices where he skied or played tennis under the pretense of delivering speeches to the Boy Scouts, and the bureau ignored Mat's allegation that Bretzing had used a bureau plane for personal Mormon Church business. The fact that Sessions had a security system and a fence installed at his home became a cause célèbre, while the legal attachés who served under him had permanent fences and security systems of their choice installed at their rented homes during their short-term assignments.

Agents complained of a protection detail that drove Sessions' wife, Alice, to public places and never stopped to consider the negative publicity that would have ensued if assassins had kidnapped, assaulted, or killed her. Agents, who first suggested it to the director, complained that the director "unethically" brought home some firewood on a bureau plane from a location he had visited. Because Sessions refused to appeal the verdict in the Hispanic civil lawsuit, all of the usual deference stopped. Many agents stood by silent, since many no doubt had observed wood, groceries, hardware, personal tools, or Amway products in the trunks of bureau cars.[23] Although Director Sessions served six years and fought back against the charges of these managers, internal dissension due to the lawsuit and other incidents proved too strong. In the end, those who plotted forced Sessions out on July 19, 1993.

57

Change is Slow

With the Civil Rights Act of 1964 and the establishment of the Equal Employment Opportunity Commission (EEOC) in 1965, one would speculate that managers, well versed in the long-standing regulations of the US Government, would have corrected equal opportunity. However, poor management decisions and predetermined investigations have created problems for employee claims. The more perfect union will never come about if the EEOC refuses to respect complaints, neglects negotiations, ignores wrongs in society, continues to discharge its authority with a defensive mentality without open discussion, refuses to acknowledge that managers make mistakes, and neglects to identify the degrees of discrimination. No one lives without discrimination, whether it is incidental or deliberate.

Our educational system is replete with underfunded school districts and discrimination against teachers and students. Unequal pay for the same work still exists. Diversity is restricted. Religious people of one faith discriminate against those of another. Religious organizations may preach forgiveness and advise loving thy neighbor, yet discriminate against those who do not share their sexual orientation.[24] Regressive political leaders resist initiating the expansion of voting rights to minority communities. Skin color affects public opinion on immigration issues.[25] Yet as Americans, we proclaim ourselves "on top" in all areas of accomplishment when compared to the rest of the world. We have room for improvement.

The common denominator is that management and employees make mistakes. Victims who perceive discrimination deserve no discredit. Victims have rights to think, see, hear, and feel what they have thought, seen, heard, and felt, and not what someone else thinks or wants them to think, see, hear, and feel.[26,27,28] These are the rights given to both supervisors and employees, and each should affirm the underlying sense of respect.

Thousands of stories highlight FBI personnel and the organization's great strides in inculcating sound values by following and believing in the FBI motto of fidelity, bravery and integrity, yet law enforcement personnel make mistakes, as does everyone in every profession. Both organizations and individuals fall out of step. How the individuals in an organization respond to a situation can either hinder its reputation or enhance its growth. "Incompetent," "treacherous," "greedy," "dishonest," "self-centered," "narrow-minded," and zealot" are epithets leveled against employees of the FBI such as Richard Miller, Robert Hanssen, Darrin McAllister, Michael Malone, Donald Sachtleben, John Connolly, Edward Preciado-Nuno, or Mary Beth Kepner.[29,30,31,32,33,34,35,36,37] The appellations cited are not those with which the FBI wishes to be associated. Most of the investigations covered by the FBI's Office of Professional Responsibility concern violations of the "four B's": Bucks, Booze, Broads, or Bucars (bureau cars).

Management relegated Hispanic agents to a segregated work environment known as the "Taco Circuit" that affected not all Spanish speakers but agents with Hispanic surnames, and these agents received forced assignments to Puerto Rico and other offices. Supervisors compelled Hispanics to translate Spanish into English, even when they spoke minimal Spanish. They found themselves delegated to investigative assignments based on their Hispanic surnames, and management directed Hispanics to work undercover assignments with no training. Management undervalued Hispanic agents' work records for their work contributions, colleagues stereotyped Hispanics by name-calling, and management promoted Hispanics at a rate much lower than Anglos.

The failings of FBI management and the letdown of the EEOC process motivated three quarters of the agency's Hispanic FBI agents; 311 of the approximate 400 supported the *Perez v. FBI* lawsuit. This number affirmed the allegations that the FBI, the agency charged with investigating discrimination and enforcing federal laws, was both in theory and in practice discriminatory in its employment practices for a perceived noble cause.[38] The Hispanic group of various experiences and high education understood unfairness by the FBI, the DOJ, and the EEOC. To identify discrimination meant displaying examples in the degrees of discrimination—that discrimination is favoritism, bias, unfair policy, disparate treatment to policy, inequitable evaluations, inaction to issues, retaliation to complaints, bigotry and breaking laws.

One expects law enforcement officers to hold themselves to a higher standard of ethics than ordinary citizens, even in equal opportunity, but management can innocently make disparate decisions. People find it difficult to believe how often their decisions affect others in an insensitive or discriminatory manner.

Discrimination is a choice, and we make choices every day. We choose foods that exclude tastes, choose clothing that excludes other styles, or choose a religion that excludes other beliefs. We root for our beliefs and cheer for our side. We are a species blessed with both rational and instinctual choices from implicit bias, yet we are wired to trust and mistrust. Mark Cuban, owner of the NBA team Dallas Mavericks, described the "fight or flight" form of discrimination[39] inherent in our amygdala as we easily fear or worry of the unfamiliar and stereotype based on our family, associations, and society.[40] Discrimination is not necessarily evil, but it can become so. When someone asks individuals if they discriminate, they would likely automatically respond that they *do not,* because the word has such negative connotations, even though a discriminating person can be a person of distinction, and yet we neglect discussing most issues on discrimination.

Bias is evident in all life, including in plants, as they accept elements and reject others.[41] We side with what we are familiar with. Bias forms from associations and professions, which can extend into discrimination. Law enforcement officers serve and protect their own first before they serve and protect the community. It is common for officers and agents to first take the side of a fellow officer and distrust Internal Affairs, although Internal Affairs represents a higher authority, i.e. the agency or policy should come before a fellow officer.

FBI management and field agents already had an "us and them" or "in or out" mentality about other law enforcement agencies. Agents, like all humans, have strong desires to be part of a group and to affirm this association publicly—come what may. Our affiliations begin as children and continue to develop through ever-expanding relationships with our teams or families. We become insiders while others are outsiders.[42] If a group member makes a poor decision, supporters or team members close ranks and continue to follow the leader and remain members of the pack.[43] The partisan silences behind the scandals at Penn State, the Catholic Church, etc., are examples of members willing to put their teams ahead of ethics.[44,45]

Group affiliation may cause us to become lazy in our thinking process, and our judgment may become impaired for the sake of the group, even when our leaders prove self-serving or even wrong.[46,47] Misstating our attributes takes little effort; making personal adjustments, or changing direction is much more difficult. It is so much simpler to wrap ourselves in our flag or hide behind letters or symbols than it is to step outside ourselves to become rational, objective observers identifying the unknown by discrimination.

Discrimination based on implicit attitudes acquired through Anglo socialization of "good ol' boy" management reinforced their power to neglect or misinterpret policy. From the comfortable venue of this position, inertia grew and made its way to Director Webster and top management, affecting operations and manifesting itself in something more than "the needs of the bureau," leading Judge Bunton to the finding of systemic discrimination.

The *Perez v. FBI* lawsuit laid bare nine days of testimony, cross-examination, and evidence of discriminatory and unfair FBI work practices. United States Magistrate Janet Ruesch, Judge Bunton, and the court understood the degrees of discrimination. Well-meaning managers and legislators produced undetected systemic policies that have unintended hidden outcomes that create damaged relationships. Although well intended, some policies have unequal and disparate circumstances that lead to anger and despair. Systemic discrimination can exist even when individual discrimination does not. No one designed the FBI's "good ol' boy" system to create animosity towards Hispanic FBI agents; on the contrary, non-Hispanics witnessed the value and the successes of Hispanic agents without hatred.

If hate were the only factor in discrimination, then perhaps Donald Sterling, the former owner of the NBA's Los Angeles Clippers, is not a racist. He expressed approval of his friend V. Stiviano having sex with black men, yet Sterling's elitist culture marginalizes racial equality by disapproving public association with blacks, even if it is Magic Johnson.[48] Likewise, the high-end storekeeper did not display hate when she dissuaded Oprah Winfrey from her free will in seeking to purchase an expensive handbag.[49] An FBI agent asked a Hispanic class member, "What's this lawsuit about? We don't hate you guys. We may hate the blacks, but we don't hate you." Too many people associate racism and discrimination with hate when they are much more complex. The *Perez v. FBI* lawsuit was not about hate. It was about Director Webster and his top management team making executive decisions that excluded Hispanic agents from receiving promotions, credit for their work, fair assignments, and led to Hispanic agents becoming locked out of the "good ol' boy" network—a network of "like-kind" comfort, favoritism, and preferences with exclusions.

Hispanic agents complained to management and then to the Equal Employment Opportunity Commission (EEOC) with no corrective actions. Individual complaints became a systemic issue. Systemic discrimination turned evil when FBI management, with the support of the EEOC and the Department of Justice (DOJ), set aside its investigative prowess to suppress the voice of Hispanics, retaliated against those agents seeking work and appraisal in a fair environment, produced invalid court exhibits, and then violated laws for a perceived noble cause.

Hispanic class members could not control FBI management's decisions, but they could control how they responded to the systemic discrimination.

As a law enforcement agency, the FBI does its job well. The specialized training, the education of its agents, the sense of purpose behind assignments, the personal responsibility of its agents, and the interest in and guidance of laws bring glory to the FBI. Agents of diverse backgrounds and cultures enjoy the glorious concept and achievements of the FBI.

Law enforcement officers investigate incidents and share a conservative approach to civil and criminal violations. When an arrest occurs, officers do not want to listen to excuses, mitigating circumstances, societal pressures, temporary insanity pleas, and other rationalizations. To officers, a crime is a crime, and a violation is a violation. After a criminal act occurs, an investigation starts; investigators conduct interviews, collect evidence, write reports, and take actions. All focus is on the incident to solve the crime.

A fraud investigation requires the finding of false representation of fact, whether by words or by conduct, by false or misleading allegations, or by concealment of a required disclosure that deceived another so that the individual acted upon it to their legal detriment. Investigations into murder, rape, and/or civil actions all follow a standard process and procedure, yet the court found that the FBI's EEO investigators followed a bankrupt process and procedure that led Hispanics to file a class action lawsuit.

Law enforcement officers, EEO investigators, and the EEOC itself know that a person who forces sex on a victim in one incident is a rapist. The same is true for a thief, killer, molester, abuser, etc. Rapists do not sexually assault everyone they meet, just as robbers do not steal from every person or place they encounter. They wait for an opportunity, and that opportunity creates the incident. However, the EEOC refused to label any authority with a finding of discrimination, even when that official attempted to ruin the career of an employee in more than one instance. Instead, the EEOC allowed discriminatory officials to hide behind a variety of declarations, and these evasions justified the EEOC's automatic decisions. Statements of association such as "my brother-in-law is black," "In the past, I selected a woman for a promotion," or "I adopted three Asian children," should be immaterial to EEOC investigators as they must instead concentrate on the facts related to the case in hand.

The facts of the incident in relation to policy, regulation, and law should be the principle focus. EEO investigators must investigate complaints with the possibility that a person has a causal connection to an incident that affects someone in a protected class. The EEOC must determine if an incident is disparate or adverse compared to a discriminatory official's past habits or in violation of established policy.[50,51,52]

The EEOC and the FBI needed changes. Within the FBI, proper training did not occur, higher-ups trumped complaints from subordinates, developing a negative cycle in which no one considered authority wrong. Program managers restricted authority, investigations, and negotiations, and they imposed sanctions that punished those trained to handle EEO complaints. Pre-set decisions continued to allow discriminatory practices and delayed implementing fairness in the workplace. Even now, the EEOC must fall back less on their findings on complaints with "No Reasonable Cause" that represent 66% of their reported statistics from 2013, or finding only 4% of complaints taken with "Reasonable Cause."[53]

When an agent filed an EEO complaint of discrimination, the investigation began with counselors who conducted restricted interviews, collected documents, and wrote reports, but management neglected to consider the side of the complainant. A discriminatory official's sterling background took precedence over the alleged incident. Deference to organizational structure or deference to a person because of his or her position should have its place, but supervisors make mistakes, as do employees. The EEOC should not claim that a person cannot possibly be a discriminatory official because there is no clear proof that he or she discriminates twenty-four hours a day, seven days a week.

It serves no purpose for the EEOC to demand crystal-clear proof that the discriminatory official is anti-black, anti-Hispanic, anti-female, anti-disabled, anti-religious, anti-gay or discriminates based on age. For the EEOC to rule against a discriminatory official, they insisted on incontrovertible proof to support the contention that the discriminatory official discriminates consistently. Clear evidence of favoritism and disparate treatment was evident, and authorities made excuses, mitigated the circumstances, rationalized why there could be no finding of discrimination, and sided with the authority figure. The FBI endorsed the same policy, justifying any wrongdoing uncovered as necessitated by "the needs of the bureau."[54]

The FBI must hire the right people and should consider psychological entrance testing that determines what actions are taken when faced with two or more values. The extensive background checks conducted by the FBI in recruiting and hiring are exhaustive. A puzzled "Who did your background?" is a common quip among FBI friends when a goof occurs. Background checks do not look for the difference between right and wrong or self-interest. While the John Quinones TV program *What Would You Do?* exemplifies the truth that some take action and some avoid involvement despite how wrong the situation is, just doing the right thing most of the time is not a high enough standard for law enforcement.[55] Judgment, and how a law enforcement officer prioritizes, selects, and responds when confronted by two or more wrongs, are important and should be tested in any selection process to identify applicants that fit the country's values.

The United States Federal Court found Director William H. Webster and the FBI guilty of systemic discrimination against Hispanic agents. The court found that the FBI and upper-level management intervened in Mat Perez's private life and failed to grant Mat, as the Special Agent in Charge of San Juan Division, the resources, financial help, support and agents his division required to address four Major Cases: a police corruption case and three other cases in which terrorists bombed United States military property, and ambushed and killed US Navy sailors by machine guns. Mat prophesied his demotion before an office inspection with predictable, predetermined results. His ASAC, Harry "Skip" Brandon, who testified that there was no discrimination, later identified retaliation by the inspection staff, "I know a hit when I see it."

The FBI lost the lawsuit by losing the core processes of execution and the essential behaviors of an organization. The alleged "needs of the bureau" served narrow interests placed over and above the well-being of the true noble cause: the organization. Management limited the capabilities of its agents and carelessly made unfair decisions regarding their people, not just Hispanics. Management disregarded its obligation to investigate realism and follow through. Contributing further was the misunderstanding of the whole concept of disparate treatment, the in-group mentality, and the FBI's unwillingness to cure itself of administrative policies gone wrong.[56]. The FBI's violation of laws, not the Hispanic lawsuit, embarrassed the bureau.

Management audacity squandered the FBI's mighty accomplishments, its reputation as the greatest law enforcement agency in the world, and the goodwill of so many, by allowing the Hispanic lawsuit to go public. After the lawsuit, FBI management made reluctant and modest improvements in promoting Hispanic agents qualified for advancement, offering a reticent opportunity.

While FBI field agents, at gatherings, often voiced their concerns about management and its unfair decisions before the 1987 lawsuit, *Mat Perez v. The FBI,* most kept mum when Hispanics certified their class action lawsuit.[57] Instead, with no investigative interest as to the cause, most Anglo agents resented Hispanic agents airing the FBI's dirty laundry, even though the lawsuit pertained to management and resulted from management's disparate decisions. Angry and proud, fellow agents failed to recognize the benefit of a system of fairness that the protected class of Hispanics could bring into the promotion process—a process about which most agents complained. Sadly, agents with badges stood silent on the sidelines, apathetic about the direction taken by top management toward violations apparent within their organization. There were no thousand points of light, no shining badges, only a dim glimmer of credentials from a few altruistic agents who had the courage to stay true to their investigative duty and oath of office.

The FBI could have led other agencies forward after this setback. It could have reviewed its management assessment program, could have reevaluated its promotion and selection systems, and reconstructed its EEO program. Instead, bitter about the court's mandate for change, management put little thought or effort into accomplishing anything greater than that which Judge Bunton ordered. The FBI and EEOC neglected to see a major flaw in the EEO program.

Freedom is the concept amplified for all Americans with the extension of free will and choices. People make choices every day from habit but rarely recognize how much their personal choices may infringe on the rights of others. Engagement in discriminatory behavior is also a choice made from free will. As a government, Americans should only restrict free will when it unfairly impinges on the rights of others. The government should protect those freedoms and impose laws on those who would stand in the way of others. The EEOC must understand the ease of disparate treatment due to our upbringing, education, and habits, or because of the groups we have joined. It is easy to cross over that line where our actions affect others and prevent our country from forming that "more perfect union" of which the preamble to the US Constitution speaks.

In terms of fairness and equality advancing for all citizens, America has advanced slowly toward the representation of the revolutionary promises of 1776 and 1789. Perhaps it would have not taken so long for the constitutional guarantees of fairness and equality to become reality if those in leadership positions had early on embraced the expanded vision in the language of our Constitution, if those in power had shown a willingness to enforce written laws, and if their actions were balanced and fair. Even seven years after passing the Civil Rights Act of 1964, the FBI continued to block women from FBI positions, although the legislation stated applicants for appointment should not be restricted to one sex. The FBI held, with no objection from the EEOC, "our policy is based on a careful evaluation of all pertinent factors germane to the operations and effectiveness of the FBI...Experience has demonstrated very clearly to us that our Special Agent position must be limited to males and our stand on this point is inalterable."[58]

In 2013, there were 983 Hispanic agents in the FBI, 262 Hispanic agents in management positions and 9 in the Senior Executive Service. Legal attaché positions now list eleven Hispanic agents in those foreign assignments.[59] The FBI has shown improvement in the promotion of Hispanics, as there was only one Hispanic in the Senior Executive Service out of about four hundred Hispanic agents when the lawsuit was filed. However, the FBI still ranks below the statistical levels of Hispanic agents in management that the Drug Enforcement Agency reached twenty-five years ago when FBI agents Bud Mullen, Jack Lawn, and Tom Kelly ran the organization.

Ethics begin at the top. Laws, values, mottos, and mission statements enmeshed in the FBI seal shaped the FBI's foundation. However, when management's actions, or lack of action, collide head-on with ethics, loyal and sworn personnel may compromise their integrity and, in thrall to fidelity, cling to the in-group, rather than to their sworn principles. It is disappointing, but not surprising, measured against our national history of discrimination, that institutions sworn to oppose discrimination have often imposed it. Mat Perez, the attorneys, the class action members, and the federal court in El Paso reoriented the FBI to balance the scales of justice in a work environment. Judge Bunton's ruling on *Perez v. FBI* benefited every agent who sought a promotion with a more transparent career board, and the bureau also witnessed a quick rise in promotions at an unprecedented rate for women after the trial.

Everyone in an organization is duty-bound to its core values. While choice and discretionary judgment are vital to any investigator or official, *No One* has the authority to compromise agency values. Investigators who, through their own inadequacy, fail to investigate an allegation of wrongdoing and act in the guise of preserving the illusion of their agency's image or that of their manager, corrupt both the agency and the official and place the integrity of all in jeopardy. The FBI's failure to investigate discrimination turned costly in the *Perez v. FBI* case, because fairness in the workplace is a matter of fundamental justice deserved by all.

"*El más terrible de todos los sentimientos es el sentimiento de tener la esperanza muerta.*" (The most terrible of all feelings is the feeling of one's hope having died.) - ***Federico García Lorca***

"A nation is formed by the willingness of each of us to share in the responsibility for upholding the common good." - ***Barbara Jordan***

About the Author

Samuel C. Martinez served twenty-six years with the Federal Bureau of Investigation as a special agent. A benefactor of the GI Bill after serving in the US Navy, he graduated from the University of Texas at El Paso before the FBI recruited him.

Over the years, the FBI assigned him to myriad postings in San Francisco, Chicago, Denver, Mexico City, Los Angeles, Washington, DC, and Montevideo, Uruguay. He worked cases involving white-collar crime, domestic terrorism, narcotics, foreign counterintelligence, and undercover assignments. While he received commendations from the FBI and other government agencies, an Equal Employment Opportunity complaint that took the FBI over twelve years to resolve in his favor, prohibited him from advancing up the FBI's ranks. He joined Mat Perez in filing an employment discrimination class action lawsuit.

After retiring from the FBI, he served as a security consultant and had a successful career in real estate. He finds his greatest joy in serving people.

Works Cited

[1] "Frontier Justice." *Futility Closet.* Retrieved from <http://www.futility-closet.com/2012/02/12/frontier-justice>

[2] "History: John Edgar Hoover." *The Federal Bureau of Investigation.* Retrieved from <http://www.fbi.gov/about-us/history/directors/hoover>

[3] "Hate Crimes." *The Federal Bureau of Investigation.* Retrieved from <http://www.fbi.gov/about-us/investigate/civilrights/hate_crimes>

[4] *Bernardo M. Perez v.Director William H. Webster, the Federal Bureau of Investigation, and Attorney General Dick Thornburgh, US Federal Court, Western District, El Paso*

[5] Martinelli, Thomas. "Unconstitutional Policing: The Ethical Challenges in Dealing with Noble Cause Corruption." *Police Chief.* Retrieved from <http://www.policechiefmagazine.org/magazine/index.cfm?fuseaction= display&article_id=1025&issue_id=102006>

[6] Soble, Ronald. "L.A. FBI Chief Quits; to Take Mormon Post." *Los Angeles Times.* 24 March 1988. Retrieved from <http://articles.latimes.com/1988-03-24/news/mn-347_1_los-angeles-office>

[7] Judgment of Judge Lucius D. bucars, Bernardo M. Perez v. FBI et al. Document. 5 May 1989.

[8] Shenon, Philip. "F.B.I. to Promote 11 Hispanic Agents in Bias Case." *The New York Times,* 20 Sept. 1990.

[9] Director airtel, Bernardo M. Perez, et al. v. FBI, et al., 21 Sept. 1992.

[10] Pimentel, Stanley. Rightful Place Seniority Panel Declaration." Document. 20 Dec. 1989.

[11] Pimentel, Stanley. "OLIA Addendum." Document. 17 Dec. 1986 and 22 Apr. 1987.

[12] Revell, Buck. "Overseas Staffing Mexico City Office, Legal Attache Program." Document. 14 Sept. 1988.

[13] Pimentel, Stanley. "Daily Press Summary Comments." 2 Aug. 1989. Taco Circuit Decision.

[14] Pimentel, Stanley. "Memo Alleging Compromised CSA." 30 Aug. 1989.

[15] Pimentel, Stanley. "Requesting Denial of IDEC Conference travel." Message to DADIC. 19 Apr. 1996.

[16] Pimentel, Stanley. "Interview Memoir of Former Special Agent of the FBI Stanley A. Pimentel." Interview. Retrieved from <http://www.nleomf.org/assets/pdfs/nlem/oral-histories/FBI_Pimentel_interview.pdf>

[17] Martinez, Sam. "Declaration of Martinez with Handwritten Changes by Hale." Document. 3 Aug. 1988.

[18] Revell, Buck, and McWeeney, Sean. "Language Requirements for the Legal Attaches." Document. 20 Sept. 1988.

[19] Revell, Buck. "Overseas Staffing Montevideo Office, Legal Attaché Program." Document. 6 Oct. 1988.

[20] Sabinson, Carlis. "Schedule of Findings, Mexico City Inspection." 17 June 1989.

[21] Vissors-Leach. "Declaration of Lynn Vissors-Leach, Rightful Place Seniority Panel." Document. 11 May 1990.

[22] "Director airtel to all field offices titled Perez v. FBI." Summary of Litigation. Document. 21 Jan. 1992.

[23] LaFraniere, Sharon. "FBI Director Sessions Accused of `Overwhelming' Improprieties." *The Tech* 112.66 (1993). Retrieved from <http://tech.mit.edu/V112/N66/sessions.66w.html>

[24] Thompson, Ian. "Op-ed: Religion Shouldn't Be an Excuse for Discrimination." *Commentary*. 21 May 2013. Retrieved from <http://www.advocate.com/commentary/2013/05/21/op-ed-religion-shouldnt-be-excuse-discrimination>

[25] Herring, Cedric, Keith, Verna, and Horton, Hayward. *Skin Deep: How Race and Complexion Matter in the "Color-Blind" Era*. Chicago: University of Illinois Press, 2004.

[26] Kane, R. *Free will and values.* Albany: State University of New York Press, 1985.
[27] Double, Richard. *The Non-Reality of Free Will.* New York: Oxford University Press, 1991.
[28] Callender, John. *Free Will and Responsibility: A Guide for Practitioners.* New York: Oxford University Press, 2010.
[29] Trahair, Richard. *Encyclopedia of Cold War Espionage, Spies, and Secret Operations.* London: Greenwood Press, 2004.
[30] Vise, David. *The Bureau and the Mole.* New York: Grove Press, 2002.
[31] Serrano, Richard. "FBI agent's journey from pulpit to prison." *Collections,* 72h. 26 December 2011. Retrieved from <http://articles.latimes.com/2011/dec/26/nation/la-na-preacher-cop-convict-20111226>
[32] Freedberg, Sydney. "Good cop, bad cop." *Special Report.* Retrieved from <http://www.sptimes.com/News/030401/Worldandnation/Good_cop__bad_cop_.shtml>
[33] "Former FBI agent, OSU-CHS visiting professor arrested in child porn investigation." *Scripps Media.* 14 May 2012. Retrieved from <http://www.kjrh.com/dpp/news/local_news/former-fbi-agent-osu-tulsa-visiting-professor-arrested-in-child-porn-investigation>
[34] Lehr, Dick, and O'Neill, Gerard. *Black Mass: The Irish Mob, the Boston FBI, and a Devil's Deal.* New York: PublicAffairs, 2000.
[35] Fitzpatrick, Robert, and Land, Jon. *Betrayal: Whitey Bulger and the FBI Agent Who Fought to Bring Him Down.* New York: Forge, 2011.
[36] Coleman, Rich. "Jury finds ex-FBI special agent guilty of manslaughter in hammer death." 21 Dec. 2010. Retrieved from <http://www.lasvegassun.com/news/2010/dec/21/jury-finds-ex-fbi-special-agent-guilty-manslaughte/#axzz2UtQfZIh9≥
[37] Murphy, Elizabeth. "Lead FBI Agent in Stevens Case Undergoing Internal Ethics Review." *Main Justice.* 9 May 2012. Retrieved from <http://www.mainjustice.com/2012/05/09/lead-fbi-agent-in-stevens-case-undergoing-internal-ethics-review/≥
[38] Martinelli, Thomas. "Unconstitutional Policing: The Ethical Challenges in Dealing with Noble Cause Corruption." *Police Chief.* Retrieved from <http://www.policechiefmagazine.org/magazine/index.cfm?fuseaction= display&article_id=1025&issue_id=102006>

[39] Blakeley, Lindsay. "Mark Cuban on Sharks, Bigotry, and What He's Really Like as a Boss." 21 May 2014. Retrieved from <http://www.inc.com/lindsay-blakely/mark-cuban-sterling-nba-entrepreneurship.html>

[40] Wright, Anthony. "Chapter 6: Limbic System: Amygdala." *University of Texas Health.* Retrieved from <http://neuroscience.uth.tmc.edu/s4/chapter06.html>

[41] Cook, Gareth. "Do Plants Think?" 5 June 2012. Retrieved from <http://www.scientificamerican.com/ article.cfm?id=do-plants-think-daniel-chamovitz>

[42] "Herd Mentality." Retrieved from <http://en.wikipedia.org/wiki/Herd_mentality>

[43] Simons, Eric. *The Secret life of Sports Fans.* New York: Overlook Press, 2013.

[44] Moushey, Bill, and Dvorchak, Robert. *Game Over: Jerry Sandusky, Penn State, and the Culture of Silence.* New York: HarperCollins, 2012.

[45] Podles, Leon. *Sacrilege: Sexual Abuse in the Catholic Church.* Crossland Press, 2008.

[46] Shaw, William. *Business Ethics.* Cengage Learning, 2013.

[47] JSTOR (Organization). *The Journal of Philosophy, Psychology and Scientific Methods.* New York: Science Press, 1904.

[48] Beyer, Lisa. "Racism Isn't Discrimination." *Bloomberg View.* 2 May 2014. Retrieved from <http://www.bloombergview.com/articles/2014-05-02/racism-isn-t-discrimination>

[49] Deverich, Amanda. "Outrage for Oprah: Racism or Classism?" *Huffington Post.* 14 August 2013. Retrieved from <http://www.huffingtonpost.com/amanda-deverich/outrage-for-oprah-racism-_b_3735326.html>

[50] Forbes, William. *The Investigation of Crime.* New York: Kaplan, 2008.

[51] Buckley, John. *Equal Employment Opportunity: 2011 Compliance Guide.* Aspen Publishers, 2011.

[52] Stalcup, George. *Equal Employment Opportunity: Pilot Projects Could Help Test Solutions to Long-Standing Concerns with the EEO Complaint Process.* GAO, 2009.

[53] EEOC. "All Statutes FY 1997-FY 2013." *Enforcement & Litigation Statistics.* Retrieved from <http://www.eeoc.gov/eeoc/statistics/enforcement/all.cfm>
[54] EEOC. "Title VII of the Civil Rights Act of 1964 Charges." *Enforcement & Litigation Statistics.* Retrieved from
<http://www.eeoc.gov/eeoc/statistics/enforcement/titlevii.cfm>
[55] ABC News. "What Would You Do?" Retrieved from <http://abcnews.go.com/WhatWouldYouDo>
[56] Bossidy, Larry, Charan, Ram and Burck, Charles. *Execution: The Discipline of Getting Things Done.* Random House, 2011. Print.
[57] Bernardo M. Perez et al. v.Director William H. Webster, the Federal Bureau of Investigation, and Attorney General Dick Thornburgh. United States District Court, W.D. Texas, El Paso Division. 15 Aug. 1988. Print.
[58] Director Hoover, letter to Dr. Adrian Chamberlain, President of Colorado State University. Document. 11 March 1971.
[59] Federal Bureau of Investigation. "A Diverse Snapshot of the FBI." *Diversity Statistics.* Retrieved from <https://www.fbijobs.gov/41.asp>

GLOSSARY OF TERMS AND ACRONYMS

ABSCAM – Operational name for the FBI's 1980 Major Case "Arab Scam" sting that eventually netted the convictions of seven members of Congress
AD – Assistant Director
ADIC – Assistant Director in Charge
ALAT – Assistant Legal Attaché
ASAC – Assistant Special Agent in Charge
AUSA – Assistant US Attorney
Bancoshares – Major Case dealing with money laundering in Miami
Bucars – FBI government cars
CDP – Career Development Program
CHOWBOAT – Major Case of bombing of one of the Navy's ships that transported chow to Vieques Island
CIA – Central Intelligence Agency
CUBIR – Major Case for the Cuban refugee exodus to Miami in 1980; the refugees were known as *los Marielitos*
DAWY – Day Agent Work Years; accumulated hours in investigative classifications
DEA – Drug Enforcement Agency
DOJ – Department of Justice
DR – Daily Reports; disciplinary form accounting for agent activity every fifteen minutes

EAD – Executive Assistant Director
EEO – Equal Employment Opportunity
EEOC – Equal Employment Opportunity Commission
EOD – Entered on Duty
EPPD – El Paso Police Department
FAA – Federal Aviation Administration
FALN – Fuerzas Armadas de Liberación Nacional; a Puerto Rican terrorist group
FBI – Federal Bureau of Investigation
FBIHQ – Federal Bureau of Investigation Headquarters
FCI – Foreign Counter Intelligence
FD-302s – Official interview reports
FGR – Federal General Regulations
GS – Government Service
GSA – General Services Administration
HAPCOA – Hispanic American Police Command Officers Association
IRS – Internal Revenue Service
KCPD – Kansas City Police Department
LAPD – Los Angeles Police Department
Legat – Legal Attaché, a foreign assignment
LULAC – League of United Latin American Citizens
Major Cases – Code-named, high priority cases of national attention requiring extra resources
MALDEF – Mexican American Legal Defense and Education Fund
MAOP – Manual of Administrative and Operational Procedures
MAP – Management Assessment Program
MAP I – First-level Management Assessment Program
MAP II – Second-level Management Assessment Program
MIOG – Manual of Investigative Operations and Guidelines
MSPB – Merit System Protection Board
NAGBOM – Major Case of the National Guard Bombing
NAVMUR – Major Case of Navy Murders at base in Puerto Rico
OLIA – Office of Liaison and International Affairs
OP – Office of Preference
OPM – Office of Personnel Management

OPR – Office of Professional Responsibility
OSM – Office Services Manager
PINS – Personnel Information Network System; agent data, training and attributes
PLA – Principal Legal Advisor
POCO – Major Case investigating corruption in the Police of Puerto Rico
PPR – Police of Puerto Rico
PT – Physical Training
QSI – Quality Service Increase, an award with a pay increase
RA – Resident Agency, a branch office of a regional division
RPS – Rightful Place Seniority
RUC – Referred upon Completion; closing of leads or investigation from a resident agency
SA – Special Agent
SAASAC – Senior Administrative Assistant Special Agent in Charge
SAC – Special Agent in Charge
SES – Senior Executive Service
SJ – San Juan
SSA – Supervisory Special Agent
SSRA – Supervisory Special Resident Agent
SWAT – Special Weapons Assault and Tactics
TDY – Temporary Duty Assignment
Three-card (3-card) – Capture of time in and out of an investigative classification
T-IIIs – Title III Wiretaps
TTA – Technically Trained Agent
UC – Undercover
UCA – Undercover Assignment
WFO – Washington Field Office

INDEX